BROTHER TRUMAN

BROTHER TRUMAN:

THE MASONIC LIFE AND PHILOSOPHY OF HARRY S. TRUMAN

BY

ALLEN E. ROBERTS

A SPECIAL MISSOURI LODGE OF RESEARCH EDITION

ANCHOR COMMUNICATIONS
Highland Springs, Virginia

Address inquiries to Anchor Communications, Drawer 70, Highland Springs, VA 23075-0070

Printed in the United States of America

Library of Congress Cataloging in Publication Data

Roberts, Allen E.
Brother Truman

Bibliography: p.
Includes index.
1. Truman, Harry S., 1884-1972—Relations with freemasons.
2. Truman, Harry S., 1884-1972—Philosophy. 3. Presidents—United States—Biography. 4. Freemasons—United States—Biography. I. Title.
E814.R65 1985 973.918'092'4 85-20140

ISBN No. 0-935633-01-4

Dedicated to

Those who seek Truth and spread the Light revealed by their research to all people everywhere, and to those who cheerfully share their knowledge and material possessions with others—

and especially Dottie

BOOKS BY ALLEN E. ROBERTS

House Undivided: The Story of Freemasonry and the Civil War
Freemasonry in Highland Springs
Sword and Trowel
Masonry Under Two Flags
Key To Freemasonry's Growth
Freemasonry's Servant
Fifty Golden Years
Brotherhood In Action
The Craft and Its Symbols
G. Washington: Master Mason
Frontier Cornerstone
Shedding Light on Leadership
A Chronicle of Virginia Research Lodge
A Daughter of the Grand Lodge of Virginia
Freemasonry In American History

MOTION PICTURES WRITTEN, PRODUCED AND DIRECTED

The Pilot
Growing the Leader
Breaking Barriers to Communication
Planning Unlocks the Door
People Make the Difference
The Brotherhood of Man
Challenge
Precious Heritage
Lonely World
Fraternally Yours
Virtue Will Triumph
Living Stones . . .
The Saga of the Holy Royal Arch of Freemasonry

FOREWORD

The Masonic life of M.W. Brother Harry S. Truman spanned a little more than sixty-three years. He passed to his eternal reward more than twelve and a half years ago, December 26, 1972. Several books have been written about President Harry S. Truman, but none about a specific phase of his life which he loved dearly—the Masonic Lodge and his activity in it.

Allen E. Roberts, Certified Administrative Manager, researcher and author of many Masonic books and articles for different Masonic publications, has applied his energetic talents to the production of this book about the Masonic life of Brother Truman. This is his third book for Missouri Lodge of Research. The first entitled *House Undivided,* the Story of Freemasonry and the Civil War, was published in 1961. It was so well received and highly praised by the membership generally, that the Lodge is fortunate to obtain his skills in researching the Masonic interests of the brother who, as Grand Master of Masons in Missouri, signed the charter of Missouri Lodge of Research on September 30, 1941.

In this fortieth year after the atomic bombing of Hiroshima, Japan, on order of President Harry S. Truman, it is altogether appropriate that this book should be written about this man and Mason from Missouri. Much reflected glory has come to Missouri and Missouri Freemasonry through the patriotic efforts of this man who saw service in the European Theater during World War I, returning as a captain and later a colonel. As a United States Senator, Vice-President and President of the United States, President Truman always endeavored to share the dignity of these, the highest stations in our land, with his people and brethren of Missouri. Without a single doubt as to the solidity of our position, we believe that Most Worshipful Brother Truman may well go down in the history of the fraternity as the most important Freemason in this century.

Right Worshipful Brother Allen E. Roberts has numerous credentials which recommend him adequately for this important assignment. For over thirty-five years he has written articles for many magazines and periodicals on Freemasonry. He is the author of the history of the Grand Lodge of Ohio, and has just completed a documentary for the Grand Lodge of Georgia. He has authored plays, books and cassettes, and a 50-year history of the Masonic Service Association. Brother Roberts is a Past District Deputy Grand Master and Past Deputy Grand Secretary of the Grand Lodge of Virginia. His many accomplishments are far too numerous to be recorded here. A review of the vast amount of Masonic endeavor he has put forth makes it altogether possible that one day a book will be written about the author.

In Freemasonry, Brother Roberts is a member of both the York and Scottish Rites, and many concordant and appendant bodies of Masonry. He has served with distinction in various capacities in all of them. He is currently President of the Philalethes Society, and holds one of its forty fellowships. The symbolic lodge holds his prime interest, and the greatest thrust of his endeavors is in that direction. In all his labors in the area of Masonic research, he seeks facts and, above all, truth. We believe these attributes are commendable, and that the readers of what follows will bear this out.

Bruce H. Hunt
Past Grand Master, Missouri

COMMENTARY FROM THE MISSOURI LODGE OF RESEARCH

Most people are acquainted with the personage of Harry S. Truman cast as a politician, and in that perspective have adjudged the man, for better or for worse, as a participant to history.

Brother Truman reveals an individual of significant contrast to the common political image afforded him by some historians. It allows brethren of the Masonic Fraternity to see Harry Truman in a new light and in a new character: as a brother Master Mason.

As an addendum to history, *Brother Truman* is a carefully researched study into the character and moral fiber of a man whose thumbprint is indelibly imprinted upon the pages of American History and within the infinite account of world affairs.

It should be of particular interest to Freemasons because Harry Truman exemplified—in his private and public life—the very essence of Masonic philosophy. His momentous decisions as a U.S. Senator and as President of the United States were, in large part, a product of Masonic morality, shaped by lessons of our ritual and experience, and performed on the stage of national and world events. These same lessons, acted out on a smaller stage, can guide the lives of countless men who have witnessed the Light of Truth that shines around our Masonic altars.

To my brother Freemasons who yearn to know whence they came, who cherish the history of our Craft and those individuals who have had a hand in writing that history, I seriously commend this book.

If we must attach some intangible value to our fraternal existence—as I feel we must in this day and age—it is necessary to judge our standards against the historical evidence. There exists no finer example of this contemporary testimony than in the life and times of Harry S. Truman. Thanks to the pen and perseverance of Allen E. Roberts, that evidence is recorded in conspicuous detail.

Brother Truman elucidates and enlightens the historical record, and in so doing performs an invaluable service to the Masonic Fraternity.

Thomas C. Warden, *Editor*
The Missouri Lodge of Research

PREFACE

Within the realms of Freemasonry a handful of men have stood out as exceptional leaders. Each decade has produced only one or two since the Grand Lodge era began in 1717. Among the thousands of great men who have been members of the Craft only a few have acknowledged their debt to the teachings of Freemasonry. One can read their autobiographies and biographies in vain to find any reference to Masonry. The few exceptions stand out vividly. One of these is Harry S. Truman.

Throughout his adult life Truman put into practice the principles taught within all Masonic Lodges. Perhaps it was because he learned the ritual of the Craft soon after he was initiated. But he went beyond the ritual; he learned and practiced what it meant. Above all, he didn't hesitate to help the Fraternity and those individuals within it. He didn't hide his membership; he spoke of it often—as you will find within the pages of this book, because much of it is written in his own words.

Friend and foe alike, for the most part, did admire and respect the principles of Truman. Many who did not share his views as a Senator and later as President have since learned he was right more often than wrong. I must honestly admit that I am one of these. I am sorry that I didn't know the man then whom now I have come to know and understand.

It wasn't until 1968, when I started work on the history of The Masonic Service Association, that I really learned what a fine and great man Truman was. As often happens, I had been brainwashed by the media, or what Truman called "the sabotage press." What I found was a man who considered others before himself; a man who was among the few who truly put into practice the teachings and philosophy of Freemasonry. He was one of the rare breed of men who actually went out of his way to help those who needed assistance, regardless of their station in life.

"President Harry S. Truman was one of my favorite Presidents of our Nation," President and Brother Gerald R. Ford told me. "I so indicated my feelings by having his portrait displayed in the Cabinet Room of the White House during my Presidency. The other two portraits were President Abraham Lincoln and

Dwight D. Eisenhower, both equally outstanding as leaders of our nation.

"President Harry S. Truman was the first I served under as a member of Congress and the first I knew personally. Although he was a Democrat and I a Republican, I supported his wise and firm foreign policy actions. We had some understandable differences on domestic policy, but his overall record was excellent."

It's easy to sit on the sidelines and criticize. This takes no effort at all. It's simple to say this or that should be done, but it's impossible to know what is correct unless one has all the facts. Too many of us, however, don't want to be confused with facts. They get in the way of the conclusions we would like to reach, or have reached.

Truman never surrounded himself with "yes men." He sought advice from all sides, as those who are truly leaders do. He listened to the arguments, then made the decision he believed correct. He publicly made a statement few have the courage to make: "The Buck Stops Here!"

Many books have been consulted, but little has been used from them, to produce this one. Many people have been interviewed. Publications throughout the Masonic world have been searched, because this is primarily the story of Harry S. Truman as a Master Mason, along with his philosophy. This is a book, however, written insofar as possible in Truman's own words. Much of the material has come from his letters, papers and journals which he thoughtfully made available for future historians at the Harry S. Truman Library in Independence, Missouri. Fortunately, he was a tireless chronicler of daily events. His letters to the girl he courted for so long and whom he finally married are priceless.

This is not, and is not intended to be, a history of his Presidency. Yet, it must of necessity cover a goodly portion of his public service, as well as the life of Harry S. Truman and his philosophy, particularly as he worked with and for Freemasonry. This philosophy, enhanced, I believe, by the teachings of Masonry, proved beneficial to the peoples of the world.

The quotations in this book are primarily from papers filed in the Harry S. Truman Library. Because of repetition the Library is not noted throughout the book. Where quotations are from other sources, they are noted in the text. Some books will be notably missing in the bibliography. This is intentional for varying reasons.

Brother Rufus Burrus, the long-time lawyer and friend of Truman, when asked if he thought Truman would like the title chosen for this book, said: "Oh, sure. He urged all those in the higher echelons of Masonry to get down to the grassroots of Masonry—the Blue Lodge, as he called it."

There are many people to thank for the opportunity that has been mine to write this book. William H. Chapman, the then Master of Missouri Lodge of Research and the present Master Earl K. Dille, who asked me to write it. Thomas C. Warden, Editor of the MLR, has been a tower of strength. He did an excellent job of editing out my many mistakes and made this more grammatically acceptable than it otherwise would have been.

Bruce H. Hunt, whom I'm privileged to call "friend" as well as "Brother," is among the last of Harry Truman's cronies. He graciously agreed to check the manuscript for historical accuracy and write the Foreword.

C. Warren Ohrvall, the Archivist at the Harry S. Truman Library, was continuously helpful from the first day this project started. He had truck loads of material ready for Dottie (my good wife) and me when we arrived at the Library. Without his assistance it's doubtful this book could have been published as soon as it was. Others at the Library were also helpful, notably: Erwin J. Mueller, Elizabeth Safly and Pauline Testerman.

Harold E. Thornton, a Past Master of Grandview Lodge who knew President Truman well, graciously shared his thoughts with me. He took me on a tour of Grandview and to the Temple of Grandview Lodge where I had the honor of sitting in the Master's chair where Truman often sat. Because of this tour I was better able to understand why the Lodge reluctantly turned down the offer of its first Master to build its temple where he wanted it. However, someday I hope the Masons of Missouri will build "Truman's Masonic Temple," follow his plans and place it close to the President's final resting place.

The folks at the Iowa Masonic Library, as always, helped. So did Dwight L. Smith of Indiana who provided me with pictures and an insight into Truman's unprecedented visit to an Indiana Lodge while battling for his political future.

Without the help of Dottie in going through thousands of papers at the Truman Library, it would have taken me weeks to search the archives. For this, and the many other things she has done for me for almost forty years, I must again say "thank you."

We could have saved hours of research time at the Truman Library had I been aware of the excellent book by Robert H. Ferrell, *Dear Bess,* because we would then have known exactly what to look for when we went through Truman's letters to his wife. Ferrell's book contains hundreds of letters not found in *Brother Truman.*

To those who shared their thoughts with me about Harry S. Truman, I owe a debt of gratitude. Notably among them is Greta Kempton, a Life Fellow of the Royal Society of Arts in London, England, and a Life Member of the Corcoran Gallery of Art in Washington. She not only told me of her unforgettable experience with the President, but gave me several copies of her portraits to use in this book.

There will be criticism of some of the material contained here. I have not attempted to gloss over the "warts" in Freemasonry that have shown up in the Masonic life of Brother Truman. Those of us who are members of the Fraternity called "Freemasonry" like to believe it has no sins. Too often we forget the system is excellent, but it is composed of human beings. These human beings too often act like people and the "warts" show through the veneer of excellence.

There are lessons for us, Freemasons and non-Masons alike, within the pages of *Brother Truman*. If we learn from these lessons (and they aren't isolated to any area), the Craft and the world will be the beneficiaries. And the Brotherhood of Man under the Fatherhood of God might become a reality.

Allen E. Roberts

Highland Springs, Virginia
September 6, 1985

CONTENTS

ILLUSTRATIONS

Youth

Behold how good and how pleasant it is for brethren to dwell together in unity!

It is like the precious ointment upon the head, that ran down upon the beard, even Aaron's beard: that went down to the skirts of his garments;

As the dew of Hermon, and as the dew that descended upon the mountains of Zion: for there the Lord commanded the blessing, even life for evermore.

—Psalm 133—

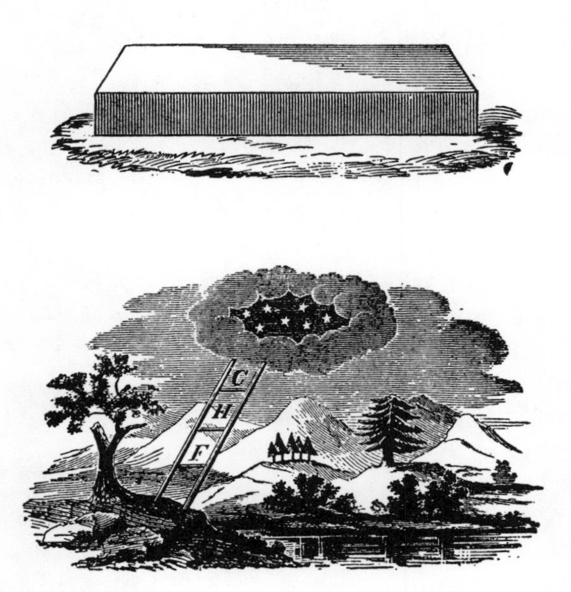

1. GROWING

God has been good to the United States of America. Throughout its brief history He has given the country the right man for the right job at the right time.

This is not to claim that every leader of this nation has been the best choice. Some have been almost disastrous. But it is to say that when a forceful leader was needed to repair the damage done by others, a man was chosen to set things on an even keel.

Harry S. Truman happened to be the right man in the right place at the right time—on several occasions. Why?

This partial tribute paid to him by Dean Acheson at a farewell dinner in June, 1953, as recorded in *Off the Record*, gives part of the answer: ". . . here we all know that the President has insisted that all the cards should be on the table. He has hated and abhorred intrigue and double-dealing. He has not tolerated yes men, but has insisted that all of us should state our opinions forthrightly and honestly. He has not been afraid of differences of opinion. Time and time again they have been brought to him, and time and time again he has done the hardest of all things—faced issues and made decisions. And all of us have known that the decisions were conscientiously and bravely made and to us these decisions were law.

"These are qualities enough to bring respect and to engender affection. But there has been more." And Acheson added: "The President has never asked any of us to do what he would not do. When the time came to fight, he threw everything into it, himself included. And what we all knew was that, however hot the fire was in front, there would never be a shot in the back."

During the Watergate fiasco, President Richard M. Nixon told John Ehrlichman: "Whatever we say about Harry Truman, while it hurt him, a lot of people admired the old bastard for standing by people who were guilty as hell, and, damn it, I am that kind of person."

People did admire the steadfast Mason from Missouri. They respected his forthright presentation of the facts as he saw them. Those who met him left his presence with a deeper understanding of his sincerity.

Nixon wrote in his *Memoirs* about his first meeting with Truman in the White House. He and three Republican freshman Congressmen were invited by President Truman to a private meeting. He made them all feel welcome, shook hands with each of them, and "spoke very earnestly about the necessity of rehabilitating Europe." He told them he was glad to see them even though they were Republicans, and added: "Some of my best friends never agree with me politically." Nixon said he included in his notes "that Truman's strength was 'his hominess, his democratic attitude, and his sincerity.' "

Truman's strength and sincerity benefited Freemasonry for over sixty years. But perhaps never more so than when he was Grand Master of Masons in Missouri. As Grand Master and a United States Senator he brought credibility to The Masonic Service Association of the United States. This came at a time when the Association was at a low point, and when the armed forces needed the values and encouragement of the Masons of the country.

This strength, sincerity and love of his fellowman that Truman had came from many sources. In his formative years these included a closely-knit family, parents and a brother and sister who shared their love. Then there were grandparents and aunts and uncles all working together. In his adult life another factor was added—Freemasonry. From the day he became a member of the Craft in 1909 he learned fully the lessons it had to share with all who would learn.

It was his love of reading, especially history, that undoubtedly made him appreciate the principles of Freemasonry. He learned while he was a boy that history had many valuable lessons to impart. "I learned from it," he wrote, "that a leader is a man who has the ability to get other people to do what they don't want to do, and like it. It takes a leader to put economic, military, and government forces to work so they will operate. I learned in those periods of history when there was no leadership, society usually groped through dark ages of one degree or another. I saw that it takes men to make history, or there would be no history."

From his earliest days in school until his death he read everything he could find in the area of history. He gave this fact credit for his love of the principles of leadership and government.

"And that boy read," said Mary Ethel (Miss Ethel) Noland, the family's historian whose mother was a sister of Harry's father. "I don't know anybody in the world that ever read as much or as constantly as he did."

The story of Harry S. Truman begins on December 28, 1881, when his parents, Martha Ellen Young and John Anderson Truman, were married. Three years later, May 8, 1884, Harry was born in Lamar, Missouri. His brother John Vivian followed on April 25, 1886. Mary Jane, their sister, was born on August 12, 1889. By this time the Trumans were living on the farm of Martha's father, Solomon Young, in Grandview, Missouri.

Solomon, a big, hard-muscled man, had been one of the early pioneers. He had driven cattle and led wagon trains over the plains to California and Utah during his younger days. In the 1870's he ran an outfitting business and advised thousands of others like him how best to make the westward trek. Harry, a young man of four, and the man in his 70's became close friends.

Truman would always remember his red-haired grandmother, who made "wonderful cookies" and who "gave us free rein." That free rein included running all over 440 acres, plus more acreage across the road. He and his brother Vivian took full advantage of the freedom, but this led to a "grand spanking" on at least one occasion. Harry dumped Vivian and another boy in a mud hole repeatedly because "it seemed a good thing to do." The wrath of the elders fell upon Harry as the ringleader because he was the eldest of the culprits.

Anderson Shippe Truman was Harry's paternal grandfather. His wife had died on February 15, 1879, before Harry's parents were married. Being alone, he lived with his son and daughter-in-law wherever they went. This included the Young farm. But during his first year there he died. It was from his grandfathers that Harry may have "inherited" his middle initial. The "S" had no name attached to it, and presumably could have meant "Solomon" or "Shippe."

The Young farm was located in Jackson County six miles north of Belton. When a railroad line was built between Kansas City and Springfield, the depot, one mile from the farm, was named Grandview. And it was a "grand view," according to Truman. It was the highest point of land in the vicinity. From it one could see for miles in any direction.

Throughout his life Truman vividly remembered his childhood. His uncle Harrison Young, who lived in Kansas City, would bring Harry and his brother "the most wonderful things to play with and all kinds of candy, nuts, and fruit." His grandfather Young would take them to the Belton Fair "in a big two-wheeled cart with high wheels." Harry would "sit in the judges' stand with Grandpa and watch the races, eat striped candy and peanuts, and have the best time a kid ever had." Later he had his own Shetland pony" and the grandest saddle to ride him with I ever saw," Truman wrote. In his *Memoirs* he added: "Vivian has just had that lovely saddle rehabilitated for his three-year-old granddaughter, sixty-five years later."

It wasn't all play, however. Apples and peaches had to be picked, dried and buried in the ground. The produce had to be harvested. With the freeze came hog-killing time. This meant sausage, souse, pickled pigs' feet and lard for the winter. Cows had to be milked, horses curried, watered and fed. Wood had to be constantly gathered, chopped and logs split for the stoves. The barns had to be kept clean, along with dozens of other chores attached to farming.

Harry's father bought a house in Independence in 1890. It became the meeting place for all the boys and girls close by. There were always ponies and horses to ride and goats to hitch to small wagons. And at this time the Truman children began attending Sunday school at the First Presbyterian Church. There he met a girl with golden curls, "and the most beautiful blue eyes," whom he would court for years. She would share his youth from the fifth grade through high school.

His mother started Harry's education early. She taught him how to read before he was five, even though his poor eyesight made reading difficult. By the time he was eight he was wearing glasses, and would wear them the rest of his life. This kept him from taking part in sports, but he found an outlet in reading. By the time he was fourteen, Harry said he thought he had read every book in the Independence Public Library.

Perhaps not surprisingly, Harry learned early to look for the strengths and weaknesses in his teachers. He then tried to give them what they expected. His high grades throughout his school years would prove that he succeeded. He later said he never had a teacher he did not like and respect. History and biographies were his greatest interests.

"The lives of the great administrators of past ages intrigued me," he wrote, "and I soon learned that the really successful ones were few and far between. I wanted to know what caused the successes or the failures of all the famous leaders of history." He was particularly interested in the development of the United States and its political leaders. He believed this was the only way to "get a solid foundation in political science and public administration."

He studied the political life of Andrew Johnson who was thrust into the Presidency. "When the same thing happened to me," he said, "I knew just how Johnson had coped with his problems, and I did not make the mistakes he made." He added:

> History taught me about the periodic waves of hysteria which started with the witch craze during colonial days, produced the abominable Alien and Sedition Acts of the 1790s, flourished again in the Know-Nothing movement, the anti-Masonic hysteria, anti-Catholicism, the Ku Klux Klan, the Red scare of 1919. When the cycle repeated itself during my administration in the form of anti-Communist hysteria and indiscriminate branding of innocent persons as subversives, I could deal with the situation calmly because I knew something about its background that students of history would know but perhaps not appreciate. When we are faced with a situation, we must know how to apply the lessons of history in a practical way.

The anti-Masonic period, he noted, began in 1826 when politicians of what would become the Know-Nothing Party used the disappearance of one William Morgan from Batavia, New York, as a "political crusade." The resulting craze almost destroyed Freemasonry, especially in the Eastern part of the United States. This is covered extensively in *Freemasonry in American History.* In this statement Truman proved he not only had learned the ritual of Masonry well, but also the history of the Craft.

His first paying job was in a drug store in Independence while he was still attending school. There he learned how to dust, sweep and keep everything clean. He also learned about something else that would prove valuable over the years—hypocrisy. Under the prescription case was an assortment of whiskey bottles. "The good church members and Anti-Saloon Leaguers would come in for their early-morning drink behind the prescription case at ten cents an ounce," he wrote. "They would wipe their mouths, peep through the observation hole in the front of the case, and depart. This procedure gave a fourteen-year-old boy quite a viewpoint on the public front of leading citizens and 'amen-corner-praying' churchmen. There were saloons aplenty around the square in Independence, and many leading men in town made no bones about going into them and buying a drink. I learned to think more highly of them than I did of the prescription-counter drinkers."

His grades began to suffer, so his father suggested he quit the job, which he did. He then started studying Latin with his aunt Ella Noland, algebra with cousin Nellie, cousin Ethel and "incidentally, my beautiful young lady with the blue eyes and golden hair." Two nights a week he took special courses in history. He was hoping to receive an appointment to West Point or Annapolis, but his poor eyesight kept that from happening.

In 1901 he graduated from high school along with Elizabeth Virginia (always called "Bess") Wallace and Charles Ross, who would remain a life-long friend of Harry's. He would later assume the important office of press secretary for the President.

The Truman family couldn't afford to send Harry to college. Money had always been a problem for the Trumans and always would be for the eldest son. Perhaps this also would be one of his strengths. But the Trumans were a proud family. Miss Ethel said: "None of us came to the colonies north of the Mason-Dixon line. If the *Mayflower* had never landed, we would still be here."

Harry became a timekeeper on the Santa Fe Railroad, working for a contractor. Most of the men earned fifteen cents an hour and worked ten-hour days; Truman earned thirty-five dollars a month and board. He also "received a very down-to-earth education in the handling of men." The education from hobos with whom he lived along the Missouri River would prove valuable in the not-too-distant future.

The job was completed in the spring of 1902 and his dad took Harry on a visit to land he owned in southern Missouri. On their return Harry went to work in the mailing room of the *Star* in Kansas City. A short time later he and his brother were employed at the National Bank of Commerce. Then Vivian left to work for the First National Bank; Harry was promoted to file clerk for the president. Later he went to work at the Union National Bank as a bookkeeper at a salary of sixty dollars a month. His room and board cost five dollars a week.

"Vivian was a much better farmer than Harry," said Miss Ethel, "because city life never appealed to Vivian for one minute. Yet, when Harry's uncle, Harrison Young, who had been working on the Young farm, wanted to quit in 1904, the Trumans moved back to Grandview. But Harry continued working at the bank for another two years before devoting full time to the farm."

Battery B of the National Guard of Kansas City was organized in 1905, and would play an important role in the life of Truman. He joined the outfit as a private. The battery was composed of sixty men, many of them influential, "who would go out to a rented armory once a week and pay a quarter for the privilege of drilling." At the summer camps Truman learned more about handling army horses and soldiers.

Then a far-reaching event occurred in 1908 that would prove influential in his life. One of his mother's cousins visited the farm. He was wearing a Masonic pin and this struck a responsive chord with Harry. The results would prove beneficial for the young man and for all of Freemasonry.

2. COURTING AND FREEMASONRY

Shortly after Truman had asked his cousin for a petition for Freemasonry, he received one from Belton Lodge No. 540, Ancient, Free and Accepted Masons. Wm. H. Waskon and Howard Lindsey endorsed the petition on which Harry listed his occupation as that of a farmer. It was received by the lodge on January 2, 1909, and Truman was elected to receive the degrees on January 30, 1909. On February 9 he was Initiated; Passed to the Degree of Fellowcraft on March 9; and Raised to the Sublime Degree of Master Mason on March 18, 1909. There was no waiting period between degrees as there is today.

In a paper at the Harry S. Truman Library he gives this account of his Masonic career:

> About a month after, the Grand Lecturer, James R. McLachlan, came to Belton for a three-day lodge of instruction. I attended all three days and accompanied the Grand Lecturer to Holden and St. Joseph, becoming almost letter perfect in the ritual in all the stations.
>
> In the fall of 1909 I was appointed a deacon, and in the fall of 1910 elected Junior Warden. I decided to organize a lodge at Grandview about this time.
>
> The Masonic Law required twenty signatures to a petition for dispensation to be presented to the Grand Master.
>
> The Grand Lodge met in St. Louis in September, 1910, and I presented the petition to the Grand Master in the spring of 1910. It was favorably acted upon and a dispensation was issued by the Grand Master with me as Master of Grandview Lodge U.D. When the Grand Lodge met in the fall I was present and a charter was issued to Grandview Lodge 618.
>
> The Deputy Grand Master, Leon Thalman, organized and put the Lodge to work in 1911. I was elected its first master and then its secretary. I was again elected master in 1916 and was the master when the War came along in 1917. While I was overseas the lodge hall burned with all the records and the Charter.
>
> When I came home from the War I kept up my interest in Masonic affairs becoming known as a ritualist and in 1924 I was appointed District Deputy Grand Master and District Deputy Grand Lecturer for the 59th District which was Jackson County outside Kansas City.

I held instruction courses in every lodge in the district in each year and held a general course of instruction for all lodges in the district with the Grand Lecturer present.

These meetings were most helpful and instructive and gave the members a chance to become better acquainted. It was also an opportunity to impress upon the membership the great lessons taught in the Old and New Testaments.

In 1930 William R. Gentry was Grand Master. He was a prominent lawyer in St. Louis and a working Republican in politics. I was presiding Judge of the County Court of Jackson County and an organization Democrat. Mr. Gentry appointed me to the first step in the Grand Lodge line. This meant that eventually, with no mishaps, I'd be Grand Master.

Some partisan Republicans in St. Louis tried to head me off when I came to the first elective office, but they failed as they did every year after that until I became the Grand Master of Missouri in September, 1940.

In the meantime I had been elected to the United States Senate in 1934. I was having the fight of my life for reelection in 1940. My political friends were in trouble, and the Governor of the State who held his office because I had been for him was trying to unseat me. So the same old St. Louis clique that tried to head me off in the Grand Lodge at the first elective office, tried again when I came up for Grand Master. They failed and I'm sure they are now sorry they tried to discredit me, because there are very few Grand Lodges who have had a President of the greatest Republic in the history of the world as a Past Grand Master.

When I became President in 1945, the Scottish Rite wanted me, of course for the 33rd Degree. I had been entitled to it for five years, but the old man who was Sovereign Grand Commander was from Kentucky and a violent anti-New Dealer. So I wasn't asked. But I didn't act the snob and tell the old man where to go when he did come around, because I wanted to top off my Masonic career with the 33rd Degree.

My Masonic career has been helpful in teaching me to get along with people, has caused me to become more familiar with the Bible and inspired me to read a great deal of history.

That's a bare-bones outline of a Masonic career which spanned sixty-three years of extremely active service to Freemasonry. And during this same period Truman was active in serving his community, state and country. Few, if any, men have equalled his devotion to what he believed to be his duty.

George Washington, whom most Freemasons revere as did Truman, could not begin to equal the Masonic service of Harry

Truman. Yet there are many parallels between the two. True, there was a century and a half's difference in time and there had been many, many changes during this period. Washington went to war immediately after becoming a Master Mason in 1753; Truman did have eight years before he entered World War I. Washington was in the forefront of building a new nation; Truman was one of the leaders in preserving what Washington and his fellow patriots had established.

Throughout the period that Truman was working for the Craft he had learned to love, he was courting the "girl with the golden curls." He was proving that when he loved it was deeply. Much of his courtship was carried out through letters to her. He didn't own an automobile and it was often inconvenient to hitch up the buggy and drive to Independence.

On June 16, 1911, he wrote: "Dear Bessie: A new Masonic Lodge is being organized at our town and they have given me the principal office. I have the big head terribly. The Deputy Grand Master was out to see us Wednesday night and handed me an awful lot of hot air. I haven't quite recovered from the effects yet."

It wasn't "hot air" the District Deputy was handing out. It was well-deserved praise. Truman had taken an immediate interest in the ritual of Masonry and he spent his waking hours studying it. His horses had to listen to him recite the lectures as he plowed his fields. At every opportunity he cornered those who could teach and would listen to his recitation.

No one is asked to be the Master of a new lodge who is unfamiliar with Masonic ritual. He should, and Truman did, know more than the ritual. He had to have leadership ability and Harry proved he had these qualities many times over.

When it came to the girl he loved, at least, he continually had an inferiority complex. On June 22, 1911, he wrote: "Say, Bessie, you'll at least let me keep on being good friends won't you? I know I am not good enough to be anything more but you don't know how I'd like to be. Maybe you think I won't wait your answer to this in suspense. Still if you turn me down, I'll not be thoroughly disappointed for it's no more than I expect.

"I have just heard that the Masonic Lodge I was telling you of is a success. There won't be two in our town. The one I belong to is in Belton six miles away. This one is in Grandview, only one mile."

For the next month Truman and several of the members of the new lodge spent as much time as possible making the building presentable. He wrote to his "friend" on July 29: "Dear Bessie: I have been working like Sam Hill on our Masonic Hall ever since I came home. We had our First Degree work last night and I conferred the first one that was put on. You see some time in the far distant future I'll be bragging about having performed that ceremony. There were about a dozen high moguls out from Kansas City and some from Belton. We had a good Ladies Aid Society time."

Being the first to confer a degree in a new lodge is certainly something to brag about. That he was able to do it with "high moguls" present speaks well of his ability.

Truman's younger brother, John Vivian, was also a Master Mason and would be the Master of Grandview Lodge in 1920. Harry told Bess about a meeting they had attended together: "Vivian and I went to the dedication of the new Masonic Temple in K.C. last night. The Grand Master and all the big guns were out. The Grand Master always wears a tall plug hat and a large gold jewel on his left breast. When he happens to be a large man he makes a very imposing figure, but a short one or a fat one is funny. The present one is tall and slim. With the high hat he looks to be about seven feet. But he's not as tall as I am when I got up against him last night. The one last year was a G.M. every inch. He was about six feet and weighed over two hundred. He also had a foghorn voice, a young-looking face, and lots of gray hair.

"They unwound yards and yards of pink tape last night and it was all very solemn. They always dedicate a Masonic Temple with corn, wine, and oil, pouring each one on with solemn invocations. This one is the finest in Missouri or most anywhere in the west. It is a York Rite Temple."

Something of his philosophy came through in a letter of October 1, 1911: "Bankers like men with overalls worn out at the knees and elbows. Uncle Harrison [Young] said there was a stranger went into the bank of Lee's Summit in the panic of 1893 and told the cashier he wanted to borrow $400 and he wanted it right away. He got the money and when the president asked the cashier why he let the man have it, he said that the man's knees and elbows were worn out through patches but the seat of his trousers was perfectly good—and he knew he'd be good for $400, and he was."

"Dear Bessie," he wrote on October 7, "I went to Lodge last night and conferred a Second Degree. It was in the New Temple and Temple Lodge, the largest Masonic Lodge in Missouri. There were only about twenty-five present though. I immediately bought a *Star* when I found I could not come over—to see if there was a Lodge meeting, because I felt not like a show after the chuckle-headed way I talked to you about not getting to come down. You can surely bet on Harry to say the wrong thing in the right place. . . .

"Corn, wine, and oil came down from King Solomon. He used them in his dedications and therefore so do we; and the Masonic fraternity does everything in form, and by ritual, that is why I said they'd unreel some pink tape."

Truman continued to keep the girl he hoped to marry informed about his Masonic activities. In his letter of November 1, 1911, he made it clear what he thought of the Fraternity: "I want an auto so badly tonight, I really don't know what to do. I have a special invitation to assist in the dedication of a new Lodge at Swope Park. I shall stay at home because I'd simply be a chunk of ice by the time I drove to 67th Street in a buggy. I couldn't go on the train because Papa and I had to pull up the carrots and beets and bury them this afternoon so they wouldn't freeze. If ever I get my debts paid and then have something left, I'm going to invest it in a benzine buggy, as the hobos say. Then I suppose I'll have the debts to pay over. Just imagine how often I'd burn the pike from here to Independence."

He never missed a meeting of his own lodge and whenever possible he visited others in the vicinity. When he didn't tell Bess in person of his adventures, he did in his frequent letters. He wasn't about to let her forget him. On December 14, 1911, he wrote: "I have been dissipating this week in Pleasant Hill. The town is wet and I really could. The Grand Lecturer of Missouri was there and Mr. Blair wanted me to go learn a lecture for him! I have a hard enough head so that when anything is pounded into it in a strong manner, it stays. That's why I got called on.

"I am very glad I was, for one of the good old brothers down there took me home with him Tuesday night and gave me quail on toast for breakfast—all I could possibly hold, with a plate full of them still on the table when I left. It was a downright shame to leave them. Even the old Lecturer himself looked at them with regret. He came over specially for breakfast. This good old brother begged me to stay Wednesday night, too, but I just had to come home. Papa says I only visit at home anyway. I am trying to make use of my time before we fire the hired men, for it'll be home for me then, sure enough. One reason why I attend these instruction Lodges is because when I visit K.C. Lodges or Independence they make it a point to call on the farmer Master to do something—and if it is bungled they say, oh well he's from the woods, it's to be expected. If it isn't, they say they won't believe I'm a farmer. I am though and I'm glad I am."

Among all of his talents, Truman was an accomplished pianist and was often asked to play for various affairs. Sometimes there were conflicts as he noted in the same letter in which he discussed his cousin who lived in Independence: "Nellie Noland called me up the other day and her voice sounded as if she were in the last stages of acute excitement. The cause was a visit from some people who had entertained her at Standardoilville. She wanted me for tomorrow night and I have a Lodge election and Third Degree that night. The people decided not to come until next week and I am very thankful. I could neither turn Nellie down nor miss the meeting. I don't know what I'd have done. Probably sent my astral body one place and my temporal the other."

With the dawn of the year 1912 Truman's Masonic activities, and courting, continued. On January 3 he wrote to Bess: "I shall have to come to Independence Saturday to swear that I have lived in Jackson County for the last five years, and if you will be home that evening I'd be most awful glad. I went to Belton from K.C. yesterday and helped them install the officers of Belton Lodge. We will do the job at Grandview on Friday. If I hadn't already lost two days this week (and I will lose another Saturday) and if it were not for that speech, I would see the same performance at Independence, but I have to stay home sometimes.

"I was Grand Marshal last night at Belton. You can see how it should be done on Thursday. I didn't do it that way. When the show was over I sneaked off to the hotel and stayed all night so I would not have to arise at an unearthly hour. Some one of the good brothers always takes me home with him when I stay in Belton. They are nearly all in business that requires their attention at an early hour. I have not had more than four hours sleep at one time since last Friday night. Therefore, the hotel."

Truman received the 4th through the 14th Degrees of the Scottish Rite, making him a member of the Lodge of Perfection, on January 24, 1912. It would be five more years before he could afford to take the other eighteen degrees. He told his pen pal all about it in a letter the following day: "The Scottish Rite has done its best to make a man of me, but they had such a grade of material to start with that they did a poor job I fear. It is the most impressive ceremony I ever saw or read of. If a man doesn't try to be better after seeing it, he has a screw loose somewhere."

At the same time he assured Bess that she had nothing to fear from him: "You shouldn't have been afraid of my getting slushy or proposing until I can urge you to come to as good a home as you have already. I don't think any man should expect a girl to go to a less comfortable home than she's used to. I'd just like to be rich for two reasons. First, to pay my debts and give Mamma a fine house to live in, and, second and greatest, I'd make love to you so hard you'd either have to say yes or knock me on the head. Still, if I thought you cared a little I'd double my efforts to amount to something and maybe would succeed. I wouldn't ask you to marry me if I didn't. Say, now, ain't I awful—I have already burned up two perfectly good sheets of stationery to keep from saying that, but this one goes."

Bess wrote Harry "one fine letter" and he answered it on January 30, 1912: "I went down to Drexel last night with Mr. [James Frank] Blair and acted as assistant district lecturer. We went down on the K.C.S. and got back at 5:50 A.M. Got four hours sleep. You ought to see me teach blockheaded Masons how to talk. (Don't ever say that to anyone, for we don't admit that there are any of the kind.) They'd have to be blockheads if I taught them. We had lots of fun. There was a big, old fat guy present who got me tickled and I lost all my high-and-mightiness in short order. We met an old fellow at the hotel who was a cow buyer and a character. He'd quarrel with anybody on any subject. He bet a dollar that Taft would be nominated and then bet two that Teddy would." Interestingly, both William Howard Taft and Theodore Roosevelt were Freemasons, and *both* were nominated.

"I have to help Mr. Blair out when it is possible for me to get away," he continued, "because he has paid my expenses a couple of times to State Lodges of Instruction. I saw his wife on the train the last time I was in town, and she said he had gone off somewhere that day. Said she guessed it was on Lodge business because he always told her where he went except when he went to Lodge."

He wrote Bess on February 27: "I am scheduled to appear in Belton this evening as assistant to the Deputy Grand Master. I am going to begin forgetting from now on. The calls are coming too thick entirely. I have to go to Freeman on Saturday, and Friday our own session comes off. That dispenses with three nights on which I receive nothing but hot air and get my hatband sprung. I am hoping that the said hatband will soon reach its greatest diameter, in which case I can stay home on at least every third evening."

"They are trying to persuade me to join a band out here," he wrote on March 12. "I think I'll draw the line though. I can stand Lodges, militia, and most anything but I guess a band is going too far."

He continued to show Bess his inferiority complex by asking her to get him out of a request to speak at a senior class affair. There were many reasons, but mainly "because the meeting is on Friday night and unless something happens to annul a Masonic meeting I'll have to stay home. If I get to go, will you honor muh with yuh company? If I don't show up by 8:00 P.M., you'll know I couldn't kill the Masonic goat and that I'm not coming."

Truman continued visiting Lodges to teach and to confer degrees. Frank Wallace, Bess' brother, caught up with him in Independence on June 30. The next day he wrote Bess, told her about the meeting, and added: "Papa says he supposes if some of the family were dying and they'd send for me to put on a degree, I'd go. Murray and also the Hon. Allen Hoyt called me up yesterday to come down and I just couldn't resist going.

"But I'd give fifty cents for a nickel's worth of sleep. I met an old man from Arkansas on the train last night who was the most interesting talker for a man that I've seen lately. I don't suppose he used the first person singular more than twice in the whole hour coming out and we talked on everything from religion to politics. He is an intense [William Jennings] Bryan man, a good Mason, and a farmer, so you see we could have a most agreeable time." Truman was a strong Bryan supporter and considered himself "one of his staunchest admirers."

Truman found that some Masons belong "in a glass cage with a plain label: the Most Exclusive Snob or Slob in America."

He told Bess on September 17, 1912: "I was in your burg last evening conferring a Third Degree. . . . Murray Colgan got his degree and of course I had to be on hand. Papa is about to hire a substitute for me. He says I am losing interest in the farm. I told him he had another guess coming, that I am only getting very thoroughly interested. I think that every month will see me stay home more, but it gets worse. What I need is a sixty-horse-power motorcar. Then I could do a day's work and run around all night."

He told her of his disappointment on November 11: "My inclination was not to work today. The Scottish Rite had one grand banquet at noon. The man who nominated W.J. Bryan in 1900 at Kansas City presided and some more distinguished members of A.A.S.R. spouted oratory. I wanted to be present so bad I almost busted. But I knew if I went today I'd never come home till Thursday evening and maybe be out some $125 and four good days' work, so I resisted the temptation and stayed home."

He made it clear that there was a lot of fun and good food to be found along with the conferring of degrees. Two automobile loads of fellows went to Belton from Grandview on April Fool's day 1913 to confer the Master Mason Degree on the son of a friend of Joe Weston. And "they sure had some spread."

The Grandview Chapter of the Order of the Eastern Star was organized in August, 1913. Harry Truman and Mrs. Nora Vanatta were chosen Worthy Patron and Worthy Matron, positions they would hold for two years. The chapter needed a piano, so in

September Grandview Lodge authorized its Master, Harry Truman, to head a committee to find such an instrument for a sum not to exceed $100. He told Bess of this adventure on September 30.

"I was in K.C. again yesterday piano shopping," he wrote. "We finally bought one from Hoffman for $125. There was a Bradbury at Olney's for $175 that was as good as new. It was surely a bargain but the tightwads out here had said we shouldn't pay over $100. I have an idea there'll be some strong, loud talk when the bill comes."

It would be interesting to know how many chapters, lodges, and appendant bodies had Truman as their pianist. In his own Eastern Star Chapter, it is said, he was often the pianist. He enjoyed playing and according to many critics, he was an accomplished musician. So was his mother and sister.

"I went to the Scottish Rite meeting last night," he wrote in the middle of November: "It was some meeting, too. There was a class of fifty-nine. I wanted to go ahead and finish up most awful but I'm not going to. Old man Thalman told me he'd lend me the money for ten years without interest if I wanted to go ahead, but I turned him down. The Scottish bodies bought $8,000 worth of new costumes this year. They are most certainly fine. A person thinks he's back in the days of the Wise King. The Eastern Star ladies served supper at six. It was a good one, too. . . . I learned another lecture last night. I can begin talking at eight o'clock and buss right straight through until 1:00 A.M. now without a break if I had to do it."

Truman wanted to go from the 14th degree to the 32nd but was still having money problems. They would increase, as would the amount of time he spent with Masonic functions.

"I've managed without any effort on my part to get this week all taken up," he wrote about November 18, 1913. "I suppose I'll have to live through it until Saturday night but you never can tell what opportunity is going to turn up for a visit to Independence. Tonight's Eastern Star; Wednesday, Ft. Peck Settlers Association; Thursday, Belton; Friday, a degree in Masonry at Lee's Summit—but thank heaven Saturday is as it should be."

Around November 25 he wrote: "About five o'clock a bunch of Masons called up and wanted to go to K.C. to Lodge. They wanted me along so they could get in. I happened to be acquainted with the big gun of the Lodge they wanted to visit. I tried to call you up but for some reason or other couldn't make connection. I guess I'll hold a Masonic Lodge of Instruction that afternoon [Sunday] or go to the Orpheum, one. I'll certainly have to do something."

Early in January, 1914, Truman, a member of the Commercial Club, was asked to audit its books. He told Bess he would never again audit books, and he disliked the club, anyway. "It doesn't please me to be tied up with a booze-selling crowd," he wrote. He tried to drop out, but the members elected him to life membership.

It was evident that not only Freemasonry was taking up his time; so were many other organizations. He told Bess of one: "I have to hold an instruction school tonight for the Woodmen. That is, I have to call it, the other boys do the instruction, because I'm not hunting learning Woodmen foolishness. My head's nearly bursting open from the strain that's been put on it by the Masons, and that's plenty for one rube."

Early in February he wrote: "I drove to Belton this morning to see Mr. Blair. It was very cold coming back, and I am shaking yet. He is going to establish a new Masonic Lodge down at Archie in Cass County and wants me to be there. It's going to be tomorrow night and I doubt very much whether I can go, but I sure want to."

Something new was added to his writing. Although Truman was constantly disparaging himself and his intelligence in letters to the girl he was still courting, he took pride in his new letterhead. Without his knowledge he had become Bureau President for Washington Township of the Jackson County Farm Bureau. He wrote: "When a person gets his own stationery and stamps furnished him he is beginning to arrive at the boodle stage. The stamps haven't been donated yet, but I have hopes. I could steal them from the Masonic Lodge but since I usually have to buy Lodge stamps myself I'd simply be in the same boat with the conductor who built himself a railroad with what failed to hang to the bell rope when he worked for the company. He became a conductor on his own railroad and knocked down so much that he broke himself up in business."

In a letter to Bess written on May 23, 1914, Truman revealed one of his ambitions: "The brass collar is going to pay our little Lodge out here a visit on Saturday evening, and since it was at his own suggestion it is a very high honor, and since it was to me he made this suggestion, and I have wanted him to stay with me I couldn't very well leave home that day without getting hopelessly in bad with the Grand Lecturer of A.F. & A.M. Therefore, and consequently I have to remain in Grandview on Saturday. The said G.L. has some strong influence with the Grand Master and I have ambitions of someday getting a start on the road to be him, and as he does the starting you can see that I don't want to lose his good opinion. Can you tell me whether it is the G.M. or G.L. I want to be? It is not *the G.L.*

"My trip to the city tomorrow has gone up in smoke. Papa is going in himself to escort our belligerent county clerk out into this neck of the woods to see the roads. I stay at home. Since I've already been gone two days and a half out of this week I can't kick much. I hope to see you Sunday evening at the usual hour. I fear the man with the brass collar will spend Sunday here and I probably can't leave until six."

Truman was finally able to buy an automobile! He called his 1910 Stafford with a brass-rimmed windshield and Prest-O-Light lamps, a "rattler." He would now be able to add "spice" about his Masonic visitations in his letters to Bess. And it would be a lot easier traveling to Independence and the Wallace home.

He was disturbed about some forms of "human nature." And he feared people were taking advantage of him because he was "an easy mark." Early in December, 1914, he told Bess: "I am going to develop a mean disposition and begin browbeating my help. It seems that the best and richest men got most of their money skinning their help and cheating ignorant people. The banker at Grandview wanted me to help him cook up a job on an old man who can't read once. That is the reason I do business with Frank Blair. His doctrine is squeeze the rich ones and give the poor man a chance. He has the biggest bank in western Missouri as a result too. He was in Grandview yesterday evening holding a Lodge of Instruction. He says every man has to have a hobby and his is Freemasonry, about as harmless a one as he could possibly have I guess. He says the only trouble he has with his hobby is his wife getting after him for being away from home so many nights."

Harry's father died during the year and the young man felt a great sense of loss. "He was an honorable man," said Truman. "If he guaranteed a horse in a horse trade that guarantee was as good as a bond. If he agreed to do a day's work for a certain amount of money he'd give good measure on the work." He expected the same from others. He taught Harry that "the expenditure of public money is a public trust and I have never changed my opinion on that subject."

With the death of his father, Harry was appointed road overseer in his place. He said he served "until the presiding judge became dissatisfied because I gave the county too much for the money." And he was appointed postmaster at Grandview. "I let a widow woman who was helping to raise and educate her younger sisters and brothers run the office as assistant postmaster and take the pay which amounted to about fifty dollars a month," said Truman.

Truman went away from home a great deal during 1915. He and a group of farmers went looking for ways to improve their farming practices. This took them to Texas, among other places. Truman kept Bess informed throughout his travels, but his fortunes didn't improve.

And from his correspondence it wasn't clear how he was progressing with his courtship. According to Miss Ethel, "Bess was the kind of a girl that the boys liked. They liked to play whatever game she liked to play. Harry wasn't any good at tennis. She was—she was really good." She also had a number of beaus. "She was a very popular girl," claimed Miss Ethel, because she did do many things well.

Actually, Harry wasn't good in sports of any kind as he readily admitted. His eyesight prevented any athletic accomplishments, yet he had other attributes that kept the "girl with the golden curls" interested in him.

Harry was blunt and to the point with everything he did. He "wasn't a person to put up a good front," said Miss Ethel. "His mother was that way. She never tried to impress people." But his mother played the piano well and children loved her, calling her "Aunt Mat" in place of Mary Ellen.

Miss Ethel was convinced "there never was but one girl in the world for Harry Truman, from the first time he saw her at the Presbyterian kindergarten. If he hadn't married Bess he never would have married at all."

"The Masonic Lodge was one enthusiasm that he has had that's been a life-long one," Miss Ethel continued, "and the Masonic Lodge has made him very well known."

The early years of Truman's career were indeed full. He had learned the ritual of the Craft thoroughly and had spent many hours teaching it to others. He had found many friends, especially Frank Blair, a District Deputy Grand Master he respected. His father had died in 1914 and the running of the farm fell mainly on his shoulders. He had become involved, in a small way, in politics.

He determined, however, at least for the moment, to make his fortune in other areas.

3. LEAD, ZINC AND OIL

Late in 1915 Harry met a fellow named Jerry Culbertson through Tom Hughes, one of his neighbors. Hughes knew Culbertson because he had been prosecuting attorney of Cass County at the same time Hughes had been sheriff. The former county employees had invested in several gold mines, none of which panned out.

Truman took over a lead and zinc mine in Oklahoma early in 1916. It was rough, dirty work. His letters to Bess revealed many of his problems with the T.C.H. Mining Co. The problems mounted to the point he had to ask his Masonic friend, Frank Blair, for help. This is evident in his letter to Bess written on May 26, 1916:

"I have been home since I wrote you, but had no chance to call up or see you. The T.C.H. Mining Co. is on its feet again. You would never guess who did it either. Mr. Frank Blair. I just couldn't see the thing go clean to pieces without some effort to save it. Jerry quit us cold and I was so discouraged I didn't know what to do. (As you well know.) Jerry assigned me his right title and interest in the concern and I went to Blair with my tale of woe. He told me I deserved to lose the whole shebang. Said I deserved a bump for going in with Culbertson. He knows him well. He finally said that if Culbertson assigned me his rights until I got my money back, he'd help. I called Culbertson and he agreed. I have paid all debts today, fired the sheriff, and we go right off the reel Monday. I tied up the superintendent's bill so he can't possibly collect before October. I am hoping he won't collect at all. If he was worth anything we'd sue him and get something back. He was the whole cause of our trouble."

His assistant was a "red-haired hoisting engineer by the name of Bill Throop. Bill was all wool and a yard wide but we couldn't make our mine pay. He asked me to raise $2,500 and buy a drilling machine and go up north of Pitcher, Oklahoma, and prospect the land up there for lead and zinc." Later Truman wrote: "I'd already put all my ready money into the Commerce mine and couldn't raise the $2,500. If I'd done it we'd both be rolling in wealth today."

And there were problems with the farm in Grandview. Men quit and his sister, Mary, had to fire others. Truman left the mine and rushed to the farm. In June he wrote Bess: "I'm thinking things will go hang down in Commerce. I'm not going to worry over it. It is necessary to save wheat, oats, and clover now. I am going to do it."

The mine was on its last legs, but Truman wasn't. He went into the oil business. Oil had become a big thing in the country and Missouri was no exception. Extensive test drilling was being done all over. So, Truman decided to team up with David H. Morgan, a man who would become a life-long friend. Morgan was a businessman with a law degree who had considerable experience in the oil business.

With a $5,000 investment, obtained from notes endorsed by his mother, Truman became a one-third partner in the Atlas-Okla Oil Lands Syndicate. This also made him secretary-treasurer of Morgan & Company, Oil Investments. He took pride in writing to Bess on November 16, 1916, on his new letterhead:

"I seem to have a grand and admirable ability for calling tails when heads come up. My luck should surely change. Sometimes I should win. I have tried to stick. Worked, really did, like thunder for ten years to get that old farm in line for some big production. Have it in shape and have had a crop failure every year. Thought I'd change my luck. Got a mine, and see what I did get. Tried again in the other long chance, oil. Still have high hopes on that, but then I'm naturally a hopeful, happy person."

The other third of the partnership was the same Jerry C. Culbertson, then a Kansas City attorney. His promotional plans called for revamping the organization. As a result the name was changed to the Morgan Oil & Refining Company, and assets of the old company were transferred to the new one.

Thousands of acres were leased by the company in Oklahoma, Kansas, Texas and Louisiana. Several test wells were dug—all dry. Others were being drilled when the war clouds that had been on the horizon since 1914 darkened.

Truman later recalled: "At the time the war came we had a well down nine hundred feet on a 320-acre lease at Eureka, Kansas. I got all patriotic and joined the army. My partners got into a fuss and let that lease go to pot. Another company took it over

Harry S. Truman during his oil well days.

[Truman Library photo]

and drilled a well on it and there was never a dry hole found on that 320 acres. It was the famous Teter Pool. If I'd stayed home and run my oil company I'd have been a millionaire. But I always did let ethics beat me out of money and I suppose I always will."

The arrogance of German leadership that began with the assassination of the crown prince of Austria in 1914 continually reached into America. The isolationists and those wanting to aid the allies were constantly at odds. President Woodrow Wilson remained neutral and pleased no one. Yet, Wilson hated the Mexican leadership and ordered American troops to blockade Mexico's coast and borders.

The sinking of the *Lusitania* in 1915 did not change Wilson's stance, although it appeared the majority of Americans wanted something done about Germany's arrogance. Many American flyers went to France and joined the Lafayette Escadrille.

Wilson won reelection to the Presidency under the slogan "He Kept Us Out of War." But when the German high command blockaded England in January 1917, Wilson severed diplomatic relations with Germany. The U-boats would put American troops in European trenches.

The country geared for war. Manpower shortages struck immediately. This affected Truman and his partners and leases were given up. Other companies took over and oil was struck in one of the sections Truman's company had started drilling in Kansas. He had again called "tails" and "heads" came up.

America's entry into the war in Europe changed the life of everyone. Lieutenant Harry S. Truman was no exception. The years of his youthful struggles reached an end. A new era began.

4. IN THE ARMY

British naval intelligence was able to decipher German codes early in the war. This helped bring President Woodrow Wilson to the Capitol to talk to a joint session of Congress on April 2, 1917. In a telegram sent by Kaiser Wilhelm to his ambassador, Arthur Zimmermann, the German foreign secretary in the United States, the global plans of the German government were made clear:

"WE INTEND TO BEGIN UNRESTRICTED SUBMARINE WARFARE. WE SHALL ENDEAVOR TO KEEP THE UNITED STATES NEUTRAL. IN THE EVENT OF THIS NOT SUCCEEDING, WE MAKE MEXICO A PROPOSAL OF ALLIANCE ON THE FOLLOWING BASIS: MAKE WAR TOGETHER, MAKE PEACE TOGETHER, GENEROUS FINANCIAL SUPPORT, AND AN UNDERSTANDING ON OUR PART THAT MEXICO IS TO RECONQUER THE LOST TERRITORY IN TEXAS, NEW MEXICO AND ARIZONA."

Most of the small contingent of American army troops and a few national guard units were then in, or on, the border of Mexico. When Wilson read the message decoded by British intelligence, he was shocked. It was then he knew he had to find a conclusive reason to enter the war on the side of the Allies. It came with the blockade of England and the threat of unrestricted sinking of shipping by German U-boats.

A cheering Congress agreed with President Wilson. Preparations for war were stepped up immediately. Thanks to the Mason, Theodore Roosevelt, the navy was a fighting force to be reckoned with. But thanks to the isolationists, an army of a mere 127,000 had to be dramatically increased. This called for a draft. It also called for everyone in the country to roll up his and her sleeves and turn a sleeping giant into a fighting war machine.

All over the country the National Guard was expanded. Missouri was no exception. Battery B in Kansas City and Battery C in Independence were enlarged into a regiment. Truman helped with the expansion that became six batteries, with supply and headquarters companies. He was elected a first lieutenant in Battery F on May 22, 1917.

In the meantime, however, Truman had been able to complete his journey to the thirty-second degree in the Scottish Rite. It took place on March 31, 1917, in Kansas City, Orient of Missouri. Two days later he was created a noble in Ararat Temple in Kansas City. He was now a Scottish Rite Mason and a Shriner.

From Kansas City in July, 1917, Truman wrote to Bess after he had returned from the Regimental Banquet, which was "a very solemn affair." The colonel had presented the men their commissions from the governor, and Truman told her he was going to give her his commission to keep "because someday it may be very valuable to someone." He then added: "I have felt like a dog all week. It seems that I have caused you to be unhappy by my enthusiastic action in getting myself sent to war. Two big tears came in Mamma's eyes last night when I started off to Lodge in my soldier clothes. You are the two people in the world that I would rather see smile and that I like to cause to smile, and here I've gone done the opposite to both of you." They all knew that Truman did not have to go to war; his bad eyesight could have kept him home, and honorably.

In another letter he wrote: "Bess, I'm dead crazy to ask you to marry me before I leave but I'm not going to because I don't think it would be right for me to ask you to tie yourself to a prospective cripple—or a sentiment." Later he added: "If you don't marry me before I go, you may be sure that I'll be just as loyal to you as if you were my wife."

At the camp near Lawton, Oklahoma, Truman was placed in charge of a makeshift canteen. These became common throughout the army, but few were in any way profitable. His was one of these.

He went into Oklahoma City to purchase supplies on September 30, 1917, and from the Lee-Huckins Hotel wrote to Bess of his adventures in the canteen business, as he would do in letters that followed. He accepted that job with the enthusiasm he tackled everything he did.

His colonel appointed him the regimental canteen officer and he brought in Sergeant Eddie Jacobson to assist him. Theirs was the only canteen to make money. Perhaps one of the reasons was because they sewed up the pockets of the clerks who were ordered to work in the canteen on a "voluntary" basis.

Truman was alarmed with the "bunch of stay-at-home plutocrats" who increased their prices for laundry by forty percent. "When a man does a day's work drilling he doesn't feel like doing a night's washing," he wrote. He was angry with the Coca Cola bottling works for refusing to sell him more than fifty cases at a time.

The canteen business continued to flourish; among his other duties, Truman branded horses, and drilled continuously. He reported the food was excellent. But several times the wind blew and the dust storms were so horrible it was almost impossible to see a horse from one end of it to the other. Even the extra-special apple dumpling the cook brought him on one of these occasions was gritty.

He finally received the picture of Bess he had been pleading for, and raved about how swelled up he got when the fellows remarked about "what a beautiful girl I have on my desk." The picture would accompany him all through France and into the White House. Today it will be found on his working desk in the Truman Library. He let her know he was happy to have his mother and Mary with him, but how disappointed he was because she couldn't be with them in Lawton for Christmas.

With the new year of 1918 came blizzards and continuing rumors of going overseas. He wrote Bess: "I wouldn't be left out of the greatest history-making epoch the world has ever seen for all there is to live for because there'd be nothing to live for under German control. When we come home a victorious army we can hold our heads up in the greatest old country on earth and make up for lost time by really living."

Early in February, 1918, Truman was able to obtain a pass and go to Oklahoma City where the "Scottish Rite are putting a class through." Later Truman added in his regular letter to Bess: "They put on all the Scottish Rite in as grand a form as I ever saw it from beginning to end. The Temple is fine and well arranged. They have a pipe organ and an organist that can play as well as Kreisler I think. They fed us three meals a day that would make [Herbert] Hoover blow up if he'd see them, and at the end they gave a dance, last night, and would let no one but soldiers dance. Then's when I wished I was a dancer."

Late in February Truman went before "an examining board not for efficiency but for promotion." He didn't expect to pass, and wouldn't learn that he had until he read about it in a newspaper while in France. He did write in March, though: "I got an underground intimation that I passed my captain's examination all right. I don't believe it though until I see the evidence from Washington."

Disaster for him almost struck. Right after the meeting with the board he was almost discharged. The doctor "turned my eyes down twice," he wrote, "and threatened to send me to division headquarters for a special examination and then didn't. I guess I can put on a real good conversation when circumstances demand it."

In a letter written early in March Truman continued to show his sense of humor had not left him. "To tell you the honest truth," he said, "I'd rather be a first lieutenant than anything else in the army except a buck private in the rear rank. He's the guy that has no responsibility and he's the guy that does the real work. I heard a good one the other day which said that a lieutenant knows nothing and does everything, a captain knows everything and does nothing, a major knows nothing and does nothing. Very true except a captain has to know everything from sealing wax to sewing machines and has to run them. He also is responsible for about $750,000 worth of material and 193 men, their lives, their morals, their clothes, and their horses, which isn't much for $200 a month and pay your own expenses."

Although there is no record of it, it is certain that Truman attended as many Masonic functions as possible while in camp. A letter to Bess indicates this:

"I have made Masons out of both Colonel [Karl D.] Klemm and Colonel [Robert M.] Danford since we've been here, so I guess maybe that helps my *drag* somewhat, although it's not supposed to. General [Lucien G.] Berry is one and I am going to help make General [Chandler] Wright one next Wednesday if he shows up as expected and I'm still here. That's one thing I've studied in the last years that has done me more good than anything, except artillery study."

Bess received a telegram on March 20 saying: "We are moving today. Your package came all right and was very fine. Will write from train." He did. And by a stroke of luck the train stopped at Rosedale, Kansas. He asked a switchman if he could use his telephone to call "my fiancee in Independence." The fellow said: "Call her. The phone's yours. But if she doesn't break the engagement at four o'clock in the morning, she really loves you." She wasn't angry, Truman reported. Then he called his mother and sister.

This is the first indication that Harry and Bess were engaged to be married. Even so, later letters gave evidence he still wasn't too sure their marriage would ever take place.

While at Camp Merritt in New Jersey Truman was able to visit New York City. There he "saw the rottenest vaudeville show" he had ever seen. "It couldn't even play at the Globe and get by in Kansas City. New York is a very much overrated burg. It merely keeps its rep by its press agents' continually harping on the wonder of it."

He bought his sixth pair of glasses from "an honest optician in New York City" who happened to be a Freemason and also belonged to the Scottish Rite. He was amazed at how well he was treated and how much less it cost him for frames and glasses than it had back home. But he still had little good to say about the city or its inhabitants. "When a New Yorker shows you the Woolworth Building or Senator Clark's house or Grant's Tomb or the Hudson River he expects you to fall dead with admiration, and if you don't he's confident your education has been overlooked."

Truman's regiment boarded the *U.S.S. George Washington* on March 30, 1918, for the trip to France, and arrived at Brest on April 13. On his last night aboard ship he wrote Bess: "The sunsets on the sea aren't half as good to see as those on our prairies at home. You see as far as the rim, which they tell me is twenty miles away. The funny part of it is we never catch up with that rim. If we could only get over it I'm sure we could go twice as fast because it would be downhill. One fellow remarked to me the other night that according to his map of the Atlantic Ocean we'd have to pull it from here to France because it would be uphill all the way. Some of the things the crew pull off are a caution to hear. Most of the best ones are unprintable but are not so bad as humorous when you hear them."

His next letter was written from a cold room in the Hotel *des Voygeurs* "Somewhere in France" on April 14, 1918. "Wine and beer are sold here, and most of the 35th Division have been in Oklahoma so long that they are trying to drink all there is here. They can't as the supply seems to be inexhaustible. Prices are marked strictly on the American plan in French money and they skin us alive. Our dinners cost us 10 francs apiece, about $1.80, so you see things are not so cheap." He signed this letter, "Yours always, Harry S. Truman, 1st Lt. 129th F.A. Det. 35th Division, A.E.F."

In his letter on the 17th he told her he had seen a Douglas Fairbanks motion picture, and "it sure was some satisfaction too I tell you. I sure do get tired of *Oui, Oui Monsieur* and *Cinq Francs, Merci Monsieur*. All I can say is *je ne comprend pas,* and I'm not sure of that."

He spent most of the month of May going to school and touring the French countryside "at the expense of the American government." On June 14 he wrote: "I am back with the regiment and a sure enough captain. Have been, it seems, some six weeks. I'll have about a bushel and a half of francs back pay coming next payday. . . . I am the adjutant of the Second Battalion, 129th F.A. A right hefty job and one that gives me precedence over all the Battery captains, even if they do out rank me. I've got to organize a regimental school and teach the balance of the officers what I learned (which won't be a whole lot)." He would later call himself "the regimental schoolteacher." Thirty days later he was made a battery commander. It was a battery composed mainly of Irish and German Catholics from Rockhurst Academy in Kansas City, Missouri. "But," he wrote, "they seem to like me pretty well and I am satisfied that, if I don't blow up with too many worries, I'll have a good Battery. I hope the best in the brigade."

What Truman didn't tell her was that these men had destroyed the careers of four former commanding officers. "I wasn't a Catholic," he later wrote, "I was a thirty-second degree [Scottish Rite] Mason. I could see my hide on the fence when I tried to run that outfit."

Although he said he was badly frightened when he took over the battery the next morning, they got along fine. And he continued to be proud of his men. "They gave me a Battery that was always in trouble and in bad, but we carried off all the credits this week," he wrote to Bess. "The men are as fine a bunch as were ever gotten together but they have been lax in discipline. Can you imagine me a hard-boiled captain of a tough Irish Battery?"

On September 1 Truman told Bess of his first fight. His battery fired 500 rounds at the Germans in thirty-six minutes. When the enemy returned the fire, his first sergeant and a few of his drivers ran away, "but my Irishmen stayed with me." The following night he returned with some of his men to retrieve the guns that were stuck in the mud. He added: "My greatest satisfaction is that my legs didn't succeed in carrying me away, although they were very anxious to do it. Both of my lieutenants are all wool and a yard wide."

He didn't tell Bess the whole story. In his *Harry S. Truman: A Pictorial Biography*, Joseph Gies records an account by a former Kansas blacksmith named Paul Shaffer who told the full story in *The Doughboys*. Shaffer had to take a message to the Truman battery. When he reached it Captain Truman "was standing there, his tin hat pushed on the back of his head, directing salvos into some spot toward the northeast. He was a banty officer in spectacles, and when he read my message he started runnin' and cussin' all at the same time, shouting for the guns to turn northwest. He ran about a hundred yards to a little knoll, and what he saw didn't need binoculars. I never heard a man cuss so well or so intelligently and I'd shoed a million mules. He was shouting back ranges and giving bearings.

"The battery didn't say a word. They must have figured the cap'n could do the cussin' for the whole outfit. It was a great sight, like the center ring in Barnum and Bailey at the close of the show, everything clockwork."

Truman ran to another area and found a "clump of woods, pretty leaves still in the autumn breeze." But behind the innocent looking scene the captain discovered a mass of Germans advancing stealthily with machine guns. "He shouted some cuss words filled with figures down to the battery, and shells started breaking into the enemy clumps." The German attack was broken up.

The blacksmith said he "never saw the cussin' captain again until I voted for him in 1948."

Two weeks later Truman continued bragging about his battery. "They win every competition they enter, yet the colonel gives us hell every chance he gets. He says that is what he is for and I guess it is. There is no other need of him that I can see. He likes me pretty well though and I get along fine with him."

It was two weeks before he got another chance to write, because he was involved in the battles of the Meuse-Argonne which started on September 26. "I shot out a German Battery," he wrote to Bess on October 6, "shot up his big observation post, and ruined another Battery when it was moving down the road. My excellent Second Lieutenant [Leslie M.] Zemer and myself were in the front of the infantry lines while I was doing it, and I saw tanks take towns and everything else that there is to see. I brought my Battery forward under fire and never lost a horse nor a man. Had shells fall on all sides and I am as sure as I am sitting here that the Lord was and is with me. I'm not yet dizzy although one or two men in the regiment are." He asked Bess to go to New York when he returned so they could get married in "the Little Church Around the Corner."

Two days later he explained one of the reasons why he had not written as often as he would have liked: "There were some three or four weeks from September 10 to October 6 that I did nothing but march at night and shoot or sleep in daylight." He said the air force got more credit than it deserved and its men are "dubbed the heroes of the war." He cautioned: "Don't you believe it, the infantry—our infantry—are the heroes of the war. There's nothing—machine guns, artillery, rifles, bayonets, mines, or anything else—that can stop them when they start. If we could keep up with them, they'd go to the Rhine in one swoop."

From the Verdun front Truman wrote again on October 30: "We sit around these Battery positions and wait for something to shoot at and make maps and do so many things that are necessary and a lot that are not that I sometimes don't know straight up from crossways." He had learned what all servicemen learn: you hurry up and wait.

On the 31st a German plane was shot down close to Truman's Battery. The next day he told Bess that when the German lieutenant stepped out of the wrecked plane, he put his hands in the air and shouted "*La guerre fini.*" "He then remarked," said Truman, "that the war would be over in ten days. I don't know what he knew about it or what anyone else knows but I am sure that most Americans will be glad when it's over and they can get back to God's country again." The German proved remarkably prophetic!

"I got a letter of Commendation, capital C, from the commanding general of the 35th Division," wrote Truman. "The ordnance repair department made a report to him that I had the best-conditioned guns after the drive that he had seen in France. The general wrote me a letter about it. My chief mechanic is to blame, not me. He knows more about guns than the French themselves. As usual, in such cases, the C.O. gets the credit. I think I shall put an endorsement on the letter stating the ability of my chief mechanic and stick it in the files anyway. I am going to keep the original letter for my own personal and private use. It will be nice to have someday if some low-browed north-end politician tries to remark that I wasn't in the war when I'm running for easter judge or something. I'll have the 'papers' and can shut him up."

It wasn't only the guns that Truman kept in good condition. One of his fellow officers was amazed at how Truman always looked neat and clean. "Dirt and cooties didn't seem to stick to him the way they did to the rest of us," the officer said. Even after weeks in the same clothes he still looked immaculate. "Moreover," he continued, "he was clean-shaven. He must have shaved with coffee, because we didn't have plain hot water."

Truman sent Bess a Christmas present of two bronze vases which he told her were "made from German 77 shell cases by a Frenchman here on the front." He also told her about a statement he read while censoring letters that nearly caused him to blow up. One of his best sergeants "said that he and the Battery had been in some very tight places and came out all right but that they had a captain that could take them to h-l and bring them all back."

On November 10 he told Bess about his censoring duties again: "I have been censoring letters today and it is some job. I had no idea that there were so many accomplished liars in any organization on earth as I have in mine. They are eternally trying to get by the censor with some big tale of their heroism and accomplishments in this war and they do it too, sometimes, especially if they put in something nice about their commanding officer and the part he took in the tale. Usually I have to tear 'em up or send them back when they tell too much or stretch the truth even beyond literary license." He also mentioned he had been hearing rumors that "the Hun is yelling for peace like a stuck hog."

November 11, 1918, Truman wrote: "I just got official notice that hostilities would cease at eleven o'clock. I knew that Germany could not stand the gaff. For all their preparedness and swashbuckling talk they cannot stand adversity."

The night of November 11-12, 1918, was hectic. Truman said the French troops became intoxicated when they appropriated a load of wine. Although he didn't mention the American troops partaking of the beverage they certainly wouldn't let such an opportunity get away. He said: "Every single one of them had to march by my bed and salute and yell, 'Vive President Wilson, Vive le capitaine d'artillerie americaine!' No sleep all night, the infantry fired Very pistols, sent up all the flares they could lay their hands on, fired rifles, pistols and whatever else would make noise, all night long."

Truman received a letter from Bess in which she was concerned because it was written with red ink. He told her: "A letter from you written with charcoal, chalk, or clay would be fine enough to send me into the seventh heaven." He still remembered his Masonic lectures.

With the end of the war Truman was able to go to Paris, Marseilles and Nice. He wrote an enthusiastic letter to Bess from the latter place. France had impressed him with its beauty where the barbaric hands of war hadn't reached. A couple of days later he was in Monte Carlo and two days from then he would "have to go back into slavery," he said, "and I'd rather be shot."

Returning to Verdun, Truman, along with the other National Guard officers, was offered an opportunity to enlist as regular army, reservists, or accept a complete discharge. "I naturally took the last event," he wrote. "I don't expect to go into anything where I can't say what I please when I please. Anyhow the emergency is over and I am ready to be a producer instead of a leach."

In most of his letters to Bess he continued to tell her of his desire for her hand in marriage. The letter he wrote from Camp La Baholle on December 14, 1918, was no different except it went into greater detail. "I've come to the conclusion," he said, "that it's not intended for me ever to be very rich, nor very poor, and I am about convinced that that will be about the happiest state a man can be. To have the finest girl in all the whole world (and to make that statement without fear of contradiction) to share my joys and troubles, mostly joys I'm hoping, to have just enough of the world's goods to make it pleasant to try for more, to own a Ford and tour the U.S.A. and France perhaps, although I've nearly promised old Miss Liberty that she'll have to turn around to see me again, and still have a nice little country home to be comfortable in—well that's really not a hard fortune to contemplate. Maybe have a little politics and some nice little dinner parties occasionally just for good measure. How does it sound to you?"

Several times he mentioned that he would like to "be on the Military Affairs Committee of the House," since he had found many things about the army he wanted to change. He wouldn't make it to the "House" but he did make it to the Senate.

Truman couldn't understand why any man would want to be in the army in peace time. "You've always got some old fossil above you whose slightest whim is law, and who generally hasn't a grain of horse sense. For my part I want to be where I can cuss 'em all I please when I please, and you can bet there are some in this man's army who are going to get cussed and more if they fool around me when I get out."

He told Bess on January 11, 1919, that a couple of his boys had fallen asleep on guard duty. Rather than "going before a summary court" they agreed to accept any punishment Truman would give them. "One of 'em is one of my Bobby's, too, and another is a nephew of the present Grand Matron of Missouri," he wrote. "The better I like 'em, the meaner I have to be to them just to show 'em that I'm impartial. You've no idea how I hate to call a man down. I'd almost rather take a beating than tell a man how good for nothing he is when he's done something he shouldn't."

Truman said he knew he was on the way home in his letter of February 18—General John J. Pershing, a Brother Mason, shook hands with him and told him so.

The happy day arrived! From Camp Mills, New York, he telegraphed: "Arrived in Camp Mills Easter afternoon. Have been eating pie and ice cream ever since. Wire me here usual address. I hope to be in Funston soon. New York gave us a grand welcome. God's country sure looks good. Harry."

His last telegram as a soldier was sent from Oklahoma at the end of May: "Expect to see you out home tomorrow." His next military service would be as Commander-in-Chief. But much would happen before that came to pass.

Manhood

Thus he shewed me: and, behold, the Lord stood upon a wall made by a plumbline, with a plumbline in his hand.

And the Lord said unto me, Amos, what seest thou? And I said, A plumbline. Then said the Lord, Behold, I will set a plumbline in the midst of my people Israel: I will not again pass by them anymore.

Amos, 7:7-8

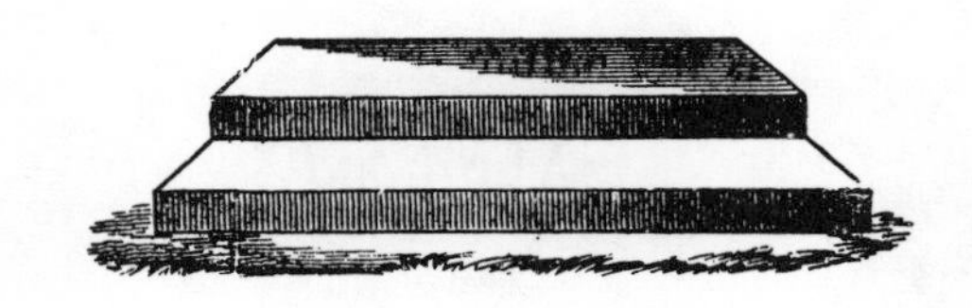

5. PRESIDING JUDGE

Bess Wallace didn't meet Harry in New York to be married in the Little Church Around the Corner, but she did meet him in Independence, Missouri. There, on June 28, 1919, the long, long courtship came to an end. They were married in Trinity Episcopal Church, and after a brief honeymoon they returned to live with her mother at 219 North Delaware Street in Independence.

Moving in with Mrs. Wallace was probably the thing to do because she needed her daughter. Then, too, Miss Ethel said that Harry's mother-in-law "liked him; she always liked him, and she favored the match from the very start. In fact, we weren't sure whether she liked him better than Bess did or not."

The Mason from Missouri lost no time getting back into the mainstream of Freemasonry. While serving his country overseas he missed the fellowship found in Masonic lodges. There was no Masonic activity for the Americans in France. This is something he would note, and help correct, twenty years later. So, soon after his return he started taking the degrees of Royal Arch Masonry, completing them and becoming a Royal Arch Mason in Orient Chapter No. 102, Kansas City, on November 19, 1919.

Truman went into business with Edward "Eddie" Jacobson, his former canteen sergeant. Their men's clothing store was opened in Kansas City in November, 1919. Truman sold equipment and stock from his farm and invested the proceeds in the haberdashery. This, along with their savings, gave them a fairly substantial business.

A month later, on December 19, 1919, Truman completed the degrees of Cryptic Masonry and became a Royal and Select Master in Shekinah Council No. 24, Kansas City.

For the first two years sales and profits in the haberdashery went well. The partners were satisfied with the business, so much so they refused an offer to sell. Then came deflation. Farm prices dropped, interest rates increased, and thousands of businesses were lost. Among them was the Truman-Jacobson haberdashery. This would come back to haunt Truman over and over again for the rest of his life. He continually had to prove that he did not enter bankruptcy, but it did cost him the loss of his farm.

It was about this time that Rufus Burrus, a precinct worker for the Democrats who would become a life-long friend and attorney of Truman, was introduced to him. Burrus met Frank Wallace, Mrs. Truman's brother, as he came out of a drug store with Truman. "Frank introduced me to Harry," said Burrus, "and he said Truman was going to be the next judge of Jackson county court. I told Harry that if Frank said so, he would be elected, because Frank always picks winners."

Burrus said he had known of Truman for years: "My grandfather's family lived next door to the Truman's when they lived on the corner of River Boulevard. My aunts were about his age. Then I lived on Delaware Street, just a block north of where his home is. That's where my father lived, and I carried a precinct book for the Democrats because Frank Wallace asked me to."

In 1922 the store closed and Truman accepted Frank's invitation to enter politics. One of the men with whom he had served in the army, James Pendergast, remembered Truman mentioning he just might be interested in entering politics. According to Burrus, Frank told James about his conversation with Truman, and James told his father, Mike Pendergast. Together they went to see Tom Pendergast, the political boss of Jackson County, and then to the Truman-Jacobson store to ask Truman to run for county judge. The elder Pendergast was impressed with Truman, mainly because he had been a captain "whose men didn't want to shoot him." Because of business reverses Truman agreed to run. And he won.

"In all the time Truman was connected with Tom Pendergast, Pendergast never asked Truman to do anything for him," said Burrus. "And I know that for a fact!"

Truman had settled down to a domestic life and stayed close to home except for yearly trips to the army reserves summer camp (he had been promoted to the rank of major; later he would become a full colonel). His attendance at Masonic Lodges didn't take him away from home for any length of time. He still saw many of his war-time buddies at American Legion conventions and meetings.

He completed the degrees in what is known as the "York Rite of Freemasonry" by becoming a Knight Templar in Palestine Commandery No. 17, Independence, on June 15, 1923. Having received his thirty-second Scottish Rite degree before he went to France, he had now completed the Masonic journey through both Rites. He had also become a member of Ararat Temple, Ancient Arabic Order of Nobles of the Mystic Shrine, on April 2, 1917. As with everything he attempted, he threw himself wholeheartedly into the various Masonic activities in the state.

Just as enthusiastically, he tackled the job to which he had been elected. He had much to learn, which was nothing new for him. Libraries had become his friend and studying had become second nature to him. But there were other aspects of the job to consider. Although there was graft and corruption all around him, he did not let it touch him. In later years all but his severest critics had to admit this was true.

The judges of Missouri county courts are administrators rather than magistrates. These courts levy taxes and authorize expenditures for state institutions and projects. Truman was familiar with these administrative affairs and with local politics. His father had been overseer in Washington Township, and when

Harry S. Truman, second from right, is sworn in as judge of the county court of Jackson County, Missouri.

[Truman Library photo]

he died in 1914 Harry succeeded him. He had been postmaster for Grandview before the war, and had been a Democratic clerk for every election since 1906.

"I became completely familiar with every road and bridge in the county," said Truman. "I visited every state institution in which the county had patients." He took his job seriously, but even so, he was defeated for reelection in 1924, the only political election he ever would lose.

On February 17, 1924, the second greatest event of his life occurred (the first was his marriage to Bess). His daughter Margaret was born. His life would never be the same again. He seldom wrote a letter to Bess without mentioning "my baby," or "young lady" and later "Margie." Eventually he added postscripts to his letters for his daughter.

In that same year the 22nd Masonic District which comprised Jackson County was divided. On the death of the District Deputy Grand Master for the newly created 59th district, Truman was appointed to that office. He was also given another office because of his proficiency in the ritual—District Lecturer. It is rare, indeed, for one man to serve in both capacities at the same time, but Truman held them until he was appointed to the Grand Lodge line.

"The Democrats who were in office after Truman was defeated didn't run the county as they should have," said Burrus. "So, Truman was asked to run for presiding judge. After he was elected in 1926 he asked me to meet him for lunch one day. He asked me to be the assistant counselor and keep things straight."

About this time Rufus Burrus received his first two degrees in Masonry. When Truman learned about this he went to the lodge the night Burrus was to receive the Master Mason degree. "He was the district deputy grand master, and when he told the Master he wanted to raise me, the Master, who had planned on doing it himself, said 'Yes, Sir.' So, Harry raised me."

Grand Master William W. Martin wrote to Truman on February 24, 1926. He had a particularly sensitive affair he wanted his District Deputy Grand Master to look into. A Mason had been tried by Mount Washington Lodge and did not like the verdict, so he appealed. The secretary of the lodge told him he had no appeal coming and the lodge reported nothing to the Grand Master or the District Deputy.

Truman investigated and reported: "I have looked into the facts in the appeal referred to and the attached correspondence and find that all the papers in the appeal were in the hands of the attorney for the Lodge at the last Grand Lodge meeting, and he failed to appear at the meeting because of his affairs being in such shape he couldn't leave.

"I have instructed the secretary to forward the papers to the Grand Secretary for reference to the Appeals and Grievances Committee. Hoping this will meet your approval." It did, and eventually the verdict of the lodge was overturned.

Truman found the county had a huge debt, and the roads and public buildings were in horrible shape. So he traveled to Chicago and St. Louis to talk to bankers about borrowing money for improvements and to pay off the debt. The county had been paying six percent interest to local banks, and when Truman talked to them about reducing the rates, they angrily refused. Truman succeeded in obtaining four percent loans from bankers in other counties and states. Later he was able to cut this to two percent.

He also took action that was not typically political; he cut the number of county employees! When the voters approved two bond issues, Truman was able to see that a new courthouse, hospital, and county home were erected. The courthouse at Independence was remodeled. "All these projects were successfully carried out," Truman said, "and without one breath of scandal, while I was presiding judge."

The connection of Truman with the Pendergast "machine" would be continually brought up by his political opponents. To set the record straight, Truman wrote in his *Memoirs*:

> Although I was to become very well acquainted with Tom Pendergast, I barely knew him when I was first elected presiding judge of the Jackson County Court. He was a power in local politics, of course, and when the bond issues for Kansas City were up for consideration I went to see him. I told him I would like very much to issue bonds for the rehabilitation of our roads in the county and for some new public buildings. A new courthouse was needed for Kansas City, and the courthouse in Independence required remodeling. A hospital was badly needed at the county home. Pendergast replied by saying that there was no possibility of the county supporting such a bond issue—that the same idea had been turned

down on two previous occasions in the last ten years. I argued, however, that if I could tell the taxpayers just how I would handle their money I was sure it would carry. My confidence was justified, too. The bonds for the county were carried with a three-fourths majority, which was much better than the city bonds did, some of which had not been carried at all.

When the first contracts were to be let, I got a telephone call from Tom Pendergast saying that he and some of his friends were very anxious to see me about those contracts. I knew very well what was in the wind, but I went to their meeting. I told them that I expected to let the contracts to the lowest bidders, just as I had promised the taxpayers I would do, and that I was setting up a bipartisan board of engineers to see that specifications were carried out according to contract, or else the public would not pay for them.

Pendergast turned to the contractors and said, "I told you he's the contrariest man in the state of Missouri." When the contractors had left, he said, "You carry out the agreement you made with the people of Jackson County." And I never heard anything from him again.

Judge Harry S. Truman signing county checks with multiple machine.
[Kansas City Journal Post photo]

All of Truman's projects were carried out successfully, and without a touch of scandal. When he ran for reelection in 1930 the voters elected him by an overwhelming majority.

His work as presiding judge and his enthusiasm as a Freemason did not go unnoticed by the leadership of the Grand Lodge of Missouri. During the Grand Lodge session in 1930, incoming Grand Master William R. Gentry had to make an appointment to the bottom of the line of officers. As most men in his situation do, he called together the officers who would immediately follow him to help him make a determination. Several names were considered, but one stood out.

It was noted that one Harry S. Truman was ritually perfect and had served continuously as a lecturer. He was twice a past master and had been instrumental in chartering a new lodge. In between serving as its master, he had been its secretary. He had served as a District Deputy Grand Master for over three years. He was active in all branches of Masonry, and had been from the beginning of his Masonic career. He had learned the ritual early and from those early days he had worked with and for several Grand Masters. This had started with Frank Blair eighteen years ago.

A large plus was the popularity of Bess Truman and her support for her husband throughout his Masonic career. She knew the benefits men found in Freemasonry because her father had been Grand Commander of the Grand Commandery in 1892.

There could have been one stumbling block: Truman was a Democrat; the leaders were Republicans. Ray V. Denslow, who was following Gentry, reminded them that politics was a forbidden subject within the walls of lodges and Grand Lodges. At any rate, Truman's actions as presiding judge were more Republican than Democratic.

They took note of the "Pendergast Machine." It only took a moment to dismiss this as not a barrier. Truman was his own man; he took orders from no one. He had proven over and over again that he lived by the principles of Freemasonry, principles that he had been teaching for twenty years. Truman was selected. The Masons of Missouri would be proud of this choice.

Before his second term as presiding judge was over he had improved the roads to the point where they were among the best in the United States. His county was one of the few in the state that was solvent.

In spite of the vast amount of work his job entailed, Truman was still able to carry out his dual duties for Freemasonry in his district and for the Grand Lodge. And he remained active with the National Guard.

During one of his yearly trips with the Guard, Truman sent a letter to his wife, probably written tongue-in-cheek. He closed this letter of July, 1932, with: "Kiss Margaret and tell her to kiss her mother for me. My address is *Colonel* Harry S. Truman, F.A. Reserve, Camp Ripley, Minn."

Colonel Harry S. Truman, left, with a friend at Fort Ripley, Missouri, during Army Reserve Training in July 1932.

[Truman Library photo]

With his second four-year term as judge coming to a close Truman had to think of the future because he couldn't run for his present office again. Bess was in Mississippi with Margaret, who was recuperating from an illness. He wrote her about an offer of two opportunities: He could run for congressman or collector. "Think of that awhile," he told her on April 23, 1933. "Congressman pays $7,500 and has to live in Washington six months a year, collector will pay $10,000 and stay at home, a political sky-power career ends with eight years collector. I have an opportunity to be a power in the nation as Congressman. I don't have to make a decision until next year."

A disturbing decision had to be made by him immediately, however: who and how many to lay off from employment. The depression had made the county's financial position difficult. On April 28, 1933, he wrote Bess: "We are discharging some two hundred people and every one of them and all his friends will try to see me. I was sick last night after the session and lost my supper but I'm going strong again this morning."

Truman attended an American Legion function in St. Joseph on May 6. On the 7th he wrote to Bess: "Tomorrow I'll be forty-nine and for all the good I've done the forty might as well be left off. Take it all together though the experience has been worthwhile. I'd like to do it again. I've been in a railroad, bank, farm, war, politics, *love* (only once and it still sticks), been busted and still am and yet I have stayed an idealist. I still believe that my sweetheart is the ideal woman and that my daughter is her duplicate. I think that for all the horrors of war it still makes a man if he's one to start with. Politics should make a thief, a roue, and a pessimist of anyone, but I don't believe I'm any of them and if I can get the Kansas City courthouse done without scandal no other judge will have done as much, and then maybe I can retire as collector and you and the young lady can take some European and South American tours when they'll do you most good; or maybe live in Washington and see all the greats and near greats in action."

He went to Washington, D.C., to check the progress of the man who was working on a statue that would adorn the new courthouse in Kansas City. From the Willard Hotel he wrote Bess: "Mr. [Charles] Keck had four Andrew Jacksons and the castings of the friezes of Law and Justice. We are going to be proud of them I tell you. We took Andy all apart and put one man on one horse, then tried him on another until there was a combination that will be unbeatable. We spent a most enjoyable morning." Jackson, the hero of the Battle of New Orleans at the end of the War of 1812, and a Past Grand Master of Masons in Tennessee, was also a hero to the folks in Missouri.

This was to be among his last acts as presiding judge because he couldn't succeed himself. The job of collector was out for him. It had been promised to someone else by the political powers. He expected to run for representative from his district; again the fates intervened. He ran for the United States Senate.

Truman's term was over, but he and the Missourians he represented could be proud of his accomplishments. His system of roads would be praised for years to come. He had shown that the lessons in building he had learned as a Freemason were not wasted. The Kansas City courthouse was a model of modernistic neoclassical design. When the voters gave him the money for building and improvements he determined it would be wisely spent.

At his own expense he had driven over 24,000 miles to look at civic structures. This journey carried him through Texas, Arkansas, Oklahoma, Louisiana, Minnesota, Colorado, Illinois and New York. He was looking for the best for his people, and many said he had found it.

He had made improvements in Independence, also. But it still held the historical setting of the beginning of the Santa Fe Trail. Miss Ethel said: "Independence has always stood for culture." Kansas City had surpassed it in population in 1883, "but Independence was the place to go if you wanted to find culture, and Kansas City was a kind of a Yankee town."

Truman campaigned in 1934 by supporting his Brother Mason, Franklin D. Roosevelt, and his policies. He traveled to a majority of the counties in Missouri, making six to sixteen speeches a day. He won the Democratic primary by 130,000 votes, and then overwhelmed his Republican opponent in the general election, as was to be expected in Missouri politics. Truman was on his way to Washington—and to immortality.

Occidental Lodge No. 163 held a farewell dinner for the Senator-elect and hundreds were present to wish him well. Many who couldn't be present sent greetings and congratulations to him. Among these was one from the Grand Secretary of the Grand Lodge of Missouri, Arthur Mather: "I have known Judge Truman for a long time and have every confidence that he will render splendid service, both to the state and nation. Will you please give him my good wishes and assure him that I, among a host of others, will watch his future career with intense interest knowing that he will never trail the banner of our ancient craft in the dust, but that he will add luster to the noble institution with which we are identified, and to the state and country of which he is so illustrious a citizen."

William R. Denslow said: "When Truman was elected to the United States Senate in 1934, he was a poor man. He was not only poor, but in debt. Before he left for Washington, a number of his friends, both political and fraternal, bought him a new Buick. . . . Truman's financial condition at that time, was, in itself, a rebuttal to the political charges that as a county court judge, with Pendergast support, he had lined his pockets with 'kickbacks.' History has proved that above all, Harry S. Truman was an honest man throughout his life."

6. JUNIOR SENATOR

Truman entered the United States Senate chambers for the first time on January 3, 1935, Although he was fifty years old he said he felt as timid as a school boy. This didn't last. He started learning the inner-workings of the upper-chamber. He was also determined to not only represent the people of Missouri but the whole country.

Immediately after he won the Democratic primary he began preparing for the duties to come. In September, 1934, he resigned his office in the Shrine line so he could conserve his time. Rufus Burrus said: "He told me that he knew he couldn't do justice to both and he wanted to be Grand Master more than the potentate of Ararat Shrine."

Truman's contributions in the Senate are too often overlooked because of his later greater responsibilities. But he did make a difference. He did it because his years on the farm and other areas had taught him how to work. His years of association with Freemasonry had taught him how to make friends and be of service to others. And this he did from the start.

Among the first of the Senators he met and liked was Burton K. Wheeler, a member of Butte Lodge No. 22, Montana. Wheeler was chairman of the Interstate Commerce Committee of the Senate and permitted Truman to sit in on his meetings. It wasn't long before the junior Senator from Missouri was made a member of this committee. Later he would become its vice chairman and eventually he would do most of the presiding and work.

Truman even found several Republican Senators he liked and respected. Among them was Arthur H. Vandenberg of Michigan who was a member of Grand River Lodge No. 34 of Michigan. In his *Memoirs* Truman recalled an occasion when he entered the Senate chambers during a heated argument. Vandenberg asked Truman to speak on the subject. He did, and the argument was settled. Vandenberg commented: "When the Senator from Missouri makes a statement like that, we can take it for the truth." That was a remark Truman never forgot.

One of the Senators Truman disliked was Huey Long of Louisiana. Whenever Long commenced one of his time-consuming filibusters, the chamber would empty. On one occasion Truman was presiding over an empty Senate while Long rambled. After Long had finally stopped talking, Truman walked across the street with him and Long asked him what he thought of his speech. "I had to listen to you because I was in the chair and couldn't walk out," Truman told him. Long never spoke to him again.

Another of Truman's friends had a run-in with Long. He was Carter Glass, a member of Hill City Lodge No. 183 of Virginia, and an excellent Masonic ritualist as was Truman. On the Senate floor, Truman remembered, Glass referred to the "horse the ancient Romans had elected to the Senate, and remarked that they had done better than the state of Louisiana—at least the Romans had sent the whole horse."

Truman had campaigned in support of the New Deal and Roosevelt's programs. He continued to support them in the Senate, thereby infuriating most of the leading national as well as Missouri newspaper publishers. He still held his own convictions and went along only with the bills he could support in principle. Against the President's wishes Truman voted in favor of payment of the soldiers bonus and even voted to override the veto.

He also favored states rights, "unless emergency conditions prevailed," so he voted to let the states control relief programs.

George Marquis and Ray Denslow paved the way Masonically for Truman in the District of Columbia. Both wrote letters to Masonic leaders they knew in and around the District. As a result the secretary of the Grand Masters' conference called on the Senator. The secretary wrote Marquis on January 18, 1935: "You will be interested in knowing that Senator Truman accepted an invitation which I extended to him to attend the dinner given in connection with the 1935 Conference of Grand Masters on February 20th and to deliver an address at that time."

In a letter to Marquis on January 21, Truman said: "I had a letter of introduction from Ray to the Grand Secretary of the Grand Lodge of the District of Columbia. He came and called on me. At the Grand Masters Conference in February, I am supposed to make a speech. I hope you'll be there to criticize." In a handwritten note at the bottom he added: "How is everything?

Senator Carter Glass, a member of Hill City Lodge No. 183, Lynchburg, Virginia, an early Senatorial friend of Truman, and who said, in speaking of Senator Long, he was sorry Louisiana did not send the whole horse to the United States Senate.

[Portrait by Greta Kempton]

Masonically & otherwise. Wish I could talk to you. This is a h- of a place."

His busy schedule kept him from attending Masonic functions in and around the District as often as he would have liked to. How many he did attend is unknown. But on June 21, 1935, he was the speaker in a local lodge. Its master was an employee in the Government Printing Office and a Missourian.

Truman wrote on June 28, 1935, to Mrs. Truman about their wedding anniversary, which he never forgot. He then added: "You see you have been married to a financial failure and the reason for that is that I have always believed in doing as I'd be done by, and to make money and keep it you must be a pirate or strike an oil well or a gold mine. Had I not been a fool patriot in 1917, I'd had the oil well. And maybe would have turned pirate and been successful. I am hoping to make a reputation as a Senator, though if I live long enough that'll make the money successes look like cheese. But you'll have to put up with a lot if I do it because I won't sell influence and I'm perfectly willing to be cussed if I'm right."

Another recorded Masonic occasion occurred in the District on April 5, 1937, when Truman had dinner with Dr. Frederick Smith, who gave him "an exact duplicate of George Washington's penknife," which he had purchased at Alexandria Lodge.

William R. Denslow, son of Truman's close friend Ray V. Denslow, was living in Washington in 1937. He had just graduated from the University of Missouri and planned on continuing graduate studies in the capital. One evening the Trumans invited Denslow to dine with them at their apartment.

"I had supposed that a U.S. Senator lived in grand style," said Denslow, "and was surprised to find the apartment to be utilitarian if not almost spartan. It was much like my own midwestern, middle class home, and I felt at ease. Mrs. Truman had cooked a delicious dinner and Margaret and I washed and dried the dishes."

With the world on the brink of war, the Neutrality Act of 1937 was passed and Truman voted in favor of it. He soon learned he had made a mistake, and admitted it, something few politicians ever do. In 1939 and again in 1941 he rectified the mistake he believed he had made earlier.

When war erupted in Europe Truman was among the minority who saw the threat to the United States and the free world. He stepped up his agitation to provide ways "that would strengthen national defense." He said: "I also voted against continuing the mandatory arms embargo, because there never should have been one in the first place. Republican Spain was lost on account of the embargo."

George Marquis sent Truman a copy of a newspaper article which had been reprinted in Missouri as taken from the Washington *Star.* Truman had given the reporter an off-the-record interview that the reporter had published, and which upset Truman. Marquis told Truman on March 6, 1939: "What I know about practical politics you could stick in your eye, and what I do not know would fill a big book, nevertheless I feel inclined to deal out advice. Get as mad as the very devil—I think I would be just that mad in your situation—but don't talk for publication except when you are as cool as a cucumber."

In assessing his first term in the Senate Truman was proud of his work that resulted in the Civil Aeronautics Act, the Transportation Act of 1940, and the Bus and Truck Act. He was also proud of his work on the Interstate Commerce Committee.

"Almost before I knew it," Truman wrote in his *Memoirs,* "my first term in the Senate was coming to a close. The years since 1935 had been the busiest and the happiest of my life, and I decided early in 1940 that I would make a fight for renomination in the August primary and for reelection in the November general election."

That wouldn't be easy. The President was supporting another man to replace Truman, and had "in a roundabout way" offered the junior Senator from Missouri a job on the Interstate Commerce Commission. Truman wanted no part of that.

Truman sent his secretary, Lieutenant Colonel (later General) and Brother Mason Harry H. Vaughan, to Missouri to set up a grass-roots campaign. He asked for, and got, thousands of volunteers throughout the state to work for Truman.

It proved to be a tough political battle. And another political battle was going on where there should be no politics. Partisan politicians were making an attempt to keep the Deputy Grand Master from becoming Grand Master of Masons in Missouri.

They were fighting against odds, though, because Truman had won two previous battles for office in the Grand Lodge, and continued to be one of the outstanding and active Freemasons in the country.

Truman had continued to work in Masonic circles throughout Missouri in spite of his back-breaking tasks in the Senate. He had attended every Grand Lodge session; he had installed the officers of several lodges; he had continued to confer degrees. Missouri Masons knew him well, and most of them were proud of his work, and they proved it—he was elected Grand Master.

However, Truman almost decided to quit soon after he was elected Junior Grand Warden. The unsavory and un-Masonic story is told in papers in the Harry S. Truman Library and the memorial edition of *The Freemason* magazine of Missouri for the spring of 1973.

Opposition to Truman as Junior Grand Warden, the first elective office in the Grand Lodge line, was unprecedented. Truman received 398 votes; his opponent 345; a plurality of only 53 votes. Many indignant letters were written to the Senator expressing the support of the writers and deploring the actions of the opposition, and many were similar to one written by a District Deputy Grand Master, Luther E. Wilhoit.

"I attended Grand Lodge in St. Louis last week and witnessed the most disgraceful thing I ever saw done in Grand Lodge," wrote Wilhoit. "In expressing myself I was informed that they didn't want Pendergast for Grand Master four years from now. In reply I told the brother that I hardly considered a man worthy of Masonry who would bring that kind of stuff into Grand Lodge."

Truman thought too highly of Freemasonry to let politics destroy it, so he considered quitting. The letters of support, and particularly one from the officers and Past Masters of his own Lodge, Grandview, helped him reconsider.

"Knowing you personally and intimately as each of us does," said the letter from Grandview, "and fully appreciating the honors you have brought to our little country lodge, we the undersigned members in good standing of Grandview Lodge No. 618 take this means of conveying to you, the knowledge of our unswerving loyalty and support in your progress toward the East in the Grand Lodge.

"May we all live to see you installed as Most Worshipful Grand Master, and may a part of the honor and glory of that occasion be reflected, as it surely will be, on your home lodge."

Ray Denslow was disconcerted to learn a rumor had been started claiming he was opposed to Truman, he said in a letter on October 1, 1938. "Anyone with any common sense would know that was false. While I cannot agree with you in some of your political views, nevertheless, I am trying to be too wide-minded to let that enter into any Masonic affairs."

Charles H. Walter, an attorney, wrote to Truman on October 17, 1938: "The purpose of my letter is to congratulate you on your advancement and to assure you that while there are a good many Republicans in our midst, and who cannot resist the temptation to resent the advancement of a Democrat, especially if he is prominent, many others will continue to support you."

Three days later Truman went to Lexington Lodge No. 149 to assist it in honoring Henry C. Chiles, the Grand Master.

Denslow asked Truman to speak in Trenton Lodge No. 111 on December 1, 1938. He did. On April 8, 1939, Truman conferred the Master Mason degree on a friend of his in Clintonville Lodge No. 482 in El Dorado Springs, Missouri.

Grand Master Henry C. Chiles had learned there was concerted opposition that would be asserted against Truman in the 1939 election. He wrote to the Senator on May 22, 1939: "Judge Ittner and Dr. Mather anticipate the fight against you is likely to be taken up again in this year's communication. They do not believe you should withdraw."

Marquis wrote to Truman on August 1, 1939: "Henry Chiles will lay the cornerstone of the Harrison County courthouse August 11th. I will be driving Henry up, and if you are at home and at liberty to go I will be glad to have you.

"Some day during the week of September 11 we will have a whale of a big meeting at Macon. There will be a district meeting of the Lodges with Wyandotte Lodge of Kansas City, Kan., conferring the Third degree. That should bring in a big crowd from all over Northeast Missouri. Then there will be a district meeting of the chapters. The big drawing card is that Henry Chiles,

Grand Master, will confer the Royal Arch degree. Altogether this will be an afternoon and evening affair. As I am propagating that affair I know we will be glad to have you present and on the program at the dinner." Truman was there.

Just before the Grand Lodge session, September 16, 1939, the cornerstone for Savannah post office was laid, and Truman was present to assist in the ritual.

As expected the 1938 group of anti-Truman members were ganging up again in 1939 to keep him from being elected Senior Grand Warden. This time, however, Truman's supporters planned on being prepared. On August 8, 1939, Marquis wrote a letter to the supporters, one of whom had always been Bruce H. Hunt: "Shall we go to the Coronado [hotel], or would it be wise to change to the Melbourne? Most of the Brass Collars will be at the Coronado, but last year the enemy had two 'headquarters' rooms at the Melbourne. We probably could not have done anything about that if we had been on the ground. One thing to consider, though, is the fact that St. Louis Masons, as a rule, prefer the Melbourne."

The election was close; Truman won by only forty-seven votes.

The new Senior Grand Warden whispered to Bruce Hunt and a couple of his long-time friends as the session was drawing to a close. He wanted them to slip away and meet him as soon as the Grand Lodge closed. They did, and it was midnight before Truman reached his hotel room. Early the next morning he was on a plane headed for Washington.

What Truman said in his acceptance speech isn't recorded, but it prompted a letter to and from E.E. Morris, the Grand Treasurer. On October 5, 1939, Morris wrote: "Thank you for your nice note of October 2nd. I am Masonically and personally so strong for you that I too regretted what I thought was your tactless acceptance of your election in the Grand Lodge, but I make so many breaks, even worse than you and which I sometimes regret with a bitter heart, that I can be tolerant and understanding of yours.

"Of course the provocation was great, that cannot be denied, but my thought was that it was the better politics to express verbally enthusiastic appreciation to the fellows that stuck to you. I hope you will not feel too badly about this. We will all do the best we can to correct it during the coming year and I believe that we can be successful though, unquestionably, there will be a strenuous fight. However much we may disagree with a man's political record, I do not believe that these things belong or should be carried into Masonic organizations or our churches.

"I hope I can still differ with a man politically, as you certainly know I differ with you, and yet have a keen appreciation of his friendship. I hope that more of our members will come to this state of mind before another election rolls around."

Marquis wrote to Truman on October 10, 1939, to tell him he was concerned about a District Deputy Grand Master who had made only one visit to the lodges in his care. He also may have been behind the opposition to Truman. Marquis suggested that when Truman became Grand Master he should "bump this gentleman next year when you appoint DDGMs and get a good Callaway County Democrat!"

The Senator congratulated "Miss Nell Page" on October 17, 1939, on her reelection in the Grand Chapter, Order of the Eastern Star. He said he was especially happy to know she had bested those who tried to do to her what had been tried on him.

Frank P. Briggs, a Missouri State Senator, wrote to Truman on November 13, 1939, to ask for his definition of "What Is This Thing Called Masonry?" Truman suggested: "Freemasonry is a system of morals which makes it easier to live with your fellow man whether he understands it or not."

An official with the Work Projects Administration didn't consider Freemasonry entitled to have its insignia on a cornerstone and refused to let one be laid with Masonic ceremonies at the post office in Ozark. Senator Truman received a frantic telegram from the Grand Master asking him to try to do something. Truman did. He sent Karl M. Vetsburg, the Grand Master, a telegram on June 17, 1940, telling him to go ahead. If there was any objection to show that official the Senator's telegram. The stone was laid on the 18th.

Truman received an invitation to meet with the Masonic Home Board, but on July 6 he wrote: "I wish I could be with you on the tenth. I am out beating the bushes for votes, however, and it just won't be possible for me to be present."

The day of reckoning arrived a year earlier than expected. In 1939 the then Deputy Grand Master resigned. This could not have happened at a worse time for Truman. It would make the year 1940 doubly crucial. He would have to fight a hard battle for reelection to the Senate as well as be nominated for Grand Master while in the heat of that battle.

To keep politics out of Masonry, Truman declined numerous invitations to speak in Masonic Lodges and Masonic functions during the the campaign for reelection. These could have helped him politically and Masonically, but he said: "I would not want the lodge or any of the brethren to become involved in a political controversy on my part. It does not belong in the lodge."

True. But it didn't stop unscrupulous characters from putting politics into the lodges. An anonymous, and cowardly, letter was sent to the 600 Missouri Lodges:

> Brethren:
>
> If Masonry is to continue to occupy an exalted position, it might be well *To Think, Look* and *Listen.*
>
> The brother in line for Grand Master, is in a position to which he can not do justice, he being a U.S. Senator.
>
> He was sponsored and practically put in that office, by the most unscrupulous racketeering boodler, that ever disgraced our State.
>
> Masonry and politics cannot and should not mix. Nor should the good citizens vote into a government or any other office a man that was created and through the power of crooked votes, was elected to the U.S. Senate by the champion of all racketeers, Tom Pendergast.
>
> The man that now seeks your vote for Grand Master and for reelection to the U.S. Senate, publicly announced, that he would stay with the sinking ship. Meaning that he would still be for Tom Pendergast, now an ex-convict and a dyed in the wool Catholic.
>
> Brethren, consider the welfare of Masonry.
>
> Let your conscience be your guide.
>
> So Mote It Be.

This cowardly act brought down the wrath of many of the Freemasons of Missouri on the unknown letter-writer. Had his identity been disclosed, without question he would not have remained a Mason. Senator Truman's office was flooded with supportive letters. Among them was one from the superintendent of schools at Bloomfield, Missouri, Elvis A. Mooney:

> . . . While your name has been before the public and you have been an official of our government there has never come to my attention any act, or failure to act on any proposition that would in any way bring disfavor to the Fraternity or have any bearing on the question raised except to do honor and to give evidence of your fitness for the highest gift within the Grand Lodge of Missouri. . . .
>
> I have very little influence in the Masonic Brotherhood of Missouri and have had very little opportunity to have much acquaintance with you as a man; however, I shall attend Grand Lodge and will rise to my feet and state my position on this outrage on a worthy brother and do all in my power to prevent this outrage on decency and good order among us. If I can be of assistance in furthering your cause so that you may serve us more fully throughout the coming year I am at your request.

The Freemason notes that Elvis A. Mooney would later have an influence in the Grand Lodge; he was appointed to the line in 1958 becoming another in the succession of appointments in the Truman line. The same magazine states that the Scottish Rite Cathedral in St. Louis was packed with one of the largest turnouts of delegates ever for an annual session of the Grand Lodge of Missouri on September 24-25, 1940. Truman was elected Grand Master by an overwhelming vote. The Republican who had appointed him to the line, Past Grand Master William R. Gentry, installed the Senator as Grand Master.

Toward the close of the Grand Lodge session, Lewis E. Smith, Grand Secretary of the Grand Lodge of Nebraska, mentioned Elliott Roosevelt, also a Mason and son of the President, had been promoted to the rank of captain simply because he was Roosevelt's son. Truman took exception to his remarks and wrote to him on September 30 to let him know the young man was thoroughly qualified.

"From what you said to me in St. Louis," Truman continued, "I have the impression that it would not make much difference what the President did, because you would not like it, anyway, and I am extremely sorry for your ultra-partisan point of view, because I like you very much.

"When I come to Nebraska, I am going to back you into a corner and make you listen to some good sound advice."

On the political scene, the Republican nominee continued to make many damaging statements about Truman. Just before the general election he did so in Wellsville, Missouri. Forrest C. Donnell, the Republican nominee for Governor and Senior Grand Warden of the Grand Lodge, was there. So was James E. Wade, evidently a reporter, who went to Donnell and asked: "If Truman is the kind of fellow Davis said he was, could he have been elected Grand Master?" Donnell replied; "No, Jim, he could not."

"That statement was promptly broadcast by Jim Wade," wrote Truman, "and it cost Davis thousands of votes."

Truman had been elected United States Senator and was reelected. Most important to him, as he would say many times, he had also been elected Grand Master of Masons in Missouri. The years ahead would add to his stature.

7. GRAND MASTER

With the November, 1940, election behind him, and the new Congress not yet in session, Truman had a little time to attend to Masonic duties. He attended to the necessary administrative affairs of the Grand Lodge, and with the Senatorial election over he felt he could again make visitations to lodges and district associations.

Immediately after the close of the Grand Lodge session, James M. Bradford, whom Truman had started in line, wrote to thank him. Truman replied on September 30: "You had been very highly recommended to me by a number of St. Louis Masons, and by my good friend, Henry C. Chiles. I was most anxious to do something for the St. Louis Masons, who had been extremely kind to me; and I am of the opinion that I picked a good candidate for Grand Master."

Lodges lost no time in trying out the new Grand Master. On September 28, 1940, the Secretary of Ivanhoe Lodge No. 446, wanted to know if the time between degrees had been shortened as it had been during the last war. Truman answered him on October 1:

> Personally, I am not in favor of any such arrangement. It seems to me that we ought to profit by what happened in the last war. We took in people by the wholesale and there were those among them who had no more business in the Masonic Lodge than I have in the Vatican. This sort of thing ought to have most careful consideration, and I am not, under any circumstances, in favor of taking down the bars as we did in 1918.

The Grand Master took action on a case that had been held over from the previous administration. On November 7 he sent a letter to the secretary of Forest Park Lodge No. 578 ordering it to prefer charges against one of its past masters. He was charged with "unmasonic conduct for refusing to obey the legal order of the Grand Master made August 26, 1940, to turn over to Doctor Arthur Mather, Grand Secretary, money of the M.S.A. of St. Louis in the sum of $1,100.67; withholding said funds; failure to obey orders of M.S.A. of St. Louis under date of September 20, 1940, to turn over said funds in conformance to the Grand Master's order." The trial was held on January 2, 1941, and the verdict was expulsion from all the rights and benefits of Freemasonry.

Carthage Lodge No. 197 wanted a cornerstone laid for a memorial hospital. Truman wrote on November 13: "It will not be possible to authorize the laying of a cornerstone for a privately-owned building. It has been the custom for Freemasonry to lay cornerstones for most public buildings, but we have not performed the ceremony for private buildings except in rare instances. I do not believe we should depart from the usual custom in this instance. Therefore, no dispensation will be issued to lay the cornerstone of a privately owned and operated hospital."

Amazingly, the Grand Master-Senator found time to do things officials with lesser responsibilities often won't do. Through an invitation, he presented a fifty-year pin to M.H. Stubblefield in Stubblefield's Lodge in November. During the same month he presented another fifty-year pin to Thomas Littlejohn in Higginsville Lodge No. 364.

In answer to a letter from Ray Denslow requesting aid for a widow, Truman wrote on November 19: "I am most happy to suggest a donation to Mrs. Johnson. How much do you think it ought to be, or should she be placed on a monthly pension basis? I remember William I. Johnson very well. He was a fine man and was a good Grand Master. As you know, my mother fell last Thursday and broke her hip. She will be eighty-eight years old next Monday."

His "official" lodge visitations began on November 20, 1940. He first went to Belton Lodge No. 450, his original Masonic home, then to Grandview Lodge No. 618, the lodge he had organized and served as its first Master.

The Grand Lodge of Texas met for its 105th annual communication on December 4, 1940. The Grand Master of Masons in Missouri was present. He was welcomed with open arms by the Grand Master of Masons in Texas, Leo Hart, and his brethren.

The *Texas Grand Lodge Magazine* recorded that Truman was presented at the altar by Past Grand Master G.R.M. Montgomery who said: "Most Worshipful Grand Master, to me has been delegated a privilege and a pleasure that comes to a Master Mason seldom, that of presenting the Grand Master of the Grand Jurisdiction of which he has the honor to be the Grand Representative near the Grand Lodge of Texas. I have the honor, sir, to present to you and through you to the Grand Lodge of Texas, Most Worshipful Brother Harry S. Truman, Most Worshipful Grand Master of the Most Worshipful Grand Lodge of Missouri."

Truman was accorded "private grand honors" and was then escorted to a seat in the East. Other distinguished guests were then received, and they were welcomed by Past Grand Master Jewel P. Lightfoot. He spoke of Truman's jurisdiction:

> I would like to reiterate one point, and to express publicly and fully, the feeling and debt of gratitude which Texas owes to the great state of Missouri and the Masons they sent from that commonwealth into the wilderness of Texas to lay the foundations of the great institutions of freedom and constitutional government that lives and rules this land. Moses Austin of Missouri established the first colony and upon his death Stephen F. Austin, his son, took up the cause and carried it to fruition. It was Stephen F. Austin who in 1827, ten years before the independence of this Republic was achieved under the leadership of General Sam Houston, petitioned the Grand Lodge of Mexico for a dispensation to establish a Masonic Lodge on this soil, and, for some unknown reason, which historians have failed to leave any record of, he never heard from that petition.

Grand Master Hart said he was delighted to have the unexpected pleasure of welcoming "one of Texas' favored sons and an outstanding national leader" to the Grand Lodge. He presented Tom Connally, a United States Senator from Texas, and invited him to "speak whatever may be upon his heart and then introduce" the distinguished guest from Missouri.

> It is an inspiration to me [said Connally] to stand before this great membership. Brother Lightfoot referred a moment ago to the conditions that this old world of ours have been plunged into in recent years. He referred to the tragic period in which we are now living and, brethren, as we contemplate the fact that in some of the fairest regions of the earth the concepts of justice have been lost sight of; when we remember that the rule of the sword and the bayonet has been substituted for the law of ethics and righteousness and fair-dealing, and fraternity among civilizations and nations and human beings, the prospect is indeed gloomy and fraught with foreboding. But there will come a time when these weary armies will wear themselves out and when the sword will be laid aside, and if when that time comes this old world as we have known it, the law of justice and righteousness and of ethics and of equity is to remain, it must be through the wisdom and through the courage of men like you who have gathered inspiration from the altars and

from the teachings and from the traditions of this great institution of ours.

It is a distinct pleasure to join in welcoming to the Most Worshipful Grand Lodge of Texas the Most Worshipful Grand Master of the Commonwealth of Missouri. It is a peculiar pleasure to introduce to you the distinguished representative of Missouri on this occasion because I have had the opportunity in the Senate of the United States to be associated with him over a period of years, and I know that there, as a servant of the people of his state, he has exemplified many of the fine qualities and many of the splendid precepts that Masonry has taught.

He is gracious, and able, a faithful and diligent public servant. He is a distinguished Mason; he is a man of the noblest and finest type and of the most admirable mold. I take very great pride in presenting to this Most Worshipful Grand Lodge, Most Worshipful Grand Master Harry S. Truman of the Most Worshipful Grand Lodge of the State of Missouri.

A part of Truman's response is recorded, and it should be noted he proved he understood Masonic terminology; he was the only one to state his title correctly.

I cannot express to you what a very great privilege it is for me as the Grand Master of Masons in Missouri to be presented at this honorable body by my friend and colleague, the Honorable Tom Connally of Texas. I want to say to you that the State of Texas, as long as Tom Connally is in the United States Senate, will be honorably and carefully represented, to the interest of this great state. He has the reputation of being the most distinguished debater in the United States Senate, and I say that advisedly, Tom. He has always had my admiration. When I went to the United States Senate, Tom Connally represented to me all that a United States Senator should be, and if I can represent Missouri one-half as well as he does Texas, I shall think I have done my public duty.

It is more than a pleasure to be here as a representative of the great State of Missouri in this great fraternity. The highest honor that has ever come to me, and that can ever come to me in my life, is to be Grand Master of the State of Missouri, and I know that your Grand Master and Past Grand Masters of Texas feel the same way. We feel that we represent a fraternity which believes in justice and truth and honorable action in your community. It represents those men who are endeavoring to be better citizens in the community, who are endeavoring to make a great country greater. This is the only institution in the world where we can meet on the level all sorts of people who want to live rightly.

We have here the honorable representative of one of the great states of Mexico. We can have here the honorable representative of any great country in the world who has taken the oath around that

> altar. This great fraternity has done more and can do more for peace and up-lift in this state than any other organization on earth, and I want to say to you that as long as three and a half million and over Freemasons are in the United States, this great Republic can't help but survive.
>
> I thank you most sincerely for this privilege. I can't express to you how much I appreciate the hospitality of Texas, and I want to say to you that at the next meeting of the Grand Lodge of Missouri, over which I shall preside, I hope that everyone of you will pay a return visit.

It was in Texas that he first made the statement he would make many times, not only in Masonic lodges but in public: "The highest honor that has ever come to me, or that can ever come to me in my life, is to be Grand Master of the State of Missouri." Even the Presidency did not change his thinking.

Professor Noel P. Gist asked the Grand Secretary for copies of the Grand Lodge *Proceedings*. He was told this was against Grand Lodge law, but he sent requests to all lodge secretaries requesting information on membership, finances, location, ownership, property, and so on. Truman sent an order to all the lodges ordering them to ignore all correspondence from that non-Masonic person who was going to use it for non-Masonic purposes.

On December 19 the Grand Master installed the officers of Northeast Lodge No. 643 in Kansas City. On the 27th he again installed the officers of his mother lodge, Grandview No. 618. He followed this by installing the officers of Grandview Chapter, Order of the Eastern Star.

Truman sent a letter to all the lodges on December 21 that would have long-lasting and beneficial effects:

> At the last annual Communication of the Grand Lodge a new section of the by-laws was adopted which authorizes the organization of Lodges of Research. By specific provision of that by-law, every Missouri Master Mason in good standing is eligible to membership in any Lodge of Research organized under the same.
>
> Brethren who have been for many years active in Masonic Research have instituted a movement looking to the organization of a Lodge of Research and at their request I am addressing this letter to all Lodges for the purpose of informing the Brethren that they are eligible to membership and that they will be welcomed to membership if they desire it.

> Any Brother interested in becoming a charter member of the proposed Lodge of Research should let it be known at once by addressing a letter to M.W. Henry C. Chiles, P.G.M., Lexington, Missouri, who will be glad of the opportunity to provide full information and further particulars.

This was the beginning of the Missouri Lodge of Research, a lodge that would grow over the years and provide excellent Masonic books and literature for Freemasons everywhere. Harry S. Truman signed its dispensation, and also its charter. In 1950, while President of the United States, he would serve as its Master.

Truman was sworn in for his second term as a Senator from Missouri on January 3, 1941. When he entered the Senate chamber the entire Senate rose and applauded him as he walked down the aisle. His peers recognized the enormous victory of the junior Senator from Missouri. He had earned the respect of most of them during his first term and this had been heightened by overcoming overwhelming odds to be able to return. He was now definitely a vital part of the "club."

Truman found that many of the isolationists, but not all by far, had come to realize the country was unprepared for war. For the first time billions of dollars were being spent to alleviate the danger to the country.

The Senator from Missouri and many of his constituents were concerned. Too much was being done in haste and without enough thought. He had learned contracts were being negotiated for supplies and munitions with big contractors, squeezing the little fellow out. This concerned him and he was determined to learn how the small businessmen could be used productively in the armament activities.

He decided he would take a close look at what was going on in the nation and began touring the country at his own expense in his automobile, not letting anyone know who he was. He found far too much work was being concentrated in a few big cities and reported what he had learned in a speech to the Senate, then called for a committee to investigate conditions and take action where necessary.

Fortunately the Senate saw the wisdom of his advice and set up the committee he recommended. He was made chairman of this new special committee to Investigate the National Defense Program. As always, he did his homework. He learned that Douglas Southall Freeman said in his biography of Robert E. Lee that the Joint Committee on the Conduct of the War between the States actually assisted the Confederacy. Truman remembered the mistakes it had made, and he avoided them.

The resulting investigation saved the country billions of dollars. It brought results that eventually helped the war effort more than any other one thing.

But in April 1941, John L. Lewis, also a Mason, called a strike of his coal miners that created a national defense bottleneck. Truman called Lewis and representatives of the mine operators before his committee. He wanted coal and was determined to get it. The committee learned that the southern coal operators were holding up a wage settlement. They were notified that if coal wasn't being mined by April 28, they, the operators, would come before the committee and explain why their wage dispute was more important than the safety of the nation. The strike was settled.

During "George Washington Week" the Grand Masters of the country met in the District of Columbia, and Truman was among them. They heard General George C. Marshall address The Masonic Service Association. He praised the delegates for their willingness to support the efforts of the Armed Forces. He also said he admired Freemasonry; his father had been a Mason. He would have liked to have been, he said, but no one had asked him to join! On December 6, 1941, Marshall and Jesse H. Jones, Secretary of Commerce, were made Masons at Sight by the Grand Master of Masons in the District of Columbia.

The Senator from Missouri was asked to make a nationwide radio broadcast on February 22, 1941, on the topic "George Washington, the Mason." This was the first time any Freemason had been asked to speak on a Masonic topic via the air waves. He did an excellent job, as would be expected. Washington was one of the men Truman admired and respected as a man, as a builder of the United States in war and peace, and as first President of the United States.

Truman's duties as Grand Master also continued. On March 10, 1941, he answered a letter received from a lodge secretary who was concerned because an entered apprentice was wearing the square and compasses insignia. The Grand Master said: "A fellow is misrepresenting the facts, of course, when he wears a Square and Compasses when he has not yet finished the first three degrees. Usually a little reasoning convinces these fellows that they are not helping themselves nor the Fraternity by being forehanded and over enthusiastic. I have had the same experiences at home, and I am sure that if you will tell these fellows just exactly what they are doing, they will stop it."

His Masonic correspondence remained heavy throughout the year and he handled it all personally. His staff was instructed to see that he received everything pertaining to Freemasonry. And the staff was also told to see that all costs concerning Masonry were charged to his personal account. Not one penny of government funds paid for his travels for Masonry, his correspondence, telegrams, or anything else.

Among the many letters the Grand Master sent to his Grand Secretary was one with which he was returning signed Grand Lodge checks. "I am enclosing the checks which you sent me for the payroll, and also the $40,000 check for the Masonic Home. The office force seems to be very much puffed up that I have the ability to sign a check for $40,000. Of course they don't understand that I don't have anything to do with whether it is good or not." It was a partial per capita payment to the Home from the membership.

The Masonic Service Association of the United States stepped up its efforts to raise funds and support for members of the armed forces. Senator Harry Truman was asked if he would address a nationwide radio audience. He agreed and used the topic "Freemasonry Helps the Armed Forces." He told those huddled around their radios on July 24, 1941, what Freemasonry was attempting to do, and that he believed it could be done by requesting only ten cents from each member of each lodge.

"In these days of big money," he said, "when even billions are a matter of course and a million is small change, I might be excused if I were apologetic for the small sum asked of the two and a half millions of Freemasons of the nation. But, as a matter of fact, I am proud that the small contributions requested can go so far and do so much. I am proud because I know why it can do so much; proud that so many devoted Masons are willing to give of their time and strength, sell their goods at cost, work for nothing or for a pittance, for the love of their fellow members of the oldest Fraternal organization in the world."

Truman said that although only Grand Lodges had been requested to help, not all money came from them. "An ex-convict in the far West, pardoned and making good after a lifetime in prison, wrote, 'I was never good enough to be a Mason, but my father was, and I want to help—here's a dollar for ten Masons who cannot pay.' And a woman, unknown to anyone in the Association, sent a check for $150 with a note saying, 'To help comfort some other woman's sons'."

Truman was criticized. The Worthy Grand Matron of the Order of the Eastern Star in Massachusetts said he should have mentioned the OES and the Rainbow Girls contributions.

He agreed. And there could have been others, such as the Order of Jobs Daughters and the Masonic Service Cadettes. The latter used this slogan: "They may not need me yet they *might,*/ I'll let my heart be just in sight./ A smile as small as mine may be/Precisely their necessity." But, as Truman pointed out to the lady: "Of course the Eastern Star should have been included, but there isn't a man in the world who can think of everything, particularly this one. I apologize, for the Star is doing a great work."

Even harsher criticism came from John H. Cowles, Grand Commander of the Scottish Rite, Southern Jurisdiction, no friend of The Masonic Service Association. Within the letter he wrote on August 16, 1941, he said:

> I read your broadcast, which somewhat surprised me. I feel positive that you do not know the true inwardness of the Masonic Service Association's work, how unnecessary it is, and how the publications it gets out fail to give all the story.
>
> Some of the statements made in your broadcast, which I am satisfied you received from Mr. Claudy, might be considered as being ridiculous.
>
> The fact of the matter is that the government itself is doing enough and plenty for the soldiers. We do not want to raise a pampered army. I went through Camp Croft at Spartanburg, S.C., and there certainly were preparations sufficient to do all for a soldier that anyone reasonably could expect.

I enclose you a copy of the plan that has been adopted by the Massachusetts Masons, which to me seems to be a sensible one, and a considerable number of other Grand Lodges have adopted something along the same line.

I enclose also a clipping from a newspaper in Tennessee which appealed to me, as I was a Captain in the Spanish-American War. I think the statement of the average pension of World War veterans being $126 is wrong. I think that is about the highest that a completely disabled war veteran gets, and that, it seems to me, is high enough.

To which Truman replied on September 9:

I read your letter of August Sixteenth with much interest and some surprise. I was a Captain in the World War, and all the fraternal connections that I received during the time I was in the service—from the time it started until May 6, 1919—was the fraternal work done by the Knights of Columbus. The reason that was so was because no one organization could speak for Freemasonry.

I discussed this situation with General Marshall and with the Chief of Naval Operations, with the Secretary of the Navy and the Secretary of War, and we came to the conclusion that if the Masonic Service Association could perform the service fraternally which we believe it can, it would fill a niche that has never been filled before in the welfare work of the Army.

So far, the work done by this organization has been entirely satisfactory. I suggested to them that they set up an organization in Rolla, Missouri for Camp Leonard Wood. That organization has been functioning very satisfactorily in my home State. The one at Jackson, South Carolina, has been entirely satisfactory.

I believe that if there is an organization through which all the Masons in the country can operate for fraternal connections with the various camps, it will prevent a situation from developing which developed in the last War. In nearly every city which was close to a training camp Masonic Lodges went into the wholesale business of conferring degrees. It was most unhealthy for the organization and caused many of our woes, and I am trying to prevent that if I can. I think that I am successfully combatting it so far as Missouri, Arkansas, Kansas, Iowa and Illinois are concerned.

I am going to recommend to the Grand Lodge of Missouri that they support the Masonic Service Association fully and completely, as the Grand Lodge of Pennsylvania and some thirty other Grand Lodges have done.

I would be most happy to discuss this whole program with you some time at your convenience, because I believe you have the wrong attitude with regard to what's intended and what should be done.

> I am absolutely against pampering soldiers, but I believe the welfare of our institution is at stake to some extent, and that every effort should be made to safeguard its interests with the armed forces.

Carl H. Claudy, executive secretary of The Masonic Service Association, invited members of Congress known to be Freemasons to a buffet dinner at the Mayflower Hotel on July 30, 1941. Claudy explained what the MSA was attempting to do for the servicemen and women being mobilized. He went into some detail about the failure of Masonry during World War I because of the lack of unity in the Craft.

This failure was something with which Truman was familiar. He had mentioned it on several occasions because he had first-hand knowledge of the lack of Masonic functions overseas. When the Senators and Congressmen agreed to organize and help in the efforts of the MSA, Harry S. Truman, Senator from Missouri and Grand Master, was elected by acclamation to preside.

In his usual capable manner, he did. Those present heard from Major Charles Coulter, director of welfare for the MSA. Then Representative Sol Bloom, who was an active Mason, offered a resolution:

> WHEREAS, a majority of the Grand Lodges of the United States, acting together through their servant organization, The Masonic Service Association, have undertaken a program of welfare work for the armed forces of the nation;
>
> AND WHEREAS, Only Freemasonry can bring Masonic comfort, aid and assistance to Masons, by visiting the sick in post and camp hospitals, reporting the well being of the sons of Masons to allay anxiety at home, provide facilities for the formation of Masonic clubs, and foster morale by providing the Masonic contacts which no other organization can supply,
>
> AND WHEREAS, This is being accomplished by money voluntarily given by Masons for Masons and without request from the public or government,
>
> NOW. THEREFORE, We, members of the Congress of the United States, who are Master Masons, heartily approve such Masonic welfare work for the armed forces of the United States, and commend these plans and activities of The Masonic Service Association to all brethren, wheresoever dispersed.

Truman, the chairman, insisted on a full discussion before he would permit a vote on the resolution. The discussion was enlightening and heartening. Those present learned that these Master Masons were not giving "lip service" to the Fraternity; they had learned the lessons of Masonry well. One Congressman became so enthused he shouted: "My Lodge has twelve hundred members. I herewith subscribe the necessary ten cents for each of them!" The resolution was unanimously adopted.

The radio address and the support of the Masons in Congress helped. Donations poured in. Before the year was over, service centers, affectionately called "Homes Away from Home," were opened in South Carolina, Florida, Alabama, Louisiana, Missouri, Oklahoma, Rhode Island and Maine. Throughout the country Freemasons were proclaiming, "Your son is my Brother!"

Not only were Freemasons raving about the service centers. An elderly chief petty officer, furiously writing a letter in a center in Newport, Rhode Island, was interrupted when a field agent greeted him. "Do you know what I'm doing?" asked the chief. "I'm giving my folks hell! I am a K. of C. My father was an Exalted K. of C., and my grandfather was an Exalted K. of C., and I went to Mass this morning and listened to a sermon on the evils of Newport; but where could I come to write a letter but to the Masonic Service Center! Believe me, I am giving my people hell!"

Truman remained chairman of the advisory committee of the Association. Along with him were several generals and admirals, plus four Senators and five Representatives: Arthur H. Vandenberg, Warren R. Austin, A.B. Chandler and Harold K. Burton were the Senators; the Representatives were Sol Bloom, Allen T. Treadway, Fritz G. Lanhan, Laurence F. Arnold and Pete Jarman.

On April 9, 1941, Truman traveled to Philadelphia, Pennsylvania, to speak in Equity Lodge No. 591. He left Philadelphia at one o'clock in the morning by plane for St. Louis. There he was met by James DeWitt and driven to Kirksville. Truman wrote a letter to DeWitt on the 16th which tells something of his perseverance.

"The plane came along at 5 a.m. [on the 11th] and I got two hours sleep on a bench," he wrote. "They took me all the way back to Philadelphia and then down to Washington. I got here at 12:30 p.m. instead of 9:30 a.m. Just three hours late." He then asked his friend to "tell the boys who acted as Masters that they did a good job and I appreciate it."

Bruce H. Hunt, a long-time friend of the Senator, recalled this visit to Kirksville:

"One of his return visits remains vivid in my memory. He came to Kirksville for a visit to the Second Masonic District. As was the custom at that time a candidate for the third degree was made available. The Grand Master was extended the courtesy of raising the candidate. This was considered the proper Masonic thing to do. No thought was given to the fact that the Grand Master had many other things on his mind, and probably had given very little thought to the precise wording of the ritual.

"I was District Lecturer of the Second Masonic District at the time. As the second section of the Master Mason Degree was about to begin Brother Truman walked over to me and said, 'Bruce, I haven't given this ritual much thought and may need some help. Stay close by.' I assured him I would do just that, and I did. However, he never needed a single word and the ritualistic perfection of the Master Mason Degree was maintained to the honor and dignity of the Grand Master."

As many a Grand Master had before and most have since, Truman found the job backbreaking. It had been particularly difficult for him. Most of his time had to be spent in Washington heading an important committee as the country prepared for war, or at least for its defense. It is little wonder he wrote to Mrs. Truman on September 18, 1941: "I'll be happy when my Masonic career ends and I can work altogether on the Senate committee, go where I please, say what I want to, and maybe do the country some good."

Six days later he again wrote to Mrs. Truman: "You should see Geo. Marquis' biography of your old man for the Grand Lodge *Proceedings*. You'd be like the old lady at the funeral of her husband, you'd have someone check to be sure it is the right corpse."

A portion of that biography written by Marquis read: "It is the opinion of this writer that Harry S. Truman represents all that is best in American manhood and citizenship. To quote a newspaper editorial, 'He was born and reared between the plow handles on a Jackson County farm.' From this rural atmosphere he has progressed step by step to heights attained by few men. In all his successes, in war and in politics, he remains unaffected by public acclaim, and is the same modest, rather retiring friendly and affable gentleman.

"Scrupulously upright in all his private dealings, he has carried that same high standard into all his public actions. Though millions of public funds have passed through his hands, no intimation of unfairness has ever been made. The late E.E. Stephens, chairman of the commission that built our State Capitol, once said to the writer that he resented newspaper comments complimenting the commission for its honesty, because that virtue was to be expected of a public official, but that he appreciated the praise of the stability and beauty of the work accomplished.

"Much more that is contained in this brief sketch could properly be said of the stability, beauty and permanence of the work wrought by Harry S. Truman. Generous to a fault, tolerant in his thoughts and actions, endowed with tremendous physical endurance, an untiring worker, devoted to his friends and fair to political opponents, he has rendered an invaluable service to his county, state and nation, in war and in peace; and to the fraternity of Freemasons he is a credit and an honor."

Again the Grand Lodge was crowded on September 30, 1941, when Grand Master Truman presided. In the introduction to the address every Grand Master everywhere is expected to make, he said:

> We are living in a period of the world's history which makes those of us who believe in morality and free government thankful that we live in the United States of America. The Masonic Fraternity on the European Continent has been suppressed. It has been suppressed because it stands for freedom of thought, and freedom of expression; for government of the people, for the people, by the people, and for freedom of worship. These great principles were established in the United States at Philadelphia in 1787, when the Constitution of the United States was written. The Constitution, and its Bill of Rights, has been a model for free governments the world over since that time. A large number of the framers of the Constitution of the United States were members of this great Fraternity of ours [thirteen were Masons].
>
> We are facing a solemn and serious period in our history; in fact, the most serious emergency we have ever faced. As Freemasons we must continually endeavor to instill appreciation of free

government, and free expression; freedom of thought and freedom of worship.

It has been my privilege, for the last seven years, to be a member of what is called the most August Deliberative Body in the world. A legislative forum where any man, who is a member, may express his views for as long and as freely as he chooses. It is the only national legislative body in the world where this privilege exists. It is a privilege guaranteed by the Constitution of the United States.

I thank God every day that I am a citizen of the greatest and freest country on earth, and that I have the privilege of worshiping as I please, of acting with complete liberty, so long as I do not infringe upon the rights of others, and of having the right to belong to any organization or Fraternity I choose, so long as it does not foster treason against the Government. We cannot really appreciate these privileges because we have always had them. But, our Brethren in Denmark, Holland, Norway, and all those other countries which have come under the heel of totalitarian dictators, are either in concentration camps, or have forsworn their liberties and their fraternal obligations.

It is a most difficult matter for me, as Grand Master of the Freemasons of the great State of Missouri—an honor which I believe is greater than any other which can come to me—to stand here and discuss this situation without getting upon political grounds. I have been extremely careful in my Grand Lodge career as a member of this Grand Lodge Line, to stay entirely clear of political actions and political utterances, where the interests of the Grand Lodge have been concerned. Brethren, we should be thankful for the privileges we enjoy. We must put forth every effort possible to maintain them with everything we have.

It has become necessary for the public welfare and the national defense of the country to train our young men for military service. Training these young men is on a universal basis. The richest of our people must serve, as well as the poorest, in the forces which are now being trained for the defense of the country.

It was my duty, in 1917 and 1918, to serve all through that emergency in the 35th Division, a National Guard Organization made up of volunteers from Missouri and Kansas. In that emergency Lodges in a great many States and in a great many cities, took down the bars, and without the proper investigation made thousands of men Freemasons who were not first Freemasons in their hearts. In this emergency, which we now face, our great Fraternity MUST NOT REPEAT that error.

In my service in France I was struck by the fact that nowhere in the welfare work for soldiers was Freemasonry represented. As your Grand Master, and as a United States Senator, it was my privilege to visit the Grand Lodge of Pennsylvania, and the Grand Lodge of the

> District of Columbia, on occasions when the Masonic welfare for the soldiers was being discussed at some length, and I am completely convinced that if the Grand Lodges of the United States would cooperate in a National organization for the Masonic welfare of our young men now in training, the welfare of the Nations, and our Fraternity, would be very materially helped. I have made a thorough investigation of the Masonic Service Association of the United States, of its personnel, and of what it proposes to do, and I have come to the conclusion that this Grand Lodge should do all it possibly can to support this Masonic Service Association for a Masonic National contact with our armed forces.
>
> Our country is facing the greatest emergency in its history. Our Masonic Fraternity must also face that emergency on a national basis.
>
> I am, therefore, suggesting that the Grand Lodge of Missouri join the Masonic Service Association and cooperate fully with the other Grand Lodges of the country for service to the soldiers in this emergency.
>
> The Grand Chapter, Royal Arch Masons of Missouri, is contributing One Thousand Dollars to this great cause. Your Grand Master is making a contribution of one-half his salary as Grand Master for the year. I hope, brethren, that this great organization will do its duty fully and completely in this national emergency.

The jurisprudence committee skirted this recommendation of the Grand Master, so the delegates didn't have an opportunity to vote to rejoin The Masonic Service Association that their Grand Lodge had quit in 1924. It would be 1944 before Missouri became a member again. The Masons of Missouri, however, did assist the Association monetarily in its efforts to help the servicemen and women of the country.

Truman concluded his address by saying: "I am sure that as long as there are three million Freemasons in the country, all good men and true, who believe in a system of morals, and the Constitution of the United States, we can safely face the future, no matter what it may bring forth."

During the evening session of the first day of the Grand Lodge session, Truman called up the officers of the Missouri Lodge of Research, constituted the lodge and installed the officers. He then presented the charter to its Master, Henry C. Chiles, Past Grand Master.

When the final gavel sounded, the 121st annual session of the Grand Lodge of Missouri came to a close. Harry S. Truman, Past

Grand Master, could do what he enjoyed best, mingle with the men on the sidelines. And his Masonic career could have come to an end in a blaze of glory. But he was too much of a Freemason for that to happen. He would remain an active Mason until the day he died.

8. WAR AND DECISIONS

Harry S. Truman, Past Grand Master, and chairman of the Senate Advisory Committee, traveled to Newport, Rhode Island, on December 1, 1941. There he formally dedicated the Masonic Service Center of The Masonic Service Association. These "homes away from home" for all members of the Armed Forces were being activated quickly throughout the country.

According to the records of the MSA and *Freemasonry's Servant,* the history of its first fifty years, each center was well equipped with comfortable chairs, pool and tennis tables, darts, various table games, newspapers, magazines, writing desks, stationery, radio and phonographs. Dances were held regularly, and the young ladies were carefully screened and sponsored by members of the Order of the Eastern Star, or a trained hostess. Everything was furnished free. And the guests were not limited to Freemasons or members of their families.

Among the early centers was one at Rolla, Missouri, headed by John Black Vrooman, who would be the first recipient of the Harry S. Truman Medal of the Grand Lodge of Missouri.

Six days after this dedication ceremony, all hell broke loose. The Japanese navy tore up Pearl Harbor, Hawaii. From December 7, 1941, on, the world would never be the same.

President Roosevelt asked a joint session of Congress for a declaration of war against the Empire of Japan. The Senate approved this unanimously; one dissenter, Jeanette Rankin of Montana, appeared in the House. This was tremendous improvement over a vote to renew the draft taken only three months earlier. In the House that bill had been approved—by one vote!

Truman wrote to his friend Ray Denslow of Missouri on December 17: "I was supposed to go to a Masonic meeting last night where two gentlemen were made Masons at sight. I got to thinking about the matter and couldn't bring myself to go, because I don't approve of such a matter, however great the recipients. I suppose the high-hats here will be somewhat put out with me because they had consulted me about the qualifications of the two men. Their qualifications were one hundred percent, but as you and I know, that just isn't the way to do it."

The two men were General George C. Marshall and Jesse H. Jones. Truman, and many other Masonic leaders, did not believe in conferring only obligations, or three quick degrees, on anyone. They were opposed to "making Masons at Sight." Truman was among the reserve officers who received a questionnaire about his availability for active duty. The long neglected reserves who had been more than neglected since World War I were finally being recognized. The war in Europe had caused the government to carefully consider shoring up its defenses.

The routine questionnaire asked if the recipient was available for active duty. Colonel Truman answered, "Yes." He noted he could leave immediately. To the question: "Are you considered essential where you are presently employed?" Truman said: "It depends on who is telling the story."

The Senator, if not the founder, certainly was one of the founders of the Reserve Officers Association. He formed the Reserve Officers Club in Kansas City which became one of the chapters of the Reserve Officers Association. Its official publication, *The Officer,* took note of his many contributions throughout the years by dedicating the May 1984 edition to Harry S. Truman.

While riding on the Missouri Pacific Railroad on December 28, 1941, Truman wrote to Mrs. Truman: "I found this in my briefcase and thought I might as well use it." The "this" was a letterhead reading: "Grand Lodge of Missouri, Ancient Free and Accepted Masons, Harry S. Truman, Grand Master."

With the United States at war the real value of the work of Truman's special committee could be seen. Billions of dollars had been saved. Work that would have been unsatisfactory was improved. All industry was aware of the "watchdog" in the United States Senate. The committee found that the automobile companies were particularly reluctant in 1941 to produce defense materials. They claimed their equipment wasn't suitable for anything but manufacturing automobiles and trucks. Truman noted: "However, when the production of automobiles was stopped, they reversed themselves and found they could convert their plants in a relatively short time."

Truman found many areas that needed big improvements. He was concerned with the airplane industry particularly. He had learned what the Army, Air Force, and Navy knew too well, that the planes being produced were of inferior quality. He learned that the inefficiency extended beyond industry and into the government. The worst culprit was the Office of Production Management. Truman recommended this be abolished and a War Production Board be set up under the direction of one man. The President agreed and the Board was established.

The special committee learned that labor unions were at fault in many instances for waste, confusion and obstructionism. An example was noted during an investigation at Fort Meade, Maryland. No one could be hired without the approval of the union, and all workers were charged a fee for work permits. In this one place alone Truman said "two hundred thousand dollars was taken in by the unions through such fees." The same conditions prevailed at other camps, the committee learned.

The number of lives of members of the Armed Forces that were saved because of Truman's committee will never be known. German submarines had sent twelve million tons of shipping to the bottom of the ocean, the committee learned. The Secretary of the Navy denied this, but when he appeared before the committee he learned its figures were correct. As a result, the shipping lanes were better protected.

An airplane manufacturer was turning out defective engines, the committee found. The company and the Army were given an opportunity to make their own inspection. They found nothing wrong. A sub-committee of the special committee went to the site and held hearings. It heard scores of witnesses, who testified that defective parts and defective engines had passed inspection at the plant and had been turned over to the Army, Truman wrote in his *Memoirs.* A second inspection by the Army proved the committee was correct. That practice was stopped.

The wingspread of the B-26 Martin bomber was found to be too short and had been responsible for several fatalities. Truman warned the company that unless this was corrected to save the lives of American airmen, no more of its planes would be purchased. The design was corrected.

Those who drive the highways owe much to Truman's committee. For example, it encouraged the development of synthetic rubber. For these, and hundreds of other improvements, this special committee caused to be made, a debt of gratitude is owed to the Mason from Missouri.

And he still found time to read about, and work for, Freemasonry. He found a story about Andrew Jackson in a Masonic history book. He took exception to some of the statements he found, and he wrote the publisher on January 8, 1942.

"I notice where you say that Andrew Jackson received his degrees at Greenville Lodge, Greenville, Tennessee in 1851," Truman wrote. "Andrew Jackson was Grand Master of Tennessee long before that, and it is not known exactly where he received his degrees, but it is recorded that he received them in North Carolina.

"He was born in 1767. You gave the date of his birth in 1808 and the place Raleigh, North Carolina. He was born in Wax Haws, and it is doubtful whether he was born north or south of the State line. There has always been a controversy between North and South Carolina about the location of the State line at the time of his birth. I don't know where you got those figures, but you certainly ought to make a correction on them.

"For your further information, if my dates are correct, Andrew Jackson died in 1845, so he couldn't possibly have received his degrees in 1851."

Truman was correct. Jackson was Grand Master in 1822. There has been speculation as to where he received his degrees but no proof. He was, however, elected an honorary member of Federal Lodge No. 1, D.C., and Jackson Lodge No. 1 of Florida. He was elected the seventh President of the United States in 1828, at the violent beginning of the anti-Masonic period. He refused to renounce his Masonic affiliation although his political advisors urged him to do so. His principles, evidently, endeared him to Truman, whose principles were just as strong.

During "Masonic Week" in Washington Truman attended the various meetings of the Masonic leadership. These included The Masonic Service Association, the George Washington Masonic National Memorial Association, the Conference of Grand Masters, and Conference of Grand Secretaries.

The National League of Masonic Clubs met in its convention in June 1942, and Truman was the featured speaker. The chairman thanked Truman in writing: "To have you present at the

Senator Truman, right, formally informs General John J. Pershing, center, a member of Lincoln Lodge No. 19, Nebraska, he has been elected an honorary member of the Grand Lodge of Missouri, as Grand Master Harris G. Johnson looks on. The ceremony took place at Walter Reed Hospital on February 15, 1942.

[Truman Library photo]

Gold Card Dinner was a pleasure, indeed, and your attendance at the Inspirational Hour on Friday evening was also a real mark of Masonry, and many of the Brothers there made mention of that fact."

Writing from Missouri on July 4, 1943, Truman was evidently pleased with what he found. "Well the gang are gathering here," he wrote. "It is a fight between Kansas City and St. Louis and it looks as if I may be able to pay some of those St. Louis guys who knifed me in 1940 in the Missouri Grand Lodge. Isn't it funny how chickens come home to some people." He added on the following day: "Have been standing in line shaking hands with hundreds of Shriners from New Hampshire to Washington State and from California to Florida. They all look at me as if I were

Jumbo in Barnum's Circus. One old guy asked if this was the real Truman or just a state senator being used for show purposes.

"It scares me to death the things they say to me and about me to the other people in the Kansas City delegation. I thought I was coming here to have a good time with a bunch of the boys from K.C. whom I know and I've turned out to be their drawing card—but at that I don't believe our man will win. Anyway he says it's some help and I hope it is, because he's a nice fellow. He gave me the honorary degree the other night for the DeMolays. I've learned something anyway. I'll know better than to be the two-headed calf."

Rufus Burrus said: "Frank Land was the man Truman supported for the National Shrine line in 1943, and Frank was elected. Frank was a good Mason and always a friend of Harry. When Frank died I went with Harry to his funeral."

When the Grand Lodge of Missouri met for its annual communication on September 28 and 29, 1942, Truman was there. So were many of his close friends. Bruce Hunt recalled how the Senator often wanted to get away from the crowd to relax. That was impossible in his own room in the hotel, so following the evening session of the Grand Lodge he walked past where Hunt was sitting and asked him what his room number was. At the close of the session Truman met Hunt in his room. Bruce was instructed to intercept all phone calls and let the callers know he wasn't to be disturbed. It was after midnight when he left for his own room. But at six in the morning Truman and Hunt met several of their close friends for breakfast.

Hunt said he usually shared a suite with another close friend of Truman, George Claude Marquis. "The living room of the suite was the scene of many late evening 'bull sessions,' where the cares of the world were laid aside," wrote Hunt. "The atmosphere was usually convivial and stories were told thick and fast. Brother Truman seldom told a story, but he greatly enjoyed hearing them. It should also be said that many an important decision concerning the business of Grand Lodge was made in this setting."

Truman was chairman for the Grand Master's address in 1942. And he had obtained the featured speaker, General Brehon B. Somervell. The Republican governor of the state, Forrest C.

Donnell, was elected Grand Master. He immediately appointed Truman to a special committee on social services at the training camps.

On the Senate floor a week later Truman asked for permission to include the speech of General Somervell in the Congressional Record. Within this speech the general said: "You may not know it but the Senator [Truman] has twice volunteered to don the uniform he wore with such distinction in the last war and is serving on the Capitol front only at the express request of the Secretary of War and the Chief of Staff who felt the need of his assistance there."

The Grand Lodge of Tennessee invited Truman to address it on January 27, 1943. He was later made an Honorary Past Grand Master.

Once again the chairman of the advisory committee of the MSA called to order a meeting of the Congressmen who were Masons on February 12, 1943. He took pleasure in introducing the executive secretary of the Association, Carl H. Claudy, who was also serving as Grand Master of Masons in the District of Columbia. Together they outlined the vast amount of work being done for the Armed Forces. They were happy to report that Freemasons in Hollywood had come to their aid. They had produced a heart-warming motion picture entitled *Your Son Is My Brother.* Claudy told the men: "The Senator did not tell you when he spoke of the Grand Lodge of Missouri contributing $7,000 when he was Grand Master, that in addition to that the Grand Master is given $500 for expenses necessary to his work as Grand Master. Instead of spending it for his expenses, he indorsed the check over to The Masonic Service Association!"

On the political scene events were taking place that would have a profound effect on the Senator from Missouri for the rest of his life. On July 12, 1943, he wrote to Mrs. Truman: "The Senator from Pennsylvania took me out into his beautiful back yard (garden in the capital) and *very confidentially* wanted to know what I thought of Henry Wallace [a Mason and the Vice President of the United States]. I told him that Henry is the best Secretary of Agriculture we ever did have. He laughed and said that is what he thinks. Then he wanted to know if I would help out the ticket if it became necessary by accepting the nomination for Vice

President. I told him in words of one syllable that I would not—that I had only recently become a Senator and that I wanted to work at it for about ten years."

Truman forgot about the conversation and went back to work with his committee in the Senate. And he didn't overlook his Freemasonry.

In September 1943, he attended the annual communication of his Grand Lodge. Again he had obtained the Monday night speaker for the Grand Lodge. This time it was Admiral George D. Murray.

During the communication, Grand Master Donnell broke into the prepared schedule to say: "I think it would be very discourteous and not at all proper if I did not at this time call to the microphone a gentleman who has come from Washington, D.C., leaving his official duties, which means simply that he has to take care of them when he returns, as they have piled up, and he has come here to pay us a fraternal visit. I take great pleasure in presenting at this time our distinguished junior United States Senator from Missouri, former Grand Master of Masons of Missouri, Honorable Harry S. Truman."

To which Truman responded: "It certainly is a very, very great courtesy for you to invite me to the microphone. I am just an ordinary member of this Grand Lodge, and it is the greatest place in the world to come, I think. I do want to take this opportunity, Governor, to again thank you for delegating me last night to introduce the principal speaker. . . . I appreciate most highly your courtesy, and while we differ politically, our friendship is just as strong as it ever was."

Claudy, Grand Master of Masons in the District of Columbia, was honored in his mother lodge, Harmony No. 17, on November 24, 1943. Truman was invited to attend, and he did.

There were no Masonic meetings In Washington in February 1944. All travel for conventions was prohibited because of shortages caused by the war. A letter announcing the cancellation of all Masonic meetings in the District was sent to all Masonic groups throughout the country. Truman personally carried a copy of this letter to the President, who was pleased to commend his brother Masons for their patriotism.

Truman addressed the Grand Lodge of New Jersey on April 19, 1944. He was sent an honorarium of $50, which he promptly endorsed and returned "with the suggestion that it go into the Masonic Home charity fund."

Rumors were running wild with the Democratic convention drawing near. It was apparent that Harry Truman was the choice of the leaders of the party for the vice presidency. Truman continued to state emphatically that he was not interested in the job. On July 13, 1944, he wrote: "Just gave Mr. [Roy] Roberts a tough interview saying I didn't want the Vice Presidency. Also told the West Virginia and Oklahoma delegations to go for Barkley. Also told [Sheridan] Downey I didn't want the California delegation. Mr. Roberts says I have it in the bag if I don't say no—and I've said it as tough as I can."

Truman had repeatedly said he was perfectly content to remain a Senator from Missouri. Mrs. Truman wasn't interested in his taking the job. In fact, she would have been content to return to Missouri. Two other Masons, however, did want it: Henry A. Wallace, the then Vice President, and James F. Byrnes of South Carolina who was often called the "assistant president." The power structure of the Democratic Party wanted neither of them; it knew the other Mason in this quartet, Franklin D. Roosevelt, was a dying man. Truman was the man the leaders wanted. Although Roosevelt leaned toward Wallace, he was still politically astute and knew what was transpiring on the political front.

At the convention Truman was cornered by Democratic and union leaders, all insisting he accept the nomination. He didn't change his mind. Then Robert E. Hannegan, the national Democratic Party chairman, handed Truman a note written by Roosevelt which said: "Bob, it's Truman. F.D.R." This puzzled the Senator because he believed the President wanted either Wallace or Douglas.

What Truman didn't know was the party leaders had met months before and Roosevelt had stated his preference for Truman. It was during that meeting that Roosevelt had handed Hannegan the note Truman had just seen.

From his hotel room, with Truman and others present, Hannegan telephoned the President, who was in San Diego, California. Hannegan told him he hadn't been able to convince Truman to accept the nomination. Roosevelt thundered into the phone so all in the room could hear: "Well, you tell him if he wants to break up the Democratic party in the middle of a war, that's his responsibility."

Truman capitulated. He became the vice presidential candidate of the Democratic Party.

He also became embroiled in a Masonic controversy concerning his friend, Ray V. Denslow, and the thirty-third degree of the Scottish Rite.

9. DEATH AND PEACE

"I send you my heartiest congratulations on your victory. I am, of course, very happy to have you run with me. Let me know your plans. I shall see you soon. Franklin D. Roosevelt," read a telegram received by Truman on July 21, 1944.

Truman visited the White House and learned he would have to do the campaigning. Roosevelt said he was so busy with war plans he had no time to spare. To find the time necessary to cover the country, something had to go. So, it was with mixed emotions the vice presidential candidate submitted his resignation as chairman of the special committee he had headed since before the war began.

While the campaigning was taking place The Masonic Service Association found that members of the Armed Forces needed more than service centers. Thousands of wounded servicemen and women were lying in veterans hospitals, many forgotten or ignored by the outside world. The Association proposed a system of hospital visitation be organized. Truman, chairman of the advisory committee, agreed fully. He, along with Generals George C. Marshall and Henry H. "Hap" Arnold, and Admiral Ernest J. King, members of the advisory committee, supported the program. A trial visitation program was started. It proved so successful it has been continued to the present time. Now dozens of non-profit organizations offer their support to what is known as "The Veterans' Administration Voluntary Services."

Truman again returned to Missouri for the annual communication of his Grand Lodge. It was held in Kansas City, September 25 and 26, 1944. This time he furnished two speakers. Senator Owen Brewster of Maine was one of them. The other was Carl H. Claudy, who not only delivered an address but presented the excellent motion picture, *Your Son Is My Brother.*

Truman also introduced a far-reaching resolution in support of his friend and mentor, Ray V. Denslow (See chapter 10).

The 1944 campaign progressed easily, Truman said. He was pleased because all of his other political campaigns had been extremely difficult. In the November election the team of

Roosevelt-Truman won 432 electoral votes to 99 for the Republicans.

For the third time Franklin D. Roosevelt had defeated brother Masons: Alfred Landon in 1936; Wendell Wilkie in 1940; and Thomas E. Dewey in 1944. Herbert Hoover, his first victim in 1932, was not a Mason but did think highly of the organization and its members.

Soon after he was sworn in as Vice President of the United States, Truman had the privilege of administering the oath to Frank P. Briggs of Missouri as a new United States Senator. Briggs had been appointed by Governor and Past Grand Master Donnell to fill the unexpired term of Truman in the Senate. The new Senator was a newspaper publisher and former state senator. He would become Grand Master of Masons in Missouri in 1957.

The new Vice President is reported to have once said the position "was as useless as a fifth teat on a cow." Now that he held the job he wanted to change that image. He told newsmen: "I want to bring the administration and Congress closer together on the methods of attaining the goal all of us have in common, and if I can create a better understanding, I feel that I can render an important public service."

During the eighty-three days he served in this office he had only one opportunity to vote in the Senate. He found that "isolationism" wasn't dead, as he had thought. An amendment to limit the Lend-Lease Bill ended in a tie. Truman voted to defeat the proposal so the program that had saved Great Britain could continue.

He also found time to work with the folks on the home front, especially servicemen and women. On one occasion he visited Washington's National Press Club Canteen. A widely-distributed photograph proved it wasn't beneath the dignity of the Vice President to entertain those present. The picture showed actress Lauren Bacall sitting on top of the piano he was playing, although the Vice President had nothing to do with that publicity stunt. It is reported Bacall's press agent saw the chance to put her in a favorable public position and pushed her onto the piano. Another picture showed Jack Benny playing his violin beside Truman at the piano.

Roosevelt had been to Yalta and returned so exhausted that Truman suggested he report to the joint session of Congress seated, something never before considered. He did, and it was apparent that he wasn't well. Gone was the forceful, confident voice. In its place was will power, perseverance and courage.

On March 30, 1945, Roosevelt left for Warm Springs, Georgia, with everything appearing to be going well in Europe and the Pacific. American and Allied forces continued to advance on all fronts. American troops crossed the Elbe River, fifty miles from Berlin, and the Germans were putting up a last-ditch stand throughout Germany. American forces were fighting suicidal Japanese attacks at Okinawa as they drew ever closer to the Empire's islands. But the President would not see victory; in Warm Springs on April 12, 1945, Franklin Delano Roosevelt died.

Truman was tired when he finished presiding over a session of the Senate on the afternoon of April 12. He walked down the long corridor to Sam Rayburn's "hideaway," called, perhaps justly, "the board of education." There he planned to relax, but Rayburn told him Steve Early, the President's press secretary, had telephoned and Truman was to call the White House immediately.

Early's voice was strained when he told the Vice President to come to the White House. Truman eluded his Secret Service guards and had his chauffeur drive him to the main entrance, as he had been instructed. From there he was taken to Mrs. Eleanor Roosevelt's study. She placed her arm around his shoulders and said quietly: "Harry, the President is dead."

When Truman could speak he asked her: "Is there anything I can do for you?"

Truman said he would never forget her understanding reply: "Is there anything we can do for *you*? For you are the one in trouble now."

As he fought off tears Truman recalled a conversation he had with Roosevelt shortly after they were nominated. Truman told the President he planned on covering the country by plane. "Don't do that, please," said Roosevelt. "Go by train. It is necessary that you take care of yourself."

Truman immediately ordered the presidential plane made ready to carry Mrs. Roosevelt to Warm Springs.

With Mrs. Truman and their daughter present, most of the members of the Cabinet and a few others, Chief Justice Harlan Fiske Stone administered the oath: "I, Harry S. Truman, do solemnly swear that I will faithfully execute the office of President of the United States, and will to the best of my ability, preserve, protect and defend the Constitution of the United States. So help me God." He then kissed the Holy Bible. The time was 7:09 p.m.

As the Cabinet was taking seats Truman made his first decision as President of the United States—the conference on the United Nations would meet as scheduled on April 25. "It was of supreme importance," he wrote in his *Memoirs,* "that we build an organization to help keep the future peace of the world."

Truman informed the Cabinet that he would certainly listen to advice, that he didn't want to be surrounded by "yes men," but he intended to make the final decisions. Although he planned on following Roosevelt's policies insofar as possible, he planned on being the President.

Secretary of War Henry L. Stimson asked to meet with the President after the others had left. It was then Truman learned for the first time about the project that had developed the atom bomb. It was then that he learned what was behind the request of Stimson to Senator Truman in 1942 to call off his investigation of two locations by his special committee. Truman had agreed because he respected Stimson as a "great American patriot and statesman." That was the only investigation Truman ever permitted to be called off.

Through all the sorrow and momentous decisions that had to be made, Truman remembered a Masonic obligation he had. Lieutenant Neville J. McMillan, son of a Past Master of Grandview Lodge No. 618, Truman's mother Lodge, had petitioned Alexandria-Washington Lodge No. 22 in Alexandria, Virginia. His petition was to be balloted on the evening of April 12. Truman sent three members of Congress who were Masons to speak for him. McMillan was elected to receive the first degree (in Virginia a man must be elected to each degree).

Truman's first official act as President was to sign a proclamation for President Roosevelt's funeral and holiday. He then went to his first military briefing, and found men he highly respected, including at least two Masons, General Marshall and Admiral

King. Truman asked Admiral William D. Leahy, who had been chief of staff to President Roosevelt, a new position that he had filled extremely well, to remain and continue in that position.

"Are you sure you want me, Mr. President? I always say what's on my mind," Leahy said.

"I want the truth," said the President, "and I want the facts at all times. I want you to stay with me and always tell me what's on your mind. You may not always agree with my decisions, but I know you will carry them out faithfully." The admiral remained.

Truman was concerned because there was now no Vice President. He felt he had to make a change in the Secretary of State. James F. Byrnes, a Mason from South Carolina, had the qualifications to serve as President should that become necessary. The President determined to make this change soon after the United Nations meeting, and he informed Byrnes of his plan so he would be prepared to take over his new duties.

Roosevelt's body lay in state in the East Room of the White House on the 14th. The following day Truman, his family and other dignitaries, boarded the funeral train for the solemn trip to Hyde Park, New York. There, on Sunday morning, Roosevelt was buried.

On Monday, April 16, 1945, Truman made his first address to a joint session of Congress. He concluded that address by saying: "At this moment I have in my heart a prayer. As I have assumed my heavy duties, I humbly pray to Almighty God in the words of King Solomon, 'Give therefore Thy servant an understanding heart to judge Thy people, that I may discern between good and bad; for who is able to judge this Thy so great a people?'

"I ask only to be a good and faithful servant of my Lord and my people."

Reporters have a way of asking nonsensical questions in times of stress. Many of these were asked of many people, high and low, throughout the country following the death of Roosevelt and Truman's ascendancy to the Presidency. His ninety-two-year-old mother was not excluded.

"I can't really be glad he's President," she said, "because I am sorry President Roosevelt is dead. If he had been voted in, I would be out waving a flag, but it doesn't seem right to be very happy or wave any flags now. Harry will get along all right. I knew Harry would be all right after I heard him give his speech this morning. I heard every word of it but Mary is going to read it to me again. Everyone who heard him talk this morning will know he's sincere and will do what's best."

From all over the world letters and telegrams poured in to the White House congratulating the new President. Thousands of Freemasons, knowing the worth of Truman perhaps better than any other group, sent along their approval and offered their prayers for his success.

Truman told Mrs. Roosevelt to take as much time as she needed to move from the White House. He and his family moved into the Blair House for the first time, but it would not be the last.

The Germans expected a reprieve, but the new Commander-in-Chief fooled them—and everyone else. Although Roosevelt had kept him in the dark about almost everything, including the atom bomb, his crash course proved that the United States had a formidable, no-nonsense leader.

Ernie Pyle, of all the war correspondents, was the best-loved by the fighting men in Europe and the Pacific. He was with them in the heat of many battles, including the long-awaited invasion that became known as "the longest day." With the war winding down in Europe, he moved to the Pacific. There, on Ie Shima, near Okinowa, he was killed.

President Truman paid tribute to Pyle on April 18, 1945: "More than any other man, he became the spokesman of the ordinary American in arms doing so many extraordinary things. It was his genius that the mass and power of our military and naval forces never obscure the men who made them."

Ernie Pyle was buried in the mountain crater of National Memorial Cemetery of the Pacific on July 19, 1945. On the 8th the President had sent a beautiful letter of condolences to Mrs. Pyle.

Six days after he became President, Truman addressed the Armed Forces around the world via radio. He told them he knew they would carry out their duties in the American tradition as he had during World War I. "I know the strain, the mud, the misery, the utter weariness of the soldier in the field," he told them. "And I know, too, his courage, his stamina, and his faith in his comrades, his country, and himself. We are depending upon each and every one of you."

Unlike Roosevelt, Truman enjoyed working with facts and figures, so he told the budget director he could remain, but policies concerning the budget would be determined by the President. He became the first President to ever present his budget to the press personally. None of his successors did until Gerald R. Ford decided to emulate Truman in 1977. Ford recalled the difference: Truman's budget called for $43 billion within 80 pages; Ford's, $394.2 billion within 955 pages.

The Soviet and Polish question quickly became a problem. From the accounts the President was receiving it was apparent that Stalin's version of "democracy" and America's were entirely different. Molotov, the Soviet Ambassador to the United States, discussed this problem with Truman on April 22. The President didn't hide his dislike of what Stalin was doing and told Molotov so—bluntly.

Molotov was shocked. "I have never been talked to like that in my life!" he said. "Carry out your agreements," answered Truman, "and you won't get talked to like that!" The President had no plans to abandon the Poles to communism, but as he would learn the matter was one he could not control.

The division of Germany, which had been agreed to by Churchill, Stalin and Roosevelt at Yalta, became a pressing problem. That Yalta agreement would haunt the world, and especially the United States, for decades.

Finally the President found time to learn more about the atom bomb. Truman listened carefully to the background briefing presented by Secretary of War Stimson. This most powerful device had been developed in laboratories in Chicago, Berkeley and New York. The giant industrial plants at Oak Ridge and Hanford had played important roles. So had the assembly center at Los Alamos. Shortly there would be available a bomb that could destroy a whole city.

The work had been performed in complete secrecy, it was thought. Although thousands of individuals in this country and Great Britain knew of the "Manhattan Project," Truman wasn't one of them until after he took the oath of office as President. He had to take a cram course in the potential of this bomb. To do this he called on many of the men who were familiar with the project so he could weigh his decision when and if he had to make one about its use.

One of the long and eagerly awaited days arrived which would always be remembered as "V-E Day." On that morning, May 8, 1945, Truman wrote to his mother and sister:

"I am sixty-one this morning, and slept in the President's room in the White House last night.

"At 9:00 o'clock this morning I must make a broadcast to the country announcing the German surrender. The papers were signed yesterday morning and hostilities will cease on all fronts at midnight tonight. Isn't that some birthday present?

"Have had one heck of a time with the Prime Minister of Great Britain. He, Stalin and the U.S. President made an agreement to release the news all at once from the three capitals at an hour that would fit us all. We agreed on 9 a.m. Washington time which is 3 p.m. London and 4 p.m. Moscow time.

"Mr. Churchill began calling me at daylight to know if we shouldn't make an immediate release without considering the Russians. He was refused and then he kept pushing me to talk to Stalin. He finally had to stick to the agreed plan—but he was mad as a wet hen.

"Things have moved at a terrific rate here since April 12. Never a day has gone by that some momentous decision didn't have to be made. So far luck has been with me."

On the day after V-E Day, Truman told a nation-wide radio audience: "We must work to bind up the wounds of a suffering world—to build an abiding peace, a peace rooted in justice and in law. We can build such a peace only by hard, toilsome, painstaking work—by understanding and working with our Allies in peace as we have in war." When the news was announced in Russia the crowds went wild. Shouts of: "Long live Truman! Long live Roosevelt's memory! Long live the great Americans!" were heard everywhere.

Mrs. Roosevelt's possessions were moved from the White House and Truman moved in. Four days later his mother and sister visited him. His mother had sent word earlier by her younger son, Vivian, to "tell Harry that if he puts me in the room with Lincoln's bed in it I'll sleep on the floor." She proved she was still a Confederate sympathizer. She wasn't given Lincoln's bed, but even though dignitaries from all over the world had slept in the one she was offered, she decided it was too big and fancy for her. She moved into an adjoining room with a smaller bed. Mary Jane, her daughter, got the fancy one.

Truman continued cramming. He wanted to meet with Churchill and Stalin, and there were many questions that troubled him: Poland, the European states, the Italian government, food and other necessities for the war-ravished countries, the war in the Pacific where it appeared continuing bombing wouldn't bring the Empire of Japan to submission, the atom bomb, among dozens of others. Before the planned meeting Truman discussed the many facets with Harry Hopkins, Averell Harriman, the ambassador to Russian, military advisors, and scores of others.

On July 6 the President boarded the *U.S.S. Augusta* for the trip to the Potsdam Conference, code named "Terminal." He had decided to travel by ship to give him time to go over the many documents that required further study. It also gave him uninterrupted time with Byrnes and Leahy.

On landing the President and his party were driven through war-torn Antwerp and along the roads to Brussels. At the airfield he boarded his plane, the *Sacred Cow,* which was waiting for him, for the flight to Berlin. From the air Truman had a first-hand view of the devastation of Germany. Stalin was delayed in arriving at the conference because of a slight heart attack, although that wasn't known until much later. Truman found time because of the delay to tour the ravaged city of Berlin.

"A more depressing sight than that of ruined buildings was the long, never ending procession of old men, women, and children wandering aimlessly along the autobahn and the country roads carrying, pushing or pulling what was left of their belongings," Truman wrote in his *Memoirs*. "In that two hour drive I saw evidence of a great world tragedy, and I was thankful that the United States had been spared the unbelievable devastation of this war."

The Potsdam Conference turned into a bargaining session of "take and give." The Russians did most of the taking; England and America the giving. Among many other things, Stalin demanded ten billion dollars from Germany in reparations. This

Truman considered exorbitant. He had no intentions of seeing American aid going through Germany into Russia.

It appeared the United States' late entry into the war was a burr in the side of Churchill as well as Stalin. The latter was still incensed because it took longer than he believed necessary for the second front he had demanded for months. Other underlying factors were brought to light, many of which would affect the world to the present day. There certainly was no unity at Potsdam.

On June 12, 1945, Truman wrote from the White House: "Just two months ago today, I was a reasonably happy and contented Vice President. Maybe you can remember that far back too. But things have changed so much it hardly seems real.

"I sit here in this old house and work on foreign affairs, read reports, and work on speeches—all the while listening to the ghosts walk up and down the hallway and even right here in the study. The floors pop and the drapes move back and forth—I can just imagine old Andy and Teddy having an argument over Franklin. Or James Buchanan [all Masons] and Franklin Pierce deciding which was the more useless to the country. And when Millard Fillmore and Chester Arthur join in for place and show the din is almost unbearable."

At Potsdam Truman told Stalin about the atom bomb which Churchill had known about for years. The Soviet leader wasn't surprised, and it would later be learned that Soviet spies had fully informed the Soviets about the Manhattan Project. In fact, it would be only a few weeks before the Soviets unlocked the secrets. Both agreed it should be used against Japan if it would shorten the war and save lives.

On July 26, 1945, Japan was given an ultimatum to surrender unconditionally or face complete destruction. Premier Suzuki announced that Japan would ignore the ultimatum. Consequently Truman ordered one of the two atom bombs dropped after August 3, weather permitting, on any one of four cities.

Colonel Paul W. Tibbets, Jr., and his crew took off in a B-29 on August 6, and the bomb was dropped on Hiroshima. This didn't bring capitulation, so on the 9th the second atom bomb was dropped on the secondary target, Nagasaki. When the total destruction of the awesome bombs could be determined from reconnaissance photos, Truman bluffed: "We are now prepared to obliterate rapidly and completely every productive enterprise the Japanese have above ground in any city." His poker playing came in handy; the bluff worked. Few, other than Truman, knew there were no more A-bombs in the American arsenal!

There is no way to determine how many American and Japanese lives were saved by the decision to drop the atom bomb. Yet, when the world was again at peace, the Monday morning quarterbacks criticized Truman for giving the order. To these he continued to say: "Let there be no mistake about it. I regarded the bomb as a military weapon and never had any doubt that it should be used." There was no criticism from those who had survived the suicidal *Kamikaze* attacks at Okinawa.

On August 15, 1945, for the first time in history, Emperor Hirohito of Japan spoke to his people by radio. He made it clear the destruction caused by the atom bomb had brought about Japan's defeat. At 7 p.m. Truman told a jubilant press corps Japan had unconditionally surrendered.

Perhaps not surprisingly, the President "suggested" to General Douglas MacArthur that the surrender documents be formally signed aboard the *U.S.S. Missouri*, a battlewagon his daughter had christened. Although V-J Day was August 14, the documents were not signed in Toyko Bay until September 2, 1945.

The *Missouri* would play another role in the life of President Truman. He made a trip to Brazil in 1947 and returned, with his wife and daughter, aboard the battleship. He was so impressed with its captain, Robert L. Dennison, he assigned him as a Presidential aide a year later. The story of the *Missouri* has not ended. Although battleships, in the "wisdom" of some military "experts," were destined for "mothballs," three have been reactivated. Among them is the battleship on whose deck the Japanese surrendered.

The Soviets, like scavengers, when the defeat of Japan was eminent, quickly entered the conflict so they could share in the spoils. However, Truman's tough policy kept the Soviets from participating in the Japanese occupation.

The need for humanitarian efforts in Europe was apparent to Truman. He had seen first-hand the devastation of war. This was

In September 1947 the Trumans visited Rio de Janeiro, Brazil, and returned aboard the battleship *U.S.S. Missouri* where the Trumans became ''shellbacks" (an honor reserved for those who cross the equator). As did "King Neptune" before him, President Truman inspected the crew.

[U.S. Navy photo/Truman Library]

perhaps one reason he met with Carl Claudy of the MSA. Claudy discussed with the President what could be done to meet the needs of Masons and others in Europe. It was noted that German and other European Freemasons had been victims of the holocaust as had the Jews. Members of the Masonic Fraternity had been murdered, sent into concentration camps, or otherwise deprived of their freedom and property. Freemasonry was the first of all organizations, including those of religious persuasions, proscribed by the Nazis. It was suggested that a Masonic commission be sent overseas to make a detailed study of the needs of those in Great Britain and on the continent.

Truman agreed. The State Department was violently opposed to this project, pointing out that it would bring demands from others for the same "privilege." The President sent a memo to his special counsel: "Mr. Grew is very much mistaken about the Masonic program. The situation that I had in mind would take in every section of that fraternity, and would represent all of the Masonic bodies. Under no other condition would the matter be considered.

"I think it can be worked out on that basis, and I am of the opinion that it would be an asset both to the State Department and to me."

If the State Department had any further objections it was wise enough to keep them quiet.

The Masonic Commission departed for Europe on August 12, 1945. It was headed by Truman's friend, Ray V. Denslow, a Past Grand Master of Masons in Missouri. With him went Past Grand Masters Claude J. McAllister of Montana and Charles H. Johnson of New York, and Justice George E. Bushnell of Michigan, who would later become Grand Commander of the Northern Masonic Jurisdiction of the Scottish Rite.

Before departing, Denslow and his companions sent a telegram to Claudy: "We depart upon our mission of Brotherhood with a strong determination to succeed and justify the confidence of The Masonic Service Association and the President of the United States for the glory and progress of American Freemasonry for world Brotherhood. Thanks for everything."

Their schedule began in London, England, on the day the Japanese decided to surrender. This delayed the mission for four days, but in less than thirty days the commission covered France, Germany, Sweden, Norway, Denmark, Netherlands, Belgium, Italy, Greece, Czechoslovakia, Scotland, and returned to London.

Everywhere the Masonic Commission found misery, devastation, hunger and all the other horrors associated with war. And the President was the first to hear the report of the commission. He made certain of that by telegraphing Denslow to come to the White House as soon as he left the *Queen Mary.*

The Freemasons of the United States quickly learned about the horrible situation. Funds poured in for the relief of the Masons of Europe, their families, and thousands in no way associated with the Fraternity.

In November, 1945, the MSA published a report entitled "Freemasonry in Europe," for the President and the Freemasons of the country. It was compiled by the special committee that had gone overseas at the request of Truman. Its findings were reported without drama, but most people learned for the first time the full extent of devastation caused by Nazism.

A portion of the lengthy report follows:

> To Hitler and Mussolini, Freemasonry was an organization which might interfere with their plans; it was a universal association of men banded together for friendliness, for cooperation, united only for the purpose of carrying on charitable activities and spreading world brotherhood. Such an organization did not fit in with the plans of Hitler and Mussolini. It was therefore selected as one of the first of those association to come beneath the hammer of the dictators. [Full details followed showing how the axis powers accomplished the abolition of Masonry.]
>
> Of all the countries visited, Sweden is the least affected by the war. The Freemasonry of the Scandinavian countries is of the highest type. . . . War conditions in Norway and Denmark created many problems for our Swedish brethren; thousands of refugees came from these two countries, and these had to be housed and fed. . . .
>
> There is a very close relationship between the peoples of Sweden and Finland. During the Russo-Finnish War the sympathies of Sweden were with Finland; many a young Swede lost his life fighting for the little country to the East to which he was united by ties of blood.

Surprisingly, Freemasonry in France was damaged less than many of the other countries. It was, however, still having problems because it was split into three parts, and the Bible was not required in the lodges. The Germans did take over all Masonic property, destroying much of it, but what could be salvaged was being returned and repaired.

Freemasonry in Norway had to submit to "terrible punishment." On July 18, 1945, a bulletin was sent by the Grand Lodge to its known members. It noted the German invaders stopped all Masonry there in September, 1940, by brute force. Its property and buildings were handed over to "quislings, the traitors of our nation, together with our Masonic furniture, books and means."

In Denmark on April 9, 1940, Hitler violated the non-aggression pact and occupied the country. The Danes never gave up but fought the Germans openly and through the underground throughout the war. The Masons managed to save much of their property by hiding it. They took pride in stating that their Grand Master, King Christian X, remained true to Masonic principles throughout the occupation.

In Greece, where Freemasonry had been strong prior to the war, the committee found the Germans had persecuted Masons from the beginning of the occupation. It was learned that there was no way to estimate the number of destitute Masons, widows and children. It was also learned that Masonic funds sent immediately after the end of the war were confiscated by a corrupt Greek official. And the Greek government wasn't sympathetic toward Freemasonry.

The committee found it wasn't welcome in Czechoslovakia. The Russians were rapidly taking over the country.

In Germany Freemasons had operated underground for years. Many of them wore a little blue flower so they could be known among their brethren. The committee found it would take a long time for legitimate Freemasonry to be revitalized in Germany.

The committee was surprised to find a Masonic lodge working in Rome, Italy, when it arrived. When the known Masons were asked what they needed, one replied: "We are poor, but we ask nothing."

The Grand Master of Holland, H. van Tongeren, was confined to a concentration camp where he died. But immediately after Holland was freed of Nazis, the Grand Lodge of the Netherlands resumed its operations. Belgium Freemasonry had always been weak, and the war had not helped this situation. Austrian

Freemasonry would have a difficult time rebounding. The country was occupied by American, English and Russian forces. The latter would permit no Masonry to exist.

"Unless one has witnessed the destruction in Europe," reported the committee, "seen the lack of clothing, of food and medicines, talked face to face with those who have undergone German occupation, one is unable to judge of the fearfulness of the past few years in Europe."

The committee strongly recommended that Freemasons in America assist *all* the peoples of the devastated countries, because it would not be right "for us to attempt to feed and clothe only our own members," and leave their neighbors naked and hungry. It suggested all aid be channeled through "established agencies charged with the supplying of food and clothing to these people."

This was done, and C.A.R.E. became the principle agency used by the MSA to help the people of war-torn Europe.

Everything that was done had the full support of President Truman. He took note of this in a letter to the Association:

"I commend the enviable record made during the war by the Association, acting as the agent for the Grand Lodges and other Masonic bodies; especially am I interested in your plans for expansion of Masonry's Hospital Visitation service. Surely Freemasonry cannot do enough for those brave men who have sacrificed so much for our beloved country.

"The European Relief Fund interests me greatly. I am convinced that nothing Freemasonry could do would more aid us all in establishing a just peace in war-torn Europe than a generous offering of relief by American brethren to distressed brethren in the occupied countries."

World War II had ended. With it came the peace, although an uneasy one, that millions throughout the world had prayed for. With the peace came responsibilities. Under the leadership of the President of the United States, not only Freemasons but most of the people of the country embarked on a program to ease the pangs of the war. They did not seek revenge and retribution as did one of its allies; they were compassionate.

The days and years ahead would provide the President with continuing world-wide problems, heartaches, and triumphs.

10. FRIENDSHIP

Truman had been an active member of the Scottish Rite of Freemasonry, Southern Jurisdiction, since January 24, 1912, when he had received the degrees through the fourteenth. He had wanted to "go all the way" to the thirty-second degree immediately, but his finances wouldn't permit it. However, on March 31, 1917, the long awaited day arrived, and he received the balance of the Scottish Rite degrees. He had long been eligible and deserving of receiving the honorary thirty-third degree, thereby making him an "Inspector General, Honorary." This is a degree only the Supreme Council of the Scottish Rite can award. Among other things, the recipient is presumed to be a leader in the community or country, moral, and a worker in Freemasonry.

The Sovereign Grand Commander of the Southern Jurisdiction was John H. Cowles of Kentucky. Truman was convinced that Cowles was antagonistic toward those who favored the "New Deal," though there may have been others in appendant bodies who also disapproved of the politics then prevailing.

Franklin Delano Roosevelt became a Master Mason in Holland Lodge No. 8 in New York City on November 14, 1911, and received the thirty-second degree on February 28, 1929. At the time he was governor of New York. He helped raise his sons, Elliott, James, and Franklin D., Jr., to the degree of Master Mason, and visited Lodges and other Masonic functions whenever possible.

Among his many Masonic honors Roosevelt had accepted the position as the first Honorary Grand Master of the Order of DeMolay; Truman would be the second. Roosevelt's physical condition and political position prevented him from participating more actively than he did, yet he was considered a good enough Mason to be elected to honorary membership in several lodges and appendant bodies. Lesser politicians and dignitaries than the President of the United States had received the thirty-third. Roosevelt, however, was a Scottish Rite member of the Northern Masonic Jurisdiction, so Cowles presumably had no control in his case.

For reasons later revealed, Cowles decided that Truman should receive this coveted thirty-third degree. Although Truman had said in his *Memoirs* he wanted it, yet he had decided to refuse it. Why?

Perhaps this letter from Cowles written on August 25, 1944, is part of the explanation:

> I received a note from you in which you stated you wanted to talk to me about an important matter. I could guess at it now, but at that time I did not know just what to think of it, for I was not aware that you knew about Brother Ray V. Denslow's criticism of our Supreme Council, particularly of myself. I have never talked to anybody about it except members of our Supreme Council, and not to all of them. We have never mentioned the matter in our *New Age* magazine or the Scottish Rite news bulletin.
>
> However, I wrote you that I was at your service at anytime and then called your office. And you did likewise, or your secretary did, and it seemed that I was out of the city when you were in the city. And you were out of the city when I was in the city. You were doing that splendid work of the special Senate committee for which you are so highly commended.

The "Denslow feud" goes back several years, according to his son, William, and others. It appears that Cowles did not appreciate some of the writings of the elder Denslow. The situation was brought to a head when Denslow wrote about Johnson's speech to the Conference of Grand Masters in 1942 in his Masonic review for the Grand Lodge of Missouri.

Melvin M. Johnson was a Past Grand Master of Masons in Massachusetts and had long been active in Freemasonry. He had researched the early history of the Craft in America and had written two books on this subject. As Grand Commander of the Northern Masonic Jurisdiction of the Scottish Rite he had continued to work with and for Symbolic Masonry. He was invited to address the Conference of Grand Masters in Washington, D.C., in February, 1942.

Johnson's assigned subject was "Do Nazi-ism, Fascism, and Communism present a danger that American Freemasonry should meet?" The question, he said, "is so indisputable as not to need discussion." How to meet the danger was open to question, but "the only ways now to meet it are to support our government 100 percent in this war and to strengthen Freemasonry itself."

"Freemasonry has but one dogma, monotheism; and it does not attempt a definition of the Supreme Being," he added. "Based upon the worship of God, we teach the love of our fellow men, both being unchangeable essentials of civilization. The two Great Commandments always have been and ever will be as immutable as that two and two are four or that the human body must ultimately die. They are basic principles of this fraternity of ours."

He continued: "[I]f Freemasonry devotes its labor and strength to hurling anathemas against competitive philosophies—whether of government, religion or other human activities—it will land, with other waste products, upon the public dump. It will survive and gain stature only if it can sell its philosophy to men."

In three fields Johnson could see a beneficial change for Freemasonry. These were 1: In the ritual, where he felt the penalties should be removed because they are traditional and not enforced, adding fuel for enemies of the Craft; 2: In the mechanical structure, where "the two principal defects are disunity and the selection of titular leaders by ladder promotion, even then giving the leaders no real opportunity to function." He condemned those Grand Lodges and other Masonic bodies that refused to join and work with The Masonic Service Association in its work for the Armed Forces. He was disdainful of the practice where one man "can get appointed or elected to a minor position in Grand Lodge" and who "will, if he lives long enough and keeps free from scandal, be Grand Master some day."

His third point, perhaps more than the other two, caused the furor which resulted in Ray V. Denslow being "disciplined." The Order of Demolay, a Masonic-sponsored organization for young men, was not being supported as Johnson felt it should be. But what disturbed him more than anything else was the action of an appendant body, which he did not name, in starting a secret drive against the adoption of the "Declaration of the Principles of Freemasonry."

In the 1939 Conference of Grand Masters "an attempt was made to draft a statement of the fundamental principles of our Craft in such a way that they could be suggested for consideration to the Grand Lodges of this country in a form which might unanimously be declared to the world," noted Johnson. "Such a declaration of principles was so carefully thought out that when, after discussion, it was finally drafted by a committee of this Conference no voice of further suggestion, amendment or opposition was heard here. The Conference was no sooner adjourned, however, than a secret drive against its adoption by Grand Lodges was initiated. One attack was made by the circulation of mimeographed documents urging opposition."

Those receiving the documents were cautioned that "these communications are strictly *personal and confidential*." Johnson added: "How does that method of submarine torpedo attack against proposed Grand Lodge legislation strike you? I refrain intentionally from indicating its source. But it is common knowledge, at least among the best informed, that the hostility of certain officers in Masonic bodies, not now responsible officers of Grand Lodges but nevertheless in a position to control honors which Grand Lodges do not grant, has had a powerful adverse effect. Do you regard it as Masonic for other bodies of our fraternity or their officers to make a secret attack upon any proposed Grand Lodge legislation, the impropriety of which attack is so clearly recognized by its makers that it is accompanied by a request to conceal its source?"

Later in the same paragraph he said: "In my judgement, no other Masonic body, directly or through its officers, has any business to intermeddle with the affairs of Grand Lodges except so far and so far only as its officers act individually as members or officers of their respective Grand Lodge jurisdictions. The acme of impropriety is covertly to use the power to grant or withhold extra-mural honor and rank as bait or threat to influence action in Grand Lodge. . . . I regard it as un-Masonic for any body, not a Grand Lodge, to flout, deny or set at naught what has been a Landmark or at least a Regulation recognized by Symbolic Freemasonry for more than two centuries since Anderson's Constitutions were promulgated in 1723."

After Johnson's lengthy address those desiring to discuss what he had said were invited to do so. Only two men present had anything to say. One was "Grand Master Carter," who absolved himself of much of what Johnson had said. The other was a "Brother Grout of Vermont," who offered "a hearty 'Amen' to everything that Brother Johnson said in his address." He wanted the address published in every Grand Lodge *Proceeding*. It wasn't. But a portion of it did appear in Denslow's review of Grand Lodges for the Grand Lodge of Missouri.

Before Denslow covered portions of Johnson's address in "The Masonic World," there was appointed a special committee of the Supreme Council of the Scottish Rite, Southern Jurisdiction. The Supreme Council in the Southern Jurisdiction is composed of no more than thirty active Scottish Rite members. The special committee, appointed by Cowles, evidently had reason to believe the Southern Jurisdiction was the culprit outlined by Johnson, although he had mentioned no organization or body by name. It took exception to what Johnson had said, and it so reported on October 22, 1943:

> These charges embody the unwarranted and unjustified implication that this Supreme Council so prostitutes its dignity as to barter the honors that it confers upon the craft in return for influence in an effort, it is alleged, to intermeddle in and control the action of Grand Masonic bodies. These charges are a reflection upon the dignity and the honor and integrity of our Supreme Council and upon the character and high purposes of Grand Commander Cowles.
>
> The reasons for this outburst by Brother Johnson are to us unfathomable and we can only ascribe them to causes which propriety and decent respect for the common amenities among Masons bound by common bounds of Brotherhood forbid discussion. They are so obviously false and so utterly ridiculous as to constitute within themselves their own complete refutation.

Within his Review Denslow wrote: "Our readers may wonder in what way an organization could engage in internal politics of a Grand Lodge? They are entitled to know." He then explained how Masonry in South and Central America "is Scottish Rite Masonry pure and simple." But "there are other matters closer to home in which Grand Lodges are interested. We refer to such organizations as the George Washington National [sic] Masonic Memorial, the Masonic Service Association and the Conference of Grand Masters. Those of our readers who have been following the trends in recent years must know that many of the active heads of the Rite are giving only lip service to the Memorial, are lukewarm to the conference of Grand Masters, and opposed to the work of the M.S.A., so much so in fact that we have searched recent issues of the official magazine to discover any mention of the fine work this association is rendering to the boys in the Armed Forces."

The review continued: "In a neighboring state a Past Grand Master who had only recently received honors made an adverse report on the work of the M.S.A. in camps. In another neighboring state a newly-honored Past Grand Master reported favorably on some questionable jurisdictions. Whether their newly-required [sic] honors influenced them or not, it would be unfair to say, but it made them liable to some very critical comment. After all, Grand Lodges, and not the Supreme Council, may be to blame, in that they have elected, or appointed, men who are too susceptible to flattery and unearned honors."

Another special committee of the Supreme Council of the Scottish Rite, Southern Jurisdiction, found Ray V. Denslow guilty of a "wilful disregard" of his vows; that he "censured and complained of the Supreme Council, and of its Grand Commander and members, not in the proper form of the Rite . . . but in writing and in print, for publication and distribution, to be read by non-Masons"; all which appeared in "The Masonic World," a part of the *Proceedings* of the Grand Lodge of Missouri.

Soon after Denslow received notice of the charges he wrote to the Grand Commander. In reply, John Cowles sent Ray Denslow the following letter on July 21, 1944:

> This will acknowledge receipt of your communication of July 4th, giving notice of your appeal to the whole Supreme Council from the decision of the Special Committee and at the approval thereof of the Lieutenant Grand Commander in the matter of the charges against you before the Supreme Council.
>
> Your notice of appeal is in apt time, and you are advised that your appeal is regularly before the Supreme Council for consideration in accordance with the provisions of a resolution of the Supreme Council concerning the case, copy of which resolution has been furnished to you.
>
> I think it proper to advise you that you will be accorded the privilege of selecting one of the Active Members of the Supreme Council to represent you in this appeal and to present your side of this case to the whole Supreme Council. The choice of this member will be left to you. If you do not care to make a choice or to express a preference as to any particular member of the Supreme Council to represent you in the appeal, it shall be my purpose to appoint for that purpose Illustrious Brother William B. Massey, 33rd degree, Sovereign Grand Inspector General in the State of Missouri, who I

> know feels very close to you, and whom I believe to be thoroughly competent to present your side of this controversy to the Supreme Council. I will be glad to hear from you as to whether or not you wish to make this choice yourself, to the end that I may notify the member of the Supreme Council you may select, in the event you wish to express a preference, and to notify Brother Massey of his appointment for this purpose in the event you do not wish to make the choice yourself.

George Marquis, a long-time friend of Truman and Ray Denslow, advised Denslow on August 1 that Cowles had "stacked the deck"; that Massey was no friend of Denslow; that Massey would take every opportunity to see that Denslow was found guilty, as Massey blamed Denslow because he had never been selected for the Grand Lodge line.

Truman had written to Ray Denslow on December 8, 1943:

> I had a very pleasant visit with Melvin Johnson the other day, riding with him from Philadelphia to New York and then from New York to Washington.
>
> We discussed a great many things, among others, the situation which faces you. Under no circumstances would I admit the rights of the Gestapo Committee to take jurisdiction. That is a matter which officially affects the Grand Lodge of Missouri, and if any one is to be tried it ought to be the Grand Lodge of Missouri. I don't think the Supreme Council of the Southern Jurisdiction can function as trial court on the fundamental organization that gives them existence, and I think it is about time we had a show-down and I am ready to go to bat on it.
>
> If you have any Grand Lodge connections in the States where the active Supreme Council members live you should begin to exert pressure on them immediately to overturn this gang who wants to act as judge and jury and prosecutor in a case over which they have no jurisdiction. It seems there will be a knock-down and drag-out between Northern and Southern Jurisdiction over the same printed matter over which they are quarreling with you.
>
> Let me know if there is anything I can do to put a stop to the situation.

William B. Massey, the Sovereign Grand Inspector General in Missouri, reprimanded Harry S. Truman, 32nd degree, for remarks he had made in support of his friend, Ray V. Denslow, 33rd degree. Massey ended his letter of reprimand written on January 24, 1944, by stating: "I presume you remember your obligation as a 32nd degree [Scottish Rite] Mason, and that you are familiar with the statutes of the Supreme Council with reference to criticism of the Supreme Council, the Grand Commander, or other officers or members of the Supreme Council, and that the same should be done, if at all, in the proper form."

Truman wasted no time in answering the reprimand. In his letter to "Honorable William B. Massey, Sovereign Grand Inspector General of Missouri," he wrote:

> Dear Brother Massey:
>
> Appreciate very much your letter of the Twenty Fourth, and for your information I don't need to be reminded by you or any one else as to what my obligations are about any Masonic bodies. I am thoroughly disgusted with the manner the Supreme Council seems to have acted in the Denslow case.
>
> I know all the facts, and if that organization is going to set itself up as Judge, Court, Jury, and Prosecutor all in one, I am through with them, and the sooner they find it out the better. If you think the Grand Lodge of Missouri cannot get along without the organization you are entirely mistaken. The Scottish Rite depends entirely on the Grand Lodges of the various States for its very existence, and I am here to tell you there are a great many of us who are not at all happy over the manner in which the Ray Denslow matter has been handled.
>
> We are fighting a war to overcome Fascist Government and I don't propose to have it operate in any organization to which I belong.

Truman wrote to Marquis on May 31, 1944: "You can rest assured I am going to get that resolution through the Grand Lodge in September and see to it that Ray gets justice. I have the old man here in Washington trying to find me. I think he is a little worried. I wish you would send me a copy of the Grand Lodge resolution and you can rest assured I will do what I can about it."

Melvin Johnson continued to be consulted in the Denslow matter. On August 1, 1944, Marquis wrote to Johnson asking if he could improve the resolution he suggested should be submitted to the Grand Lodge of Missouri. Marquis wanted a resolution "asserting the absolute supremecy of Grand Lodge," which Harry Truman said he would present. "We are agreed that your resolution covers well the point of Grand Lodge sovereignty," Marquis wrote, "but we think that it should be preceded by a concise statement of the facts as relate to the present controversy calling names and making the entire matter so plain that the mine run of representatives will thoroughly understand what it is all about, even those who are there from the country Lodges for the first time."

Past Grand Master Harry S. Truman took time out from campaigning for the Roosevelt-Truman Democratic ticket to be present for the Annual communication of the Grand Lodge of Missouri in September, 1944. On the morning of the first day he asked for, and received, permission to submit a resolution. It contained a lengthy preamble setting forth Masonic law, according to Albert G. Mackey, regarding committees on correspondence. This preamble ended by stating: "Your Reviewer was performing a Masonic duty, assigned to him by this Grand Lodge, in reporting to you these facts. Whether or not anybody *was* attempting to dominate the Grand Lodges, you are entitled to know that such charges were made in the conference of Grand Masters, a Masonic forum of public opinion. The Grand Lodge of Missouri will never consent to be dominated by so called higher bodies, either York or Scottish, and in order to set up a policy for future procedure this resolution is hereby offered as setting forth its power and sovereignty:

> The Grand Lodge of Ancient, Free and Accepted Masons of Missouri is hereby declared to be the sole, supreme and final Masonic authority, within its territorial jurisdiction, to determine what is and what is not Masonic; and to fix the conditions under which any person or organization may be regarded as Masonic, or to remain so regarded. As such, its Masonic Acts, and those of its officers, are not open to question by any other organization, and subject only to the civil government for any infraction of civil law.
>
> The Masonic acts and doings of its officers and members, by its authority, are its acts; and, likewise, free from question or review, except by itself. When any of its officers, or members, perform any act in the lawful discharge of duties to the Grand Lodge, it shall be un-Masonic for any other body, claiming to act Masonically, to reprimand or otherwise discipline such officer or member; and if done shall disentitle such body to be further regarded as Masonic.

The resolution was referred to the jurisprudence committee for study, which is normal. It was held over until 1945, and then 1946. Indications are that it was never acted on.

Rumors of this controversy were circulated throughout the Masonic world for years. Ray's son, William R. Denslow, was asked about it on many occasions, and explained the dispute in an item that appeared in the Spring, 1973, edition of *The Royal Arch Mason* magazine. Stewart M.L. Pollard reprinted it in *The Lighter Side of Masonry* in 1983:

> For many years my late father, Ray V. Denslow, fought a running battle with Bro. John H. Cowles, the sovereign grand commander of the Supreme Council of the Scottish Rite, Southern Jurisdiction (1921-1953). Dad held an honorary 33rd degree for may years, but was unequivocally opposed to the autocratic ways of Cowles. Words led to words, letters to letters, and finally published articles. Cowles, however, had the "top card"—he withdrew Dad's 33rd degree!
>
> But it was a new ball game when Truman became President in 1945, following the death of Roosevelt. The Southern Jurisdiction of the Scottish Rite wanted to give him a 33rd degree. Truman called my father to ask his advice. As I remember, my father encouraged him to accept it "for the good of the Fraternity." He [Truman] wrote Dad on May 17, 1945 saying—"I sure appreciate it very much (Dad's advice), and I believe we know how to handle it when the time comes. The Greeks don't fool me" (alluding to the old cliche "beware of Greeks bearing gifts").
>
> Truman told Cowles that he wouldn't accept the 33rd degree until Dad's was returned. Shortly, my father was removed from purgatory and again enthroned.

In the midst of the Denslow controversy another began. Charles S. Coulter, who was director of welfare for the MSA, wrote a nasty letter to every Grand Lodge in the country. A copy was sent to members of the Advisory Committee of the Association. Truman wrote to him on March 2, 1944:

> Dear Major Coulter:
>
> I have just received the open letter to the Grand Masters which bore your typewritten signature at the bottom. I am certainly sorry this sort of thing has to happen in our organization. The main difficulty we have been up against in getting things done in this war effort has been personality which evidently cannot be kept down. A fuss between you and Claudy can only make the situation much harder to handle.
>
> Everyone on the outside seems to think people in our organization have no difficulty in getting along, but when the Sovereign Grand Commander of the Northern Jurisdiction and the Sovereign Grand Commander of the Southern Jurisdiction are persecuting the Grand High Priest of the United States, and when you and Claudy are at each others throats over personal matters I don't see how you can expect us in the legislative branch of the government to be of any usefulness to you.

> I regret exceedingly that you have seen fit to send out such a letter, and I cannot for the life of me see what difference it makes who is responsible for getting the job done as long as the job is done for the benefit of the soldiers who are doing the fighting.

The General Grand High Priest Truman referred to was Ray V. Denslow, the subject of the Cowles controversy. Denslow served as Grand Master of Masons in Missouri in 1931 and was one of the "Republicans" who supported the appointment of the "Democrat" Harry S. Truman to the Grand Lodge line. Denslow served Missouri as the Grand High Priest of the Grand Chapter, Royal Arch Masons, in 1919. He was General Grand High Priest of the General Grand Chapter, Royal Arch Masons, International, from 1942 to 1945. He was Grand Secretary of the Grand Chapter, Grand Recorder of the Council of Royal and Select Masters, and the Grand Commandery of Knight Templars from 1923 until his death on September 10, 1960. He was the author of several Masonic books, and the foreign correspondent and author of *The Masonic World* since 1933. He was the Masonic advisor to Harry S. Truman from the day Truman started in the Grand Lodge line. He was also the backbone of the Missouri Lodge of Research.

On October 19, 1945, Harry S. Truman was invested with the thirty-third degree of the Scottish Rite. He became the first President to receive this degree, but he wouldn't be the last. There were three hundred forty-eight others designated to receive it at the same time. Among them was General Hap Arnold and General James Doolittle.

The feud didn't end with the conferral of the thirty-third degree. A Mason named Henry P. Fry sent a copy of the *Virginia Masonic Herald* containing a sketch of the President to John Cowles. Fry suggested it be reprinted in the *New Age,* the Southern Jurisdiction's magazine. In a letter to Truman, Fry said: "Yesterday I received a letter from Mr. Cowles in which he flatly declined to reprint the article. In highly incendiary language he denounced the President for his civil rights program, for the repeal of the Taft-Hartley Act and other measures. He stated that the President was made a 33rd degree Scottish Rite Mason soley because of his Masonic record and not because of his political position or life, which, said Cowles, he owed entirely to the Pendergast machine.

"The Scottish Rite is not real Masonry but a collateral body that devotes itself in political matters. John H. Cowles has often appeared before Congressional committees in opposition to various measures.

"I regard Cowles' letter to me as highly uncalled for, in bad taste, rude and bad mannered. Our article was not political or eulogistic of the President. It was purely factual and gave a complete sketch of one of the country's most distinguished Masons, who also happens to be the President of the United States," concluded Fry.

Truman took a realistic view of this "thirty-third and last degree" throughout his life. Earl J. Wallace of California asked Truman for his Masonic history, particularly information on the thirty-third degree. Truman answered him on May 29, 1957:

"The thirty-third degree was conferred on me, not for any merit or work in the Scottish Rite, but because I was President of the United States. John Coles [sic] and I were not particularly friendly. He was a captain in the Spanish-American War, and I was a captain in World War I. He was a backward-looking, conservative Kentucky democrat, and I looked the other way. Nevertheless we always got along. He conferred the thirty-third degree on me because it was a good advertising stunt for the Scottish Rite. I did not object because I thought very highly of the Scottish Rite. I also felt I should do something for the old man before he died."

The same fellow was highly elated when he wrote to tell Truman on June 13: "The local Democratic Central Committee has furnished me with a colored reproduction of [the] painting by Greta Kempton of yourself which is excellent and I have made arrangements with a local painter (who belongs to the craft) to paint a 33rd degree white cap to place on the picture from which I can secure a wonderful color slide."

Truman's deflating answer on July 10, 1957, was to the point: "In reply to your letter of June 13th. I have never worn a thirty-third degree white cap in my life.

"The only regalia I have ever worn is that belonging to the office of Grand Master of Missouri."

11. THE FIRST PRESIDENTIAL TERM

The President continually received requests for him to sign Scottish Rite certificates, aprons, cards, and everything else imaginable. The office staff insisted on a decision as to what the President would and would not sign. It was decided that there would be no signatures on these mementos, because they would be time consuming. All would be sent back with a polite note by one of the secretaries. This would usually say: "While the President treasures his membership in the Masonic fraternity, he receives so many similar requests he is obliged to limit . . ."

Solicitation for funds was unbelievable. Requests for "a few words to report at our meeting," "for a congratulatory letter for my work," and hundreds of other schemes flooded the White House mail room. The President received bulletins, pictures, newsletters, periodicals, advertisements, and on and on. And most of these items were saved and will be found in the Harry S. Truman Library. Truman believed that everything a President touched should become a part of his record.

The demand for the President's time was also unbelievable. An entered apprentice wrote to ask Truman to coach him! And if he couldn't, to find someone who would. Hundreds asked for a few minutes to meet with him to present him with certificates, or something of like nature. Others just wanted to be able to say they had shaken his hand.

All Masonic mail was given to the President for whatever action he wanted to take. This became his practice from the first day he entered the Senate and it continued throughout his Presidency. Much of this he answered immediately, but if there was some question with which he wasn't familiar he would send it to someone who was. This was usually Ray V. Denslow of Missouri. Often Truman dictated a full reply; at other times he would write a word or two in the margin for one of his secretaries. A typical notation might be: "A nice pleasant no. HST."

Thousands of children were named in his honor during his eight years in office, and he was usually informed of this by proud parents. To all of them Truman sent a polite, and proud, letter.

He continued to be as active as possible in Freemasonry. But moving any President from place to place poses problems in security that are overwhelming. Because of this, Truman left many decisions to his Secret Service.

He did make exceptions, though, and on several occasions. One took place on October 11, 1945. The Neville J. McMillan whose petition was balloted on in Alexandria-Washington Lodge No. 22 on April 12, was to be raised to the sublime degree of Master Mason. When Truman received this notice he wrote at the bottom to his appointments secretary: "Matt: I'd like to go. This boy's father is my good friend. In fact I took him through and he served as Master of my little Lodge. The boy's brother was killed in the Pacific. HST."

Secret Service agents swarmed all over the George Washington Masonic National Memorial, the home of the lodge, on October 11. Every square inch was searched, and guards were posted at every entrance. Although no notice had been given to the press or anyone else, an overflow crowd was present when the lodge was opened at 7:30 p.m. The ever present grapevine had worked overtime.

The President and Secret Service men who were Masons were escorted to the altar. Past Grand Master Truman was then escorted to the East where he received the honors due his office. After the young man was made a Master Mason, Truman spoke to the lodge. He remained to talk with and meet the Masons who were there. He signed dues cards and other pieces of paper for all who asked. It appeared he would stay the whole night through, but the Secret Service finally insisted he go home.

A couple of days later the President sent the Master of the lodge a note saying, "I enjoyed the visit and wish it were possible for me to make more of them. Neville McMillan is a good young man—just as his father was before him."

In 1943, while Truman was a Senator, the Northern Masonic Jurisdiction of the Scottish Rite wanted to present him with the exclusive Gourgas Medal. His Senatorial duties prevented him from receiving it. Again in 1944 it was impossible for him to be present to receive it.

The rose garden at the White House on November 21, 1945, held many Masonic dignitaries when Melvin M. Johnson, Grand

Commander of the Northern Masonic Jurisdiction of the Scottish Rite, presented President Harry S. Truman with the Gourgas Medal. In his presentation Johnson said he was particularly happy to be able to address the President as "Ill. Harry S. Truman, 33rd degree." It had been only a month earlier that Truman had received this degree.

Johnson explained that his jurisdiction had created this award in 1938. It was named for James Joseph Gourgas who was "the dominant member of the group which, in 1813, established the Northern Supreme Council." Gourgas was credited with preserving the Scottish Rite "during the dark days of anti-Masonry." Johnson, for one, believed the Rite would have disappeared from the United States had it not been for the perseverance of Gourgas.

The medal is the highest award the jurisdiction has and is to be awarded in recognition of "notably distinguished service in the cause of Freemasonry, humanity, or country." He continued:

> In 1943, the Sovereign Grand Commander of the Northern Supreme Council felt confident that no civilian officer of the United States was performing more distinguished service than yourself, in your conception and leadership of the Committee of the United States Senate commonly known as the "Truman Committee." You made it clear to your fellow citizens that its leadership was intelligent, courageous, impartial and effective. You won the admiration, respect and confidence of all honorable men of whatever race, politics or religion. The public service rendered by the Truman Committee demonstrated the functioning of our political system at its best. It gave us continued faith in and hope for the future of democracy in government at a time when that future was obscure.
>
> When you were invited to attend our Annual Meeting in September, 1943, to receive the Gourgas Medal, you replied that an imperative duty to the Grand Lodge, of which you were then the immediate Past Grand Master, required your presence at its meeting at the very time of our Supreme Council session. The invitation was renewed for the following year, but then you were a candidate for the Vice President of the United States. Naturally, you felt that it would not be wise or in good taste to subject yourself or the Fraternity to the adverse criticism that might be made in the heat of a campaign.
>
> You now occupy the most exalted civic station in the world. You are here because your fellow citizens believe in you and in your ability to measure up to the high responsibilities of the office should it fall to your lot to serve in you present capacity. Now we come to you. We do not expect you to attend upon us.

> Today you are not only honored by the Supreme Council for the Northern Masonic Jurisdiction to the extent of our ability, but you honor it and our entire world-wide Fraternity for accepting this decoration. You are the first President to receive the Thirty-third and Last Degree. You are the first person to receive the Gourgas Medal.
>
> In behalf of the Ancient Accepted Scottish Rite for the Northern Masonic Jurisdiction of the United States, and particularly its Supreme Council, I am proud and happy to present this decoration to you as our token of appreciation of the notably distinguished service which you have rendered to your Country and to Humanity. And may God give you strength and wisdom for all the tasks that lie ahead.

There are several notable references in that address. The award, the first of its kind ever to be presented, went to *Senator Truman*. It was authorized long before Truman was considered for the thirty-third degree. It took note of his work as a Senator, and stressed what he had done for the American people. It was an address that Truman could look back on with pride, one that could soften the nasty blows of his detractors then and in later years. It was something that came unsolicited and because it was known that he was living by the principles taught in Freemasonry.

Truman thanked Johnson: "I appreciate this more than anything I have ever received. I have given a lot of medals to other men, but this is the first that anyone has given me."

The President spoke personally with each of those present then gave each a book of matches. The message on the cover read: "Swiped from Harry S. Truman!"

While Truman was home in Independence for Christmas in 1945, he was invited to become a member of Mary Conclave No. 5 of the Red Cross of Constantine. He accepted and was initiated into the order after breakfast in the home of his friend, Nat D. Jackson. Each of the men present signed the Bible on which Truman was obligated. The Bible was later presented to the Grand Imperial Council of the order.

The "New Deal" became the "Fair Deal" as Truman attempted to convert the country from a war to a peace standard. He asked for programs many found far too liberal, such as an increase in the minimum wage, federal housing, aid to education, medical aid, the St. Lawrence Seaway, nationalization of atomic energy, and others. It appeared that most businessmen opposed his plans; labor and some consumer groups supported him, but there was nothing general about this support or opposition.

When the coal miners struck, the President ordered the mines seized in May 1946, after talking with John L. Lewis six times between March and then. Along with the seizure the administration continued discussions with the parties on both sides. The mines continued operating until November 21, then a strike was called against the government. Lewis refused to comply with an injunction the President had requested ordering the miners to return to work. On December 4, Lewis was found guilty of civil and criminal contempt of court and fined $3,500,000. His men returned to the mines.

Criticism from labor unions flooded the White House. To a letter he received from D.B. Robinson, president of the Brotherhood of Locomotive Firemen and Enginemen, he replied in part:

"We used the weapons that we had at hand in order to fight a rebellion against the Government and I am here to tell you that I expect to use whatever powers the President and the Government have, when the law and the Government are defied by an arbitrary dictator, such as Lewis. . . .

"I am going to need all the help and cooperation I can possibly get to keep labor from getting its throat cut in this Congress. When [Philip] Murray [of the CIO] and [William] Green [of the AFL] and able leaders, like yourself, condone the action of Lewis you are not helping yourselves either with me or with the Congress."

Later Jerry Marsengill wrote an article entitled "Going to the Dogs" for *The Royal Arch Mason* about the confrontation:

> When two Masons, highly placed in their respective spheres, began barking at each other, it seemed for awhile as if the country were "going to the dogs."
>
> State Senator Neal Bishop of Denver, Colorado, suggested to President Harry S. Truman, Past Grand Master of Missouri, that he appoint John Lewellyn Lewis, president of the United Mine Workers and one of the founders of the CIO, as ambassador to Moscow.
>
> His reason was that Lewis, many times standing alone, had been one of the first labor leaders to recognize the communist con-

> spiracy, and one of the first to speak out against the danger of communist infiltration of labor unions.
>
> Truman, however, remembering the critical time in WWII when Lewis made himself a national villain by calling a coal strike, was not overly pleased with the suggestion. The peppery Missourian, never noted for his tact and diplomacy, snapped: "I wouldn't appoint John L. Lewis dogcatcher!"
>
> The flamboyant Welshman, hearing of Truman's remark, glared through his bushy brows like an old lion looking from some jungle thicket, and wrote to Senator Bishop: "Conceivably it is true that the president's choice of words was again unfortunate. One could, however, persuade one's self that he was thinking only in terms of problems of state and had no intent to belittle or sneer gratuitously at a private citizen. Assuredly, the president of the United States would not permit his personal feelings to sway his judgement on appointments to public office.
>
> "A presidential appointment to the Office of Dogcatcher would postulate creation of a new federal bureau with its accompanying personnel of thousands of employees and, in consequence, an increase to the tax burden. Naturally, the first duty of the Bureau of the Dog, if staffed by the undersigned, would be to collect and impound the sad dogs, the intellectual poodle dogs and the pusillanimous pups which now infect our State Department. This would be gravely disturbing and would, perhaps, cause profound unrest throughout our national canine fraternity.
>
> "The President could ill afford to have more brains in the Dog Department than in the Department of State, and, from this standpoint, his remarks to you are eminently justified."
>
> President Truman's further remarks on learning of this eloquent epistle, inscribed by a brother Mason, have not been preserved. Remembering the capabilities of Brother Truman for pungent and earthly language, perhaps both of the old warriors were willing to "let sleeping dogs lie."

Another Freemason who could use pungent language on occasion was Winston Churchill, the man who guided Great Britain through its darkest hours. The shooting crisis over, the British didn't feel they needed him any longer. Others, however, like his brother Mason, General Harry Vaughan, felt differently. When the general was asked to find an outstanding speaker for the graduating class of Westminster College in Fulton, Missouri, he called on Churchill.

Truman was with Churchill at Fulton in March 1946 when the former British Prime Minister made a prophetic statement which would be remembered for decades. "From Stettin in the Baltic to Trieste in the Adriatic, an iron curtain has descended across the continent," he said. "Behind that line lie all the capitals of the ancient states of central and eastern Europe."

Surprisingly, for one of the few times in American history, most of the people realized there was a communist conspiracy to control the world. They began to agree with and support the President as he attempted to block further Russian advances.

The "Truman Doctrine" saved Greece and Turkey in 1947 when the British government, almost bankrupt, had to quit giving them financial assistance. Unless America took over, the chance of those countries going over to the communist block was strong. Truman convinced Congress and the American people the Greeks and Turks were worth saving, and it could be done by generously giving them military and other aid. The Americans agreed, so Turkey was able to retain possession of The Straits, and the anti-communists won the civil war in Greece.

Then came the "Marshall Plan," or "European Recovery Act," brought into being because the communists were using American relief funds to strengthen communism. George Marshall said of this Truman-Marshall plan: "Our policy is directed not against any country or doctrine but against hunger, poverty, desperation, and chaos. Its purpose should be the revival of a working economy in the world so as to permit the emergence of political and social conditions in which free institutions can exist." The Plan put controls on where and how American funds were spent.

American aid to Europe did eventually revitalize the depressed countries on the continent. Russia was invited to participate, but Stalin walked out calling it a capitalist scheme.

Truman's unswerving firmness removed the Soviet threat from Iran. That country would support Freemasonry until a religious fanatic called the Ayatollah Ruhollah Khomeini, working from France, was able to overthrow the Shah, Mohammed Reza Pahlevi, a Freemason. This occurred in 1979 during the Carter Presidency.

Frank S. Land was the founder of the Order of DeMolay, an organization for young men sponsored by Freemasons. He was also a close friend of the President. In this capacity he urged the

President to make every effort to be present at the George Washington Masonic National Memorial on February 22, 1946.

This Memorial had been erected by Freemasons of the United States to the memory of the first President of the nation. George Washington had been initiated into Freemasonry in the Lodge at Fredericksburg, Virginia, before he was twenty-one, the accepted age today. He received the next two degrees in 1752 in the same lodge, and remained a Mason until he died. He had been proposed during the War for American Independence as the General Grand Master of Masons in the country, an office that has never existed. He was the charter Master of Alexandria Lodge No. 22 (now Washington-Alexandria Lodge) when it left the Grand Lodge of Pennsylvania. When he died in 1799 he was buried at Mount Vernon with Masonic rites.

The Memorial now holds plaques depicting all the Presidents who were Freemasons. In 1946 Truman's was to be added. "Mel Johnson is going to make the presentation, and all the Grand Masters of the nation, as well as members of the Memorial Association, and Grand Secretaries will be present as well as a host of others," Land added in his letter to the President.

"The reason for my urging you to do this is apparent," continued Land. "I have expressed to you many times the thought that your great prominence in Masonry and being President has done something for American Masonry that cannot be measured by ordinary standards. You have put new life and prestige into the order that is tremendously heartening to the ordinary Mason and Masonic leader. Masonry has 'closed its ranks' so to speak. Men everywhere, because of your leadership, are letting it be known as never before that they take pride in being members of the Order. There are now nearly three million Masons in this nation in good standing. Your connection with the Fraternity has reached down into the grass roots of the Craft.

"When these national meetings are held next month in Washington, the leadership of this entire body of men will be present and it seems to me that it would be a great opportunity for you to give to these leaders some task that could not be presumed to be politics that would materially strengthen your hands in every town and hamlet of the nation. I am not day-dreaming in this, because I know that I am in a position to gauge the trend of thinking among Masons. You have captured their devotion and interest, and let us not lose it. You have become the head and front of Masonic endeavor in this nation, something that has never happened before in our national history."

Frank Land was telling the truth. Freemasons throughout the country, whatever their political persuasion, admired and respected the Mason from Missouri. He was one of them. He did not seek honors; these came to him because he deserved them. And they were not empty honors to Truman as they were to many who received them, and many who would receive them in later years. He gave all Freemasonry something in return.

The meetings of the national Masonic leadership of which Land spoke had been taking place in the nation's capital each year for over fifteen years. These would continue, but in recent years they would move periodically to other states.

Truman was continually concerned about the way the press and partisan politicians treated his family, especially the women. Pot shots had been taken against him through his sister, Mary Jane. She had long been interested in the Order of the Eastern Star. Because of her work a large majority wanted her as the Grand Worthy Matron. On September 20, 1946, he closed his letter to his mother and sister by saying: "Hope you'll continue to feel in good health. Hope also you have a nice time in Milwaukee. But don't, for goodness sake, let that bunch of trash entice you into the Grand O.E.S. again. They'll simply mistreat you again for malicious political purposes against your brother." In spite of her brother's warning, Mary Jane did begin the journey to the Grand East in the Order. In 1950 she became the Grand Worthy Matron and the President made it a point to be present for her installation.

On the same day, September 20, 1946, Truman felt he had to decline an invitation to attend a Masonic meeting because of the same press of business he had just told his mother and sister about. "I appreciate most highly your letter of the eighteenth about the Grand Encampment of Knights Templar, Houston, Texas," he wrote to Marquis, "and goodness knows I'd like to come but that date is bad.

"October twenty-seventh is just about a week before the election— I've cancelled all campaign speeches; have cancelled my usual trip to southeast Missouri and I fear if I'd make an appearance in Texas that close to election they would make something out of it. We will just have to call it off until a year when there is no campaign."

Truman changed his mind about Henry Wallace and fired him from his job as Secretary of Commerce on September 21, 1946. Wallace had shown far too much sympathy for the Soviets, many people believed. The news of this action caused the stock market to go up twenty points and Truman said he received "an avalanche of telegrams from Maine to California agreeing with the action." But Truman was also called "a traitor to F.D.R. and a warmonger." Charles C. Ross told Truman he had proved he'd rather be right than President. Truman told him: "I'd rather be anything than President."

An item in the Kansas City *Times* on November 2, 1946, tells of another incident in the life of the President:

"After leaving his mother's home last night, President Truman paid a visit to the Grandview Masonic Lodge No. 618. While Eddie Wray, the Master of the fraternal organization, was supposed to be the only one apprised of the visit, somehow a rumor had spread around among the Masons of Washington Township and a good crowd was on hand.

"The meeting was called for the purpose of conferring the second degree in the Blue Lodge on Harry A. Truman, son of his brother Vivian Truman and a nephew of the President.

"In the ceremony, the President took the role of Worshipful Master and his brother performed the duties of Senior Warden. Following the ceremony, a social period was held 'in which Mr. Truman visited with his fellow Masons' before starting the journey home to Independence."

Back in Washington Truman found everything was "normal." There were decisions to make constantly, letters to answer and initiate, and then there were the constant protests. One of these he wrote about to his wife.

A group of men who had refused to bear arms in the war marched outside the White House. Truman didn't think highly of them. He wrote to Mrs. Truman on December 22, 1946: "The only one of 'em I ever came in contact with, whom I thought to be on the level, was the little skinny pharmacist's mate to whom I gave the Congressional Medal of Honor out in the back yard of the White House. He'd carried wounded man after wounded man to safety from under fire at the front and finally was shot himself and still kept working on the other wounded. He said he thought he could serve the Lord acceptably under fire if he himself didn't try to kill anybody. He did his heroic job on Okinawa."

Truman told his wife about the "experts" on foreign policy: "Had to listen to Burt Wheeler for one whole hour tell me all about South America. He went down there on a special mission ($10,000 fee and expenses) but he knows all about Brazil, Uruguay, Argentina and Chile. Another funny one. Senators and ex-Senators go to S.A., Germany, Japan, China, spend two or three days and know all about the countries and know all the answers. Guess I'm dumb."

The November, 1946, elections were a disaster for the Democrats. Among the Republicans swept into office to make up the Eightieth Congress was Richard M. Nixon. In his *Memoirs* Nixon recalled his first visit inside the White House which occurred on February 18, 1947. Four months later Nixon returned, one of four Republican Congressmen to be invited to the Oval Office.

"Truman made us all feel welcome and relaxed as we shook hands with him," wrote Nixon. "We sat around the desk, and he spoke very earnestly about the necessity of rehabilitating Europe and emphasized his concern that peaceful German production should be encouraged. He said he was glad to see us even though we were Republicans, because he always considered it necessary for the two parties to cooperate in foreign affairs. He said, 'Some of my best friends never agree with me politically!' "

After the lengthy discussion of world affairs, Nixon concluded: "Truman's strength was his hominess, his democratic attitude, and his sincerity."

"By a companion's count," read an item in *Newsweek* magazine for November, 1947, "not one in 20 strollers recognized the black-hatted figure walking briskly up Pennsylvania Avenue in Washington last Thursday evening, November 6. As his Secret Service guard trailed him discreetly, President Truman walked the three blocks from the White House to the Masonic Temple and, once inside, donned the traditional white apron. Reason:

Capt. Thomas J. Burns, assistant White House physician, was taking the Lodge's third degree. Though some of the officiating Masons flubbed their lines during the initiation ceremonies, all noticed that Former Grand Master Truman of the Missouri Grand Lodge recited his, after a 12-year lapse, without missing a syllable. Later the President chuckled: 'I thought Burns' eyes would pop out. Wish I could get out this way more often.' "

The Masonic Service Association's Hospital Visitation program had worked so well that other voluntary organizations joined in working with America's hospitalized veterans. This humanitarian effort was aided considerably when on January 3, 1946, President Truman signed the law that created the Veterans Administration's Department of Medicine.

Earlier the President had asked the Mason and General Omar N. Bradley to head the Veterans Administration. He did, and with the full support of Truman began a mammoth hospital construction program. The President's contribution to the veterans did not go unnoticed. On October 19, 1975, the VA hospital at Columbia, Missouri, was renamed the Harry S. Truman Memorial Hospital.

In 1945 the President had proposed the military services be united under a Department of National Defense. From his days in World War I, through his experience in the Senate where he had found no unity of purpose, he tried to bring constructive management from the chaos. It took two years of arguments, but on February 26, 1947, he was pleased to sign the "National Security Act."

The spring of 1948 found Truman's popularity as President so low just about everyone firmly believed the next occupant of the White House would be a Republican. Why this was so is difficult to evaluate. People were working; they were eating as well, if not better than ever before. The wartime boom had continued. The administration had done a good job under the most trying of conditions and times.

Perhaps Truman's popularity was at a low ebb because of the nation's press, which he heartily disliked. Some of the stories told about him in the media were slanderous and outright falsehoods. Among other things he was accused of being "soft on communism," a charge any thinking person should know was utterly false. Yet the media almost accomplished its purpose to destroy his credibility, as it would others to follow him.

Truman had almost fired Byrnes as Secretary of State because he had not been as forceful with the Soviets as the President had demanded he be. On January 5, 1946, he bluntly discussed the many things Byrnes wasn't doing, among them keeping the President fully informed. He ended that conference by stating: "I'm tired of babying the Soviets!"

James F. Byrnes did resign a short time later, and wrote a book called *Frankly Speaking*. About it Truman wrote on October 13, 1947: "The story is accurate though on the facts. Roosevelt and I only play minor roles, however, such as approving things put up to us by Mr. Byrnes. You know there is an old saying, 'Oh! that mine enemy would write a book.' Well I wish my so-called friends would quit trying to write one."

Hiram Lodge No. 10 in the District of Columbia had agreed to confer degrees on two fellowcrafts as a courtesy for two Missouri Lodges. The President was invited to participate in the conferring of the Master Mason degree on November 6, 1947. He not only participated, acting as Master he made them Master Masons according to the ritual of the Grand Lodge of Missouri.

A memo written by Truman in December, 1947, and unearthed by Wes Cook, a Past Grand Master of Masons in Missouri, reveals the makeup of his "Kitchen Cabinet" which consisted of secretaries for "politics, probabilities, gossip columns, prohibition, hard drink, pussy footers." In his memo he added "a Secretary for Inflation." His duties? "I have given him the worry of convincing the people that no matter how high the prices go or how low wages become there is not any danger to things temporal or ethereal. I'm of the opinion he'll take a real load off my mind—if Congress doesn't."

He didn't stop there. He added: "I've appointed a Secretary of Reaction. I want him to abolish flying machines and tell me how to restore oxcarts, oarboats and sailing ships. What a load he'll take off my mind if he'll put the atom back together so it can't be broken up. What a worry that will abolish for both me and Vishinsky."

Then he added another member of this "Cabinet"—"a Secretary for Semantics." Truman considered this "a most important post. He is to furnish me 40 and 50 dollar words. Tell me how to say yes and no in the same sentence with a contradiction. He's to tell me the combination of words that will put me against inflation in San Francisco and for it in New York. He's to show me how to keep silent—and say everything. You can very well see how he can save me an immense amount of worry.

"Its a great addition to the Kitchen Cabinet and I'm sure would be of great use to my successor if the [Chicago] *Tribune* should by unforeseen chances get its wish [to send him home in 1948]."

The President couldn't attend the conferences during "Masonic Week" in Washington, so he wrote from the White House on February 19, 1948: "We live in a world torn by jealousy, hatred, greed and avarice, in which, alas, the true spirit of brotherhood is sadly missing.

"In sending hearty greetings to my brothers of the Conference of Grand Masters of Masons in North America, may I urge all to work to bring back in the world the spirit of charity, kindness and brotherly love."

Perhaps Truman's admonition had some affect. Another movement by appendant bodies to control the Grand Lodges was stopped. According to Ray Denslow's report to the Grand Lodge of Missouri, the major appendant bodies endeavored to take over administration of the George Washington Masonic National Memorial Association. Melvin Johnson of the Northern Masonic Jurisdiction, notably, said: "I do not believe in the dilution of our membership. I believe that this organization should be controlled by the Grand Lodges of the various jurisdictions, . . . the Grand Lodges represent every Mason, every one of them." The proposition lost.

At 6:00 p.m. Washington time on May 14, 1948, the State of Israel declared its independence. Eleven minutes later the United States recognized Israel. Then Truman endeavored to work with it and the Arab countries toward the development of the whole Middle East, offering American aid. It didn't work, but the President did manage to hold the friendship of Great Britain, Israel and the Arab countries.

Five years later, on October 20, 1953, the Freemasons of Israel formed a Grand Lodge which was constituted by the Grand

Mrs. Truman and Greta Kempton, the artist who painted the White House portrait of President Truman, the portrait of Truman in his Masonic regalia, and other portraits of the Truman family, at the opening of the Corcoran Gallery of Art in Washington, D.C.

[Photographer unknown]

Lodge of Scotland. Masonry in Israel has remained strong and viable ever since.

There were misgivings when Truman determined to run for the Presidency, but the Democratic Convention had to go along with the incumbent. Yet until the morning of the day after the election few of the political pundits, poll-takers, and those in the media, gave him the slightest chance of winning.

Many of his advisors opposed his determination to use an airlift to aid the Berliners who were being blockaded by the Soviets. Among those opposing his decision was James V. Forrestal, who Truman said "wanted to hedge—he always does. He's constantly sending me alibi memos which I return with directions and the facts. We'll stay in Berlin—come what may." Forrestal enlisted the aid of others to try to persuade the President to get out of the Berlin situation. Truman noted this in his diary on July 19, 1948, and added: "I don't pass the buck, nor do I alibi out of any decision I make."

Without question, supplies were scarce; so was the equipment, manpower and everything else that would be needed for an airlift to keep the Berliners alive. But the President managed to see that everything was provided that "couldn't be furnished."

The aircraft used in what Americans called "Operation Vittles" and the Germans termed *die Luftbreuecke* ("air bridge") were many and as varied as human ingenuity. They began flying on June 12, 1948, carrying about 6,000 tons a day, but this was gradually increased as the people involved became more efficient. Before the airlift ended on May 12, 1949, the United States-British planes were delivering about 700,000 tons. During the period of Soviet inhumanity to man American aircraft carried almost two million tons of supplies into Berlin.

Much has been written in recent years about certain individuals who proclaimed and worked for the integration of the races. Most have forgotten that it was Harry S. Truman who worked for equality when it was considered political suicide. He told Ernest W. Roberts this in a letter on August 18, 1948: "I am not asking for social equality, because no such thing exists, but I am asking for equality of opportunity for all human beings and, as long as I stay here, I am going to continue that fight. . . . and if that ends up in my failure to be reelected, that failure will be in a good cause." And he had the courage of his convictions: when he spoke to an integrated audience in Dallas he stated unequivocally that blacks have the same rights as whites.

In the less than four years he had been President, Truman had accomplished more under the worst of conditions than most Presidents did in eight years. He believed his job wasn't completed, and felt the Republicans would destroy what he had accomplished, so he wanted four more years.

12. THE CAMPAIGN

President Harry S. Truman not only had to fight the Republicans in the 1948 campaign for the Presidency, he had to overcome a drastic split in the Democratic Party. Henry A. Wallace was running on the Progressive ticket and J. Strom Thurmond on the States Rights Democratic ticket. Each of these candidates, along with Republican Thomas E. Dewey, was a Freemason.

Truman had another handicap the other candidates didn't have; he had to manage the federal government during a continuing hectic period.

Recollections of the 1948 Campaign by William J. Bray is an oral history done for the Harry S. Truman Library. Bray was with the President and his staff throughout the campaign. His first-hand account is revealing, though at times understated. He recalled: "Many of Truman's supporters were disturbed at the beginning of the Presidential campaign for 1948. All the polls and newspapers predicted a landslide election for Thomas Dewey, the Republican candidate. Money for the Democratic campaign was scarce. Several of his friends met with the President and he assured them he was going to go down fighting.

"The first campaign trip was scheduled to have its initial speech at Rock Island, Illinois, at 5:45 a.m. While they were on the way to Rock Island, the group in Chicago insisted on a conference with the President. That would mean it would take place at 2 a.m. and his staff didn't think the President was up to such a schedule. The President insisted the train stop at Chicago and meet with the delegation. It did. The conference was held and the President still arrived at Rock Island on time."

They expected to find a small group waiting for their arrival, but over 4,000 were there. Truman spoke for ten minutes to an enthusiastic crowd. His staff was heartened, because it felt if that many would come out that early they could surely expect many more at more reasonable hours. The train then rolled into Iowa and there were tremendous crowds everywhere it went, and the President was highly pleased with the enthusiastic reception of his speeches.

President Harry S. Truman as he began the 1948 campaign that he was given no chance to win.

[Abbie Rowe photo for the National Park Service]

At Dexter, Iowa, people came by every means of transportation possible. "It was quite a sight to see this mass of humanity assembled to hear the President's first major speech on the farm situation," said Bray. "It was boiling hot; the temperature was between 110 and 115 degrees. After he spoke the President stepped down from the platform to demonstrate that he could still plow a straight furrow. This was a pleasant surprise to the crowd."

The crowds continued throughout Missouri and Colorado. In Denver Truman learned there was a veterans' hospital close by and he insisted on visiting the patients, "despite the fact that this visit delayed us since we were running very close to our established schedule."

The President would never make a political speech on Sunday. He would bring his family out onto the platform and say "hello," but that's as far as he would go.

At Salt Lake City the President "recognized a familiar face in the crowd. It was his old friend the barber from Battery 'D.' Mr. Truman waved to him to come aboard the train. Then he suggested that this old friend ride the train to Salt Lake City. He told the President that he had gotten married just the day before, so the President invited his wife along and advised me to bring them back to his private car when the train started to move," Bray related. The staff was alarmed when the visitors stayed with the President all the way to Salt Lake City, and even went with him to his hotel suite. Finally, politely but firmly, they had to remind the couple the President had speeches to make.

When they arrived in California the crowds continued to be enormous. "The size was beyond the expectations of those of us on the train," wrote Bray. The President kept up the pace by taking twenty-minute naps.

James Roosevelt, a Mason and one of Franklin's sons, met the President on the way to Los Angeles. He was astonished at the size of the crowds the President was attracting in Southern California. According to his mother, James was not one of Truman's supporters.

In Phoenix, Arizona, Truman drew much larger crowds than Dewey had when he was there earlier.

"The President was shown the low cost housing project that [John Nance] Garner had built," said Bray. The former Vice President of the United States "had been against the government spending money for housing projects because he felt that private financing could do the job, and he was happy to show the President the results of his personal undertaking along this line."

In San Antonio, Texas, the President attended a small Baptist church rather than the much larger one he was expected to visit.

Crowds continued to gather around the President, in spite of newspaper reports that Dewey was a ten-to-one favorite to win the election. As they continued across Texas, "the crowds seemed to grow and the people seemed very pleased with what the President was talking about," reported Bray.

The President made major speeches at Dallas and in the ball park at Bonham, Texas. An impromptu reception at the home of Sam Rayburn, the Speaker of the House, found thousands lining the roads to Rayburn's home hoping to be able to shake the hand of the President.

"Another of the many interesting developments on this trip was the desire of many Masons to have their certificates of membership in the Masonic order endorsed by the President," said Bray. "This of course he was happy to do, but the number of requests became so great that we had to insist that people leave the certificates with us and we would return them by mail after the President had time to sign them. Usually the first order of business after the train left the town was to place these certificates before the President for his signature."

A problem arose during the campaign in Texas. Walter Bedell Smith, the ambassador to Moscow, had to meet with the President as soon as possible. "Secrecy was important," said Bray. "What Smith wanted to report was that the Soviets refused to end the Berlin blockade and had walked out of the conference that they were having on the subject. An impasse had developed between the Soviets and the Western powers over the Soviet blockade. The Soviets refused to end the blockade and the Westerners refused to be deterred by it. Smith said the situation was serious."

Crowds continued to swell larger from town to town. "At Marietta we picked up some of the leading citizens and top political figures in the state. They rode with us to Oklahoma City. The crowds greeting the President on the way to Oklahoma City were so enthusiastic that the train was two hours late in arriving." There he was to give a major radio speech and the time had already been set. "People along the route from the train to the ball park were wondering why the President's car had gone so fast that the President couldn't wave to anybody. Fortunately Mrs. Truman and Margaret, in another car, drove slowly along the same route, which helped to make up for the loss the people felt because they hardly saw their President. It was announced that the President would return to his train along the same route. After his speech he did so and the situation was rectified."

The lack of money in the Democratic coffers remained a problem; it was only an hour before the scheduled broadcast that they were able raise the funds to pay for the radio time.

They spent a full day in Missouri and arrived at Mount Vernon, Illinois, the following day. The President and his staff took a motor caravan to the downstate region, and the Republican governor refused to provide police protection for the President. "The only help we got was from some of the county or local police," Bray said. "Because of the large crowds that came to see the President, we had trouble holding to our itinerary."

Adlai Stevenson gave the President little help, and appeared to be putting as much distance between himself and Truman as possible. As the trip progressed the President departed from his prepared text more frequently. "He seemed more persuasive when speaking extemporaneously," noted Bray. "This caused people at every stop to shout 'give 'em hell, Harry.' To this remark the President would reply: 'I'm not going to give 'em hell, but just tell them the truth.' "

Into Indiana and then Kentucky the campaign train went. Through West Virginia it traveled late at night, but the crowds remained tremendous all along the way. The first leg of the campaign ended on October 2, 1948, when the train arrived back in Washington. "President Truman's constant reminder about 'the do-nothing Eightieth Congress' had a tremendous effect on the people he talked to during his trip," said Bray. "This was proven by the results in November."

One newspaper reporter noted: "On the Dewey train the newspaper men played bridge and drank martinis and manhattans. On the Truman train they played poker and drank Scotch and bourbon."

On October 10, 1948, the Presidential party left Washington at 8 p.m. to start its travel through six states, West Virginia, Ohio, Indiana, Illinois, Wisconsin, and Minnesota. Again enthusiastic crowds greeted the President wherever the train stopped or passed. The hour appeared to make no difference. At Milwaukee, where he made a major speech, the ball park was filled to capacity. Two days before, the same park was half empty when Governor Dewey delivered a speech.

Bray relates an excellent first-hand and little-known account of an unusual Masonic event that took place in Indiana during this 1948 Presidential campaign of Harry S. Truman:

> At Kokomo a very interesting incident occurred. When the President had finished speaking and people started to come over to the rear platform of the train to shake hands, he noticed in the crowd a boy wearing a sailor suit—the uniform of the United States Navy. The President recognized him as a member of the crew of the *Williamsburg*, the Presidential yacht which was docked on the Potomac River in Washington.
>
> The President motioned to the boy to come up and shake hands, which the young man did. The President asked what he was doing in Kokomo. The young man said he was home to visit his family and also to be inducted into the Masons. This made the President very happy because he was a Mason himself. He asked the young man when the induction would take place. The sailor said he planned to take the train which would follow the President's train and travel to a little town about eight miles from Indianapolis where the Masonic lodge would induct him.
>
> The President invited the young man to ride the President's train to Indianapolis. He said he would be glad to take the youngster along. The youngster said his father was going with him, so the President told him to get his father and get on the train. And he instructed us to bring the boy and his father back to the President's private car for a visit as soon as the train started to move.
>
> During the visit the boy's father said it certainly would be nice if the President could attend his son's induction into the Masonic order. The President replied by saying there was nothing he would like to do better than to participate in the boy's induction, but he was traveling on a tight schedule and arrangements had already been made that would occupy every minute of his visit that night to Indianapolis. When the visit concluded, the boy and his father

moved forward to the club car and the train moved on to Tipton, Indiana, where the President spoke from the rear platform.

As the train left Tipton the President called several of us back to his car for a conference. He informed us that after thinking things over he had decided that after the ceremonies ended at Indianapolis that evening he would like to go out to this little town and attend the installation of the boy from the *Williamsburg* into the Masonic order.

We apprised the President that this would be impossible because of the tight schedule we were following and also because the President had indicated that he wanted no publicity about this matter, we advised him that the newspaper people traveling with the President would probably get the story and make much of it. **The President was insistent. He said he was not interested in the details, but to work it out and bring it about.**

Moving the President from one section of the country to another is not a simple task. There are many factors involved because of the security precautions necessary for the President's protection in all places. Therefore, when the train arrived in Maplesville, Indiana, for another platform speech, several of the Secret Service men left the train to put into adoption a plan which had been drawn whereby the President could participate in the ceremonies.

We arrived in Indianapolis in the late afternoon and proceeded to the Indiana Hotel. Along the route there were cheering crowds. At the hotel a big reception was arranged for the President, after which he proceeded to the Indianapolis Athletic Club where dinner was served, and he made some brief remarks. At 8:30 the party left for the Indiana War Memorial where the President made a major speech. Following the speech the party returned in cars to the train.

The car in which the President was supposed to arrive at the head of the procession, however, was occupied by two members of his party and his personal secret service body guard, Henry Nicholson. The car containing the President and several Secret Service people proceeded to this little town where the President had indicated that he wished to be at the installation of the boy from the *Williamsburg.*

Advance members of the Secret Service had already proceeded to this town to notify the local police and Masonic officials of the President's expected attendance. They were pledged to secrecy. When the procession of cars which left the Indiana War Memorial arrived back at the railroad station in Indianapolis, the car which apparently contained the President drew up to the rear of his private car and agent Nicholson walked out to inform everyone that "that will be all for this evening." He announced that the train would be leaving the station in about an hour and a half.

> The President was then in the Masonic lodge in the community near Indianapolis. About an hour later the President returned to his railroad car very much pleased that "maybe" he had made several people happy. Of course he had made many, many people happy. Especially the boy and his father. It was not until two days later that word "leaked out" about the President's detour and it did not make the press feel very happy. They had missed quite a scoop.

"October 15, 1948, bids fair to become a legendary date at Beech Grove Lodge No. 694," reported the *Indiana Freemason* in November. "Years hence, Brethren now youngsters in the service of this Marion County Lodge will revel in telling their grandchildren how back in '48 they 'sat in Lodge' with a President of the United States—and how they participated in the ceremony of receiving him before a Masonic altar. For on that date President Harry S. Truman, Past Grand Master of Missouri, took time out from the demands of a strenuous political campaign to partake of Masonic fellowship—and to witness the Master Mason degree, conferred by Beech Grove Lodge."

The second section of the Master Mason degree was delayed while over three hundred men patiently waited until the President could arrive. When he did, he signed the Lodge register and was then escorted to a preparation room for an examination to determine if he really was a Master Mason, simply because "this is the way things are always done in Freemasonry." He told the committee, among whom Past Grand Master Dwight L. Smith was a member, "Shoot some questions at me if you like; I used to be a district lecturer in Missouri." And the committee was amazed at his Masonic proficiency.

When he was presented in the Lodge it was, at his specific request, as "Harry S. Truman, Past Grand Master of Masons in Missouri." After he had received the honors of the Craft in the East he was asked to address the Lodge. He did:

> Masonry has always meant much in my life. I have been Worshipful Master of a Lodge, Secretary of a Lodge, district lecturer and district deputy, and have held all the offices in the Grand Lodge of Missouri. When I served as Grand Master in 1941 I was at that time a United States Senator, and found it necessary to "commute" by plane between Washington and Missouri—but even with all this I managed to make an average number of visitations.
>
> Although I hold the highest civil honor in the world, I have always regarded my rank and title as a Past Grand Master of

President Truman addresses the members and visitors of Beech Grove Lodge No. 694, Indiana, on October 15, 1948, during his campaign for the Presidency of the United States.

[Photo courtesy of Dwight L. Smith]

> Masons as the greatest honor that has ever come to me. I value it above all others because to be a Grand Master of Masons one must be more than a good public relations man—he must have a background based upon the noblest of principles, and he must bear the respect and esteem of the good men who make up the Craft.
>
> Freemasonry takes good men and endeavors to make them better. Its principles, which are taught in the Book which we open on our altars, are the principles which make for good citizenship and upright living. During my life I have made a study of the Bible, and the more I have studied it the more I have been convinced that its lessons, which we teach around our Masonic altars, are the lessons mankind must learn if civilization is to endure.

Indiana's Grand Secretary, Past Grand Master Dwight L. Smith, was then called on to convey the greetings of Indiana Masons to the President. He expressed the pleasure of all Hoosiers on being able to welcome so distinguished a Brother. He concluded by saying: "I don't know how the brethren will feel about you on November 2, but you may be very sure they are 100 percent for you tonight."

Truman said he would like to remain for the conferral of the degree, so he sat in the East beside Carlisle Bauermeister, uncle of candidate Donald Earl Bauermeister, the sailor from the *Williamsburg.* The acting Master was visibly nervous, but Truman, an old hand at setting nervous men at ease, patted his arm and whispered: "Now don't pay any attention to me; just go ahead as if I weren't here."

When the ceremony was over Truman was asked to present a ring to the candidate. He did and said: "This is a beautiful ring given by your parents, and I hope you will wear it with pride that you are a Freemason. Regardless of the number of additional degrees you may receive in the future, regardless of the different emblems you may be entitled to wear, I hope you will always wear this.

"The Square and Compass[es are] the essence of Masonry. All other bodies, while helpful and valuable, are but elaborations on the great lesson of life, death and immortality through which you have passed. The Square and Compass[es are] the emblem of Freemasonry and may these emblems ever remind you of the proud title that is yours—a man and Mason."

[Indiana is one of the few jurisdictions that uses "compass" instead of "compasses." Although the Indiana account used its

Past Grand Master Harry S. Truman presents Donald Earl Bauermeister, a sailor on the Presidential Yacht *Williamsburg* with a Masonic ring, a gift from the parents of the young man.

[Photo courtesy of Dwight L. Smith]

accepted term, Truman was an excellent ritualist and would have used the Missouri term of "compasses."]

After posing for pictures, the President asked to be excused so he could return to his train. He was, and as he removed his apron he asked if he could keep it as a memento of his visit in Indiana. He received enthusiastic permission.

Outside the Lodge room he was asked to pose for a formal portrait. Then he was joined by two Indiana political leaders who asked him to pose with them. The photo was taken and he was asked to pose again. He agreed. They shifted his hands so his Masonic ring was covered. Truman looked at them and asked: "Is that the reason you're taking the photo over?"

"Yes," they answered, and explained there are Democrats opposed to Masonry. "Then to hell with it!" said Truman as he walked away without posing with them for the second picture.

The Kansas City *Star* reported on October 16, 1948, from Indianapolis, Indiana: "President Truman took a sudden leave of absence from his campaign train last night to drive to suburban Beech Grove to attend a Masonic lodge ceremony for a sailor on the President's yacht. The sailor, Donald Earl Bauermeister, showed up in a crowd at Noblesville, Ind., yesterday afternoon when Mr. Truman spoke there. Mr. Truman spotted him, called him over and invited him to ride to Indianapolis. Bauermeister told the President he was to get the third, or Blue lodge, degree in Masonry last night. Chas. G. Ross, presidential secretary, said Mr. Truman told the sailor he would like to sit in. Arrangements were made for him to attend the ceremony at Masonic Lodge 694 at Beech Grove. The rites were delayed until the President had finished a campaign speech here and had time to drive to Beech Grove."

Mrs. John Bauermeister, the young man's mother, wrote to the President on December 18. She thanked him "for the time you spared, on October 15, 1948, to be present at the raising to a Master Mason of our son, Don." She added: "I also wish to thank your daughter for the beautiful orchid she sent to me. I still have it, and hope to keep it always."

When the President arrived at the train the party left Indianapolis to travel through Ohio and into West Virginia. It returned to Washington at 4 p.m. Saturday, October 16, 1948.

On October 22 the Presidential party went to Pennsylvania. The crowds were again encouraging. The final trip of the campaign started on October 24 when the President left Washington at 9:30 p.m. The odds remained the same—Dewey ten-to-one. At Gary, Indiana, a large crowd cheered the President heartily. Chicago was the next stop, and the Democratic organization greeted the President with a stupendous fireworks display. The next major stop was South Bend, Indiana.

Then came Cleveland and Toledo, Ohio, followed by Albany, New York, where thousands stood in a pouring rain to hear the President speak. The campaign then went on to Boston, Massachusetts.

Police estimated the crowd along the parade route at over a quarter million people. Throughout the cities in Massachusetts there continued to be record crowds.

The Democratic Party in New York was in the hands of Liberals controlled by Henry Wallace, and would not release enough money to rent Madison Square Garden. But a group of liberals

President Truman on the stage of the Chicago Stadium on October 25, 1948.
[Truman Library photo]

did come to the President's rescue and the Garden was obtained. Even so, the Democrats couldn't sell enough tickets to begin to fill the seats. The gates were thrown open and thousands followed the motorcade into the Garden.

The campaign ended in St. Louis where Truman gave a completely extemporaneous speech that many who had traveled all the way with him said was his best. They then went to Independence to await the decision of the voters.

Being in Independence also gave the President a few moments to relax with his Masonic brethren. A breakfast was held on November 1 by Mary Conclave, Red Cross of Constantine, in Kansas City. Truman, as could be expected, was asked to say a few words. He did, and concluded by saying: "Boys, I'm not a betting man myself, but if any of you want to make a little easy money, just bet on me to win tomorrow." William Denslow remembered that statement well. In fact, he remembered the whole day.

"November 1, 1948—the day before the election—was filled with Masonic activity in Kansas City, honoring Mr. Truman," said Denslow. "It began with a breakfast given by Mary Conclave, Red Cross of Constantine, for its most honored member. There were 45 guests present in the Florentine Room of the Kansas City Club. A cardinal rule for all who are in the same room with a President is to keep your hands out of your pockets. One good companion innocently sauntered in with both hands in his pockets and was immediately nailed to the wall by two Secret Service agents."

"That day was selected by Ararat Shrine Temple for a ceremonial in honor of the Chief Executive," continued Denslow. "The Shrine gave a dinner in his honor at the Kansas City Club in the evening with 386 present, both Shriners and non-Shriners, Democrats and Republicans." The President then spoke of his activities during the campaign: "As you men undoubtedly know, buck-passing stops at the White House. The President has to make decisions. I made a lot of them—and I tried to make good ones. Some persons may not agree with me. History will tell who was right.

"I'm going to wind up this campaign at 9:30 o'clock tonight with a nonpolitical speech. If you fellows would like to hear what a real nonpolitical speech sounds like, tune in on me. I'll be on four networks."

The President continued: "I've traveled 31,100 miles in this campaign. Some people have expressed wonder that I could do all that traveling and make some two hundred eighty or two hundred ninety appearances before thousands of persons. I'm just hitting my stride when I'm out among the people. It feels so good to be out of that White House jail that I'm just going good."

Many of those present wanted their programs autographed by the President. He agreed to sign them if they would submit them with their name and address so he could return them by mail. When Denslow received his it said: "Bill—Your father was a friend when I *needed* a friend." Denslow noted that "seemed to epitomize Mr. Truman's idea of friendship."

Denslow said Truman "delighted in introducing my father among Washington politicos as 'my damned Republican friend.' Dad, a rock-bound Republican, always said that he never voted for Truman—but I know that he did! They were close friends until my father's death in 1960, and I am happy to say that during these years the friendship spilled over to include me."

Throughout the long night of November 2-3, 1948, Truman slept while commentators, reporters, poll takers, and even the home folks in Independence predicted Dewey would be the next President. Truman, bright and cheerful, joined his dreary-eyed supporters in the Muehlebach Hotel in Kansas City at 6 a.m. At 10:14 a.m. Missouri time, Thomas E. Dewey finally conceded he had lost. The whistles blew and the bells finally rang throughout Kansas City and Independence. The home town boy had pulled off an upset.

The campaign train, now renamed the "Victory Special," left for Washington on the morning of November 4. When it stopped at St. Louis someone handed Truman a copy of the Chicago *Tribune* whose headline proudly proclaimed in huge black type, "DEWEY DEFEATS TRUMAN." The picture of a laughing Truman holding up that paper was recorded for posterity. In Washington, where only a meager few had seen the campaign train off, thousands welcomed the "Victory Special."

Hundreds of thousands lined the route to the White House, which Truman often called "the great white jail," and an untold number of bands played "We're Just Wild About Harry." As they passed the Washington Post building they were greeted with a large sign reading: "MR. PRESIDENT, WE ARE READY TO EAT CROW WHENEVER YOU ARE READY TO SERVE IT."

Harry Truman had proven to the world that he *was* a great man, President, husband, father, and Freemason.

13. THE SECOND TERM

The President's opponents were not able to defeat him at the polls, so again they began taking pot shots at his family. His sister, Mary Jane, was disturbed by some ugly statements she had heard, and told the President so. He cautioned her on November 14, 1948: "You must not get touchy about things in your Chapter O.E.S. or anywhere else. Don't read Doris Fleeson and those fool columnists. No one pays any attention to them at all. Now if you go around all the time expecting someone to do you a bad turn you can always find them doing it. . . . Hope you have a nice time at all your meetings now and keep going. Pay no attention to supposed slights and think only of the nice treatment. Where would we have been if I'd paid attention to the smart alecks."

The President told several Freemasons in Missouri that he would like to do something for the Masons of his state. Several of them persuaded him to sit for his portrait in the regalia of a Grand Master of Masons in Missouri.

"It seems to me a rather egotistical thing to do," Truman wrote to Ray Denslow, "but since the Grand Lodge seems to want it and Secretary [John] Snyder became interested in it I believe we will get as good a picture as the subject under consideration can produce."

Truman had asked Ray Denslow for his advice about the manner in which he should pose for the Masonic portrait. Denslow answered him on November 20, 1948.

On November 24, 1948, Truman again wrote to Denslow: "Thanks a lot for yours of the 20th and the enclosures. Everything arrived in good shape and we are going to work on the picture tomorrow morning." The "everything" consisted of a Grand Master's collar with the jewel and Denslow's Past Grand Master's apron. The hat, gavel, and everything else he had on hand.

A young portrait artist named Greta Kempton of New York City had been commissioned by the Masons of Missouri to paint the portrait of the country's outstanding Freemason. Miss Kempton was considered by many the outstanding portrait artist in the

John W. Snyder, Secretary of the Treasury, a member of Steele Lodge No. 634, Missouri, who encouraged President Truman to have his portrait painted in his Masonic regalia.

[Portrait by Greta Kempton]

country. Her finished portrait of President Truman proved to be another jewel in her crown of artistic achievement.

Greta Kempton had painted, among many other portraits, those of John W. Snyder, Secretary of the Treasury, his wife and daughter. Through the Snyders the Trumans learned of her outstanding work, and she was commissioned to paint a portrait of the President. So well was this accepted, it became the official White House portrait.

It was little wonder then that the young lady again met the President of the United States on the morning of November 25 as the artist chosen by the Masons of Missouri. They determined how and where he should pose, and as they were ready to start Truman said, "Wait a minute! Where's my hat?"

"He rushed out," said Miss Kempton, "and came back with a tall silk hat. When I saw the way he was carrying it, I said, 'stop! Please don't move. Hold the hat just like that!' He said, 'Oh, it's the correct way it's supposed to be held.' It was the way he was resting the top hat on his forearm—the way he was clutching it—that struck me—a perfect pose. We had a lot of fun over that hat."

The President told Miss Kempton he wanted her to concentrate on the gold collar, the gavel and the apron. "Those are the things that seemed to him the most important." That she concentrated on every portion of the portrait is evident in the finished project.

Miss Kempton was on an assignment in St. Louis, Missouri, when Truman agreed to the request for a Masonic portrait, so she was contacted while there. Being a stickler for detail, she asked to see the room in the Masonic Temple where Truman had presided. There she sketched the details that would be missing in the White House where she would work. Among the first things she noted was the letter "G" centered on the wall where the chair of the presiding officer sat. She said: "I knew the 'G' had to be an important part of the background; so did the chair. Later the President told me the 'G' stood for God."

"We didn't pose too long at a time because of the press of business in the White House," continued Miss Kempton. "During the sittings he explained to me the principles of Masonry. I was very impressed because he mentioned so many of my own ideals. He certainly impressed me because you don't hear many people talk that way. And to hear this from a man of his stature was an amazing thing."

She added: "It really was wonderful the way he asked questions about the techniques of painting as he watched me mix colors. He was inquisitive about everything. I could readily understand how he became President and why he was such a good one.

"I loved the way he held his gavel. Even now I can hear it when he bangs it down." She took the apron, collar and gavel to her studio where she worked many hours on their intricate details. She said these were challenging hours which she enjoyed.

"After the portrait was finished," she said with well-deserved pride, "he was just bubbling—he couldn't wait for the next day. He said, 'Wait until the fellows see this! Their eyes will pop out!' Then he told me that being Grand Master meant more to him than anything, 'and now having this portrait shall be the biggest honor I'll ever have.' The way he said it made me feel very humble. Later he told me that he would always have a soft spot in his heart for that Masonic portrait."

Life magazine took note of the portrait on December 6, 1948, and in an article entitled "Back in Stride" appeared a piece of misleading reporting: "The President also found time to sit three times for an oil portrait showing him in all the regalia to which he is entitled as a Master Mason of the 33rd degree: silk hat, apron, heavy rings on his fingers. When his picture is finished it will occupy a place of honor in the Masonic Grand Lodge of Missouri at St. Louis."

A brief check of the facts by the reporter would have revealed there is no such thing as a "Master Mason of the 33rd degree," nor is a 33rd degree *Scottish Rite Mason* entitled to wear the regalia Truman wore for the portrait unless he had earned that right in a Grand Lodge. A close inspection of the portrait fails to disclose any rings, heavy or otherwise.

Life rectified its error in its edition of March 28, 1949. It carried one of the finest tributes to the oldest fraternal organization in existence. Never before had there appeared in a national publication anything like this tribute to Freemasonry.

Underneath the full page color reproduction of the Kempton portrait it was recorded: "IN FULL REGALIA Mason Harry Truman pounds gavel in new portrait by Greta Kempton which hangs in the Grand Lodge at St. Louis. This is the way Mr. Truman dressed for meetings as Missouri Grand Master in 1940 [and 1941]. Symbol of office is right-angled square suspended from his neck. He also wears Masonic apron with eye and face of sun."

Later the article added: "Americans who have grown used to seeing pictures of Harry Truman in everything from tails to swim suit got still another view. This time he appeared in a brand new portrait as a Grand Master."

The cover of the magazine depicted all the Grand Masters in the United States. It also carried a 1935 photograph of Franklin D. Roosevelt in a Masonic apron along with his sons James and Franklin, Jr., and Fiorello La Guardia, a long-time mayor of New York City. Another page carried a photo of the giant-sized statue of George Washington, in "Plasticine form," along with the creator, Bryant Baker. It said the statue was seventeen feet three inches high and cost one hundred thousand dollars. Also pictured was the twelve-foot replica of the chair Washington is said to have used, which would be behind the statue.

The Kempton portrait was "officially" unveiled on September 27, 1949, during the Grand Lodge session in St. Louis, and was presented by the President to his own Grand Lodge of Missouri. It was unveiled by Deputy Grand Master James M. Bradford, the man whom Grand Master Truman started in the Grand Lodge line, and whom the President would later install as Grand Master. During this ceremony the organ appropriately and quietly played "God Bless America."

This portrait has resided on permanent loan prominently in the Harry S. Truman Library in Independence, Missouri, since its opening.

The White House had been in deplorable condition for longer than anyone knew. In 1947, with numerous guests present, the President noted the chandelier above their heads shaking. He had it checked out the next morning and then removed. Repairs were started but were never satisfactorily completed. So, immediately after the campaign, the Trumans moved into the Blair House so the "great white jail" could be thoroughly overhauled.

Although the White House had been remodeled several times, the work had been botched. Most of the floors still "sagged and moved like a ship at sea." It was found that burned-out timbers, evidently partial survivors from the War of 1812, had been reused.

On February 17, 1948, Truman was elected an honorary member of Hiram Lodge No. 10 in the District of Columbia. The President expressed his appreciation of this honor. During 1949 he was elected an honorary member of the Grand Lodge of Florida. Florida Masons knew him well because he had his "summer White House" at Key West which he visited as often as possible.

Columbia Lodge No. 2397, London, England, notified the President that he had been elected an Honorary Member on January 29. On April 9, 1949, Truman wrote to the Lodge:

President Truman, center, is presented a life membership in the Grand Lodge of Florida.

[U.S. Navy photo, Truman Library]

"I am deeply appreciative of the action of Columbia Lodge of Free and Accepted Masons, No. 2397 in the Register of the Grand Lodge of England, in conferring on me Honorary Membership in that Lodge.

"I count it a rare privilege to be included in the noble company of my predecessors in office who have received this signal fraternal honor. After all, the teachings and tenets of our ancient craft which promote good will and the spirit of amity among the brethren, should also be a vehicle of good will between nations.

"I am mindful as I write that the roots of American Masonry are sunk deep in English soil and tradition since our earliest lodges derived their authority and were erected under charters from the Grand Lodge of the Mother Country.

"To you and to all the brethren who joined with you in the letter of February fourteenth last, I send fraternal greetings."

The touchy situation in Germany had finally eased. The New York *Times* for May 12, 1949, reported from Berlin: "Just as the morning sun rose over the jagged skyline of this broken but defiant city a Soviet zone locomotive chugged wearily into the British sector hauling the first train to reach Berlin from the West in 328 days. Arrival of the train completed the relief of the city from the iron vise of the Soviet blockade." Truman's patience and courage had won! So had the heroic American and British pilots who braved untenable conditions to keep the planes taking off and landing on the average of one a minute. So had the men and women who loaded the planes and those who kept them in flying condition. It was a triumph of freedom over tyranny.

The President, perhaps because of his good friend Frank S. Land, addressed the Imperial Council session of the Shrine at Soldier Field in Chicago on July 19, 1949. It was a speech many of his listeners remembered for years as he discussed foreign policy decisions past, present and for the future. He hoped he would see the "creation of a world in which we, and all people, can live and prosper in peace."

No fez was worn by Truman during the parade, or after, and it is said there were those who chided him for not wearing one. To them he is reported to have said: "I appeared here as the President of the United States, not a Shriner."

President Harry S. Truman with Freemasons from all over the country at the Shriners parade in Chicago.

[Truman Library photo]

The China situation created problems for the President throughout the early years of his second term. In an attempt to forcefully inform the Ambassador to China, Patrick J. Hurley, what he wanted done, the President called Hurley to Washington. They met, along with Secretary of State James Byrnes, on November 27, 1945, and the President informed both that it "would be our policy to support Chiang Kai-shek but that we would not be driven into fighting Chiang's battles for him."

Hurley agreed to return to China immediately because the situation was worsening. To the President's surprise, two hours later he received a phone call informing him Hurley had attacked the administration and then resigned.

Truman wrote in his *Memoirs*: "I went to the telephone in the Red Room of the White House and called the general at his home in Leesburg [Virginia]. Without any preparation I told him: 'General, I want you to go to China for me.' Marshall said only, 'Yes, Mr. President,' and hung up abruptly.

"When General Marshall came to the White House two days later to discuss his mission with Byrnes and me, I asked him why he had hung up on me without asking any questions. The reason, he explained to me, was that Mrs. Marshall and he had just driven up to the house, and he had been in the process of unloading some of their belongings when the phone rang. He had not wanted Mrs. Marshall, who was concerned about his health, to know how short-lived their retirement would be, and so he had hung up before she might hear any part of the conversation. He expected to break the news to her gradually, but when he turned on the radio a few minutes later, the very first thing she heard was the news flash announcing the general's mission.

" 'There was the devil to pay,' he confessed."

Marshall and Harry Truman were unable to save the China that was once controlled by Chiang Kai-shek. In the Congress those who had opposed everything the President had proposed raised the cry that the administration had "sold out China." Nothing could have been further from the truth.

Looking at the situation from the perspective of today is Jane Wu, a young lady from Shanghai. She has been studying foreign relations for her doctorate in history, and earned her Master's Degree for her thesis on George Marshall. Among the research centers where she has studied for considerable periods of time is the Harry S. Truman Library.

Miss Wu said neither Harry Truman or George Marshall particularly liked Chiang Kai-shek "but backed him as the lesser of two evils." Chiang's "situation was hopeless," Miss Wu continued. "He would take no advice from Marshall. His whole regime was so corrupted there was nothing that could save it. I don't think Truman expected Marshall to be successful, but they were caught in a dilemma. Chiang's brothers-in-law, P.V. Soong and H.H. Kung, were so corrupt most of the money went into their pockets. Truman, who hated corruption, found this out and was furious. But on the hill there was a lot of support from the powerful China Lobby in Congress. In 1952 Truman had this lobby investigated.

"Chiang went to Formosa in 1949. Northern China fell first, and most of the weapons the communists captured were American-made. These weapons had not gone to the troops who really fought; they went to the favored troops, most of whom surrendered without a fight. The fighting generals and admirals did not get enough weapons to really fight."

"Things changed for Chaing when he went to Formosa. He had learned his lessons well," said Miss Wu.

Bruce H. Hunt, a long-time personal friend of Truman, had breakfast with the President in September, 1949, when he returned to St. Louis to install his appointment to the Grand Lodge line as Grand Master. Hunt told Truman about his three-year-old daughter's refusal to let a doctor examine her. The next day she had no trouble with another doctor. Her mother asked her why. "Well, Mother," she said, "he was not a real doctor anyway, he was a Dewey, and I didn't want him to look at me." The first doctor had a mustache; the second didn't. The President enjoyed the story and said: "Suzanne has the right idea."

The President was attending the Grand Lodge of Missouri for at least two reasons: to present his Masonic portrait to the Masons of Missouri, and to install his friend. The portrait was unveiled, and later the installation of James M. Bradford as Grand Master followed, but Hunt said it wasn't without incident. Not all the Secret Service men were Masons. The presiding Grand Master refused to entertain a suggestion that the Grand Lodge be put at ease for the installation. This information was conveyed to Truman. The President told them not to worry, he would handle the situation.

Two thousand Masons waited for the President of the United States, one of their own Past Grand Masters, to enter through the double doors of the inner assembly. The doors opened; the organ struck up a rousing march; the Masons stood and cheered; and a smiling Truman was escorted into the auditorium and to the East. There he was handed the gavel from the Grand Master, and he immediately declared the Grand Lodge called from labor. The President's aides, staff and Secret Service men entered.

Truman's long-time friend, Ray V. Denslow, Past Grand Master, acted as the installing marshal, and the installation proceeded. According to *The Freemason*, the Missouri Grand Lodge magazine, it was partly "official ceremony of the Grand Lodge, but mostly 'Trumanese.' " During the installation of Bradford as Grand Master, Truman said:

> This is a thing I have looked forward to for a long time. I remember very well when the M.W. Bro. William R. Gentry installed me at that altar under like circumstances.
>
> **I considered that, and still consider it, the highest honor that has ever come to me.**
>
> As Grand Master of Masons of this State, you are entirely familiar with all the ritual from beginning to end. You are entirely familiar with the charges which are given to a Master of the Lodge, and you are entirely familiar with the duties which you, as Grand Master of this great Jurisdiction, will have to pursue.
>
> I know that you will do the job well and creditably, to yourself and to the Grand Lodge. If I hadn't thought that in the beginning, I would not have appointed you to the Grand Lodge. For that reason, I am going to ask you to say to this Grand Lodge that you expect to pursue the customs and policies of the Grand Lodge of this great State of Missouri, through your entire incumbency as Grand Master; and that you will turn the Grand Lodge over to your successor in as good condition, or better—I hope—than it is today.

After installing the other officers, Truman said:

> Before I take off this hat and surrender this gavel to the Grand Master—who has a right to take it away from me now—I want to present to him and to the Grand Lodge of Missouri a special gavel, for his use in presiding over this Grand Lodge when it is convened at its next regular session.
>
> This gavel has some history attached to it. It is made of wood out of an elm tree which was known on the national old trails road as the Van Buren elm.
>
> The Van Buren history is interesting because in his second attempt to be nominated for President in Baltimore, he did not receive a two-thirds majority. He did receive a majority of the delegates there present, but the anti-Masons were strong enough in his own state to beat him. I thought the Most Worshipful Grand Master would be happy to use this gavel, which I am going to present to the Grand Lodge.
>
> Now I would like, under the circumstances, on account of the necessity of my again becoming President of the United States in about three minutes, I would like to have your permission to retire.

"I consider it, and still consider it, the highest honor that ever came to me," Truman is quoted as saying in an article in *Time* on October 10, 1949. He was referring to his election as Grand Master of Masons in Missouri in 1940. A *Newsweek* letter-writer said angrily: "If Mr. Truman doesn't consider being President of the

U.S. a far greater honor, the voters should return him to his Missouri Masons in 1952."

An editor replied: "We think President Truman was right. The position of Grand Master was never sought after by Mr. Truman; it came unsolicited. It is our belief that if Mr. Truman had never served the Grand Lodge of Missouri as Grand Master, he would never have been considered as a United States Senator, or President of the United States. Mr. Truman has a right to feel as he does. Politics did not enter into his Masonic election; his first position in the Grand Lodge of Missouri was an appointment by a Republican, the appointment being concurred in by *two other Republicans!*"

On October 25, 1949, Grand Master Bradford wrote to thank the President for installing him. "My recent installation by you as Grand Master was an historic event," Bradford stated, "the recollection of which will be my most cherished memory." Bradford's wife, Edna, beat her husband to it, though. On September 30 she had written to thank the President for starting her husband in line and for then installing him as Grand Master.

On January 1, 1950, John Cowles asked Truman for a block of wood from the White House to make a gavel. This was referred to the buildings department which refused because it was "not possible under P.L. 397."

Truman learned that his good friend and Masonic brother Hap Arnold had died, so he wrote in his diary on January 15, 1950: "The first of the big five to go. A grand man, a great commander and one of the original U.S. Air Force. He was a good friend of mine—a great loss."

For years the young men of the Order of DeMolay had been raising funds to pay for a gigantic bronze statue of George Washington to adorn the entrance to the George Washington Masonic National Memorial. The day for its dedication arrived and on Wednesday, February 22, 1950, thousands gathered on Shooters Hill, Alexandria, Virginia, to hear the President of the United States speak to them and a nation-wide radio audience at its unveiling.

Truman began his talk by saying: "It is a privilege to dedicate this inspiring statue of George Washington.

"This is the climax of many years of planning and effort. I congratulate particularly the Order of DeMolay, whose contributions have made this statue a reality. This heroic likeness of our first President makes even more impressive the entrance hall of this temple. It is altogether fitting that this work should stand in the community that Washington did so much to build, and so near his own home at Mount Vernon."

The President then made a major foreign policy address in which he praised the American system of government and condemned that of communism. He closed his address by stating:

"The progress we have made in this country since the days of George Washington is proof of the vitality and truth of the ideals he fought for. We must be no less firm, no less resolute, no less steadfast than he was. We move upon a greater stage than he did, but our problems are fundamentally the same problems that faced the first President of this Nation—to make democracy work and defend it from its enemies.

"George Washington sought guidance from Almighty God as he faced these tasks in his time; let us be guided today by Divine Providence as we strive for lasting peace with freedom and justice for all mankind."

The President received a Masonic plaque on February 27 from "A Free Acceptive Mason to another." Rose Conway, Truman's personal secretary, got a chuckle out of that.

George Marquis informed the President on April 1, 1950, that the Missouri Lodge of Research had twelve shelves of books in the Jackson County Public Library. He suggested that "it would be a gracious gesture for your mother and the children of David W. Wallace, who was Grand Commander in 1892, to present his sword to be placed in the cabinet with the McDowell sword." Truman responded on April 17:

> The Wallace boys gave me the Knight Templar swords of my father-in-law and I am sure that they will be happy to have them placed as you suggest. The first time I am home I'll see that you get possession of them. There are two swords—one of them is a gold-plated one and the other is the ordinary dress sword. Ben Wallace inherited them and when he died Miss Carrie gave them to George. George and Frank gave them to me the last time I was at home thinking I would appreciate them more than anybody else in the family and, of course, I do.

President Harry S. Truman leaving the George Washington Masonic National Memorial after his dedication and major policy address at the unveiling of the George Washington statue, which was a gift from the Order of DeMolay.
[Photographer unknown]

> I think your suggestion is a good one and we will proceed to carry it out.

Truman later had the swords polished and turned over to the lodge so they could be displayed with the Masonic mementos in the Jackson County Public Library.

Work on the rebuilding of the White House brought all kinds of requests to the President. A Masonic lodge needed a new building and asked for "about 100 bricks from the old White House to dispose of as souvenirs to help raise money for the building." Another lodge requested "a piece of pine lumber big enough to make one or two gavels for use in the Lodge." All such pleas were referred to another department.

Even Frank Land and George Marquis were not reluctant to make a request. Marquis asked Land to ask the President for "a cabinet or chest that might be among the historical objects being taken out of the White House and available for distribution by the Commission on Renovation of the White House." This was wanted for the special display room at the public library.

"I have been absolutely against the souvenir business on the White House program," wrote Truman on May 25. "The matter, however, is in the hands of the Commission and I have not heard of any decisions on their part as set out in the clipping you sent me from The Kansas City Star. I certainly am not in favor of making a racket out of the wreck of the White House. I'll talk with you about it sometime when I have an opportunity to see you."

Dean Acheson, who had succeeded George Marshall as secretary of state, made a fateful statement in January, 1950. He announced that Korea and Formosa were outside the perimeter the United States felt obligated to defend. Since the end of World War II Korea had been divided at the "38th parallel" and all efforts by the United States to get the Soviets to agree to unification were rebuffed. The Soviets, who controlled the portion north of the parallel, treated its section as it did East Berlin.

In 1947 the Joint Chiefs of Staff, of which Dwight Eisenhower was a member, recommended United States forces be removed from Korea. In February, 1949, Douglas MacArthur favored prompt removal of what American forces remained in South Korea. So, on June 29, 1949, all American troops, except for about five hundred advisors, were removed from the new Republic of Korea.

Acheson's statement that the United States would not defend the southern part of Korea brought North Korean troops, equipped with Soviet tanks and arms, into South Korea on June 25, 1950. Truman acted quickly, although the United States, as had always been the case, was not prepared for war. He requested and got a special meeting of the United Nations Security Council, and at the same time he ordered General Douglas MacArthur to speed up naval and air support for South Korea.

Surprisingly, the Security Council voted to condemn the aggressors, and called on all member nations to support the decision. It was, and would remain, the only time the United Nations condemned anything connected with the Soviets. This feat was accomplished in this case only because the Soviets were absent. They had boycotted the United Nations because it had seated Nationalist China as a member.

Truman had progressed through the line of Missouri Lodge of Research and the time had arrived for him to become its Master. He would be unable to be present, so he authorized Dr. Solon Cameron, the Master, on September 18, 1950, to accept Truman's election to that office. He asked the doctor to speak to the members on his behalf.

"I hope you will say to the Brethren who are assembled for the usual breakfast before the Grand Lodge that I regret exceedingly that I can't be present," wrote Truman. "I hope the session will be a successful one and I am sure that it will be because Jim Bradford is Grand Master."

Throughout the year that followed, Truman was kept informed about who had made contributions to the lodge. As its Master, he wrote dozens of letters of appreciation on White House stationery to the contributors. This method worked. Hundreds of books and other items were received by the lodge.

The day Mary Jane Truman, the President's sister, had long awaited, finally arrived. She was elected Worthy Grand Matron of the Grand Chapter, Order of the Eastern Star, in Missouri. Harry S. Truman, Past Grand Master and President of the United States, along with his brother, J. Vivian, proudly escorted their sister to the East. According to reports, several thousand were involved in this meeting which took place in Kiel Auditorium in St. Louis on October 11, 1950.

Immediately after the event, Truman and his staff continued the journey to Wake Island to meet with General MacArthur. That meeting has been widely reported in thousands of newspapers and dozens of books. The President returned to Washington believing he and MacArthur were in complete accord. To Truman's dismay, he soon learned he was wrong.

On November 1, 1950, two Puerto Ricans tried to assassinate President Truman at the Blair House. One of them and one of the guards, Leslie Coffelt, a member of Potomac Lodge No. 5, D.C., were killed. Two other guards were wounded as was the other would-be assassin. The wounded Puerto Rican was sentenced to life in prison, but in 1979 President Carter freed him along with three other Puerto Ricans. This assassination attempt changed the life of Truman and all future Presidents. He, and they, would never be free to walk alone again. Truman's open style was over.

A saddened President attended the Masonic graveside service of Coffelt. Later he wrote to Potomac Lodge:

> I want to thank the entire membership of Potomac Lodge No. 5, F.& A.M., for your kind expression of gratitude for my personal safety. My deepest concern is that Officer Leslie Coffelt, a member of your lodge, made the supreme sacrifice and two other valiant White House Guards were badly wounded in my defense. We all grieve the loss of Brother Coffelt, a brave and heroic man, but we have reason to be proud of him and take pride in his devotion to duty.

Truman took note of the increased security in his diary on November 5: "Because two crackpots or crazy men tried to shoot me a few days ago my good and efficient guards are nervous. So I'm trying to be as helpful as I can. Would like very much to take a walk this morning but the S.S. say that there are more crackpots around and the 'Boss' and Margaret are worried about me—so I won't take my usual walk. It's hell to be President of the Greatest Most Powerful Nation on Earth—I'd rather be 'first in the Iberian Village.' "

Twelve days later he added to his tale of woe in a letter to his cousin Ethel: "I'm sorry I didn't get to talk to you and Nellie [Noland, Ethel's sister] at the dinner or after it. But I'm really a prisoner now. I'm like the '600' and the cannon—only mine are guards and they are trying to keep me out of the 'mouth of hell.' Everybody is much more worried and jittery than I am. I've always thought that if I could get my hands on a would-be assassin he'd never try it again. But I guess that's impossible. The grand guards who were hurt in the attempt on me didn't have a fair chance. The one who was killed was just cold bloodedly murdered before he could do anything. But his assassin did not live but a couple of minutes—one of the S.S. men put a bullet in one ear and it came out the other. I stuck my head out the upstairs window to see what was going on. One of the guards yelled 'Get back.' I did, then dressed and went down stairs. I was the only calm one in the house. You see I've been shot at by experts and unless your name's on the bullet you needn't be afraid—and that of course you can't find out, so why worry?"

Truman made it clear that he could do as he pleased, but he didn't want any more guards killed, so "I conform—a hard thing for a Truman to do."

Carl Claudy wrote to Truman on December 5, 1950, saying he was highly incensed about a Voice of America broadcast made on September 24, 1950. A man named Mikel asked questions of a fellow named Ernst about Freemasonry. One of the questions and answers that upset Claudy was: "What role do the Freemasons play in the United States?"

Ernst's answer: "The whole organization of Freemasons are really nothing but an organization which does not claim to pursue any secret political aims and purposes. Its main objectives lie in the pursuit of ethical and humanitarian ideals."

Mikel replied: "Well, that is a very fine defense argument for the Freemasons, but now it is our purpose to give some information about their standing in America."

"Well, here in America the Freemasons are only one of the many 'secret orders' to belong to which provides the basis for a good many so-called jokes among the Americans. I say 'jokes' because they may be the main basis for the Freemasons, that is why so many Americans become members of the Freemasons, the Odd Fellows, the Elks, the Kiwanis, the B'nai B'rith and other lodges and orders that are organized according to similar principles. In the first place you have a good excuse for remaining away from home two or three times a month. Then, too, you meet in the lodges people with whom you can carry on a pleasant conversation and who, because they get to know you so much better, may prefer you in their business dealings."

Another man named Carolus answered a question concerning titles: "It is perhaps true that many an American regards himself as highly flattered whenever anyone addresses him with a pompous and high sounding title. Not that he is looking for titles, but because it differentiates him somewhat from those with whom he otherwise is just so, so. . . . All at once he becomes the 'worshipful and serene grand keeper of the seal' of the fraternity or something similar. In everyone of these secret orders and lodges there are numberless degrees and ranks. Even the Freemasons do not have three degrees in America as in Germany, but thirty-three, and I mean thirty-three degrees. In itself, however, that is all quite harmless and nothing at all mysterious or out of the way lurks in the background. But it flatters one's vanity."

Truman answered Claudy's complaint on December 7: "Dear Carl: I appreciate yours of the fifth enclosing me a transcript of a broadcast by the 'Voice of America.' I don't believe that any discourtesy was intended. If you will read the broadcast very carefully you will find that it is not far from the facts and, as you know very well, I am in a better position to judge that than most anybody else in the country."

On December 22, 1950, Truman wrote in his diary: "Frank Land had a dinner for the Red Cross of Constantine. He asked Roy Roberts, editor of the Kansas City *Star*, to speak. Made an ass of himself, and I gave him a kick where it would do the most good to anybody else—but his anatomy is so surrounded with lard that he didn't feel the kick!"

The meeting Truman referred to was held in the ballroom of the Hotel Muehlebach in Kansas City. The dress was tuxedo with cordon and jewel, and ladies were included. The notice of the meeting informed those invited: "The Secret Service will want a list of the names and addresses of all those from your Conclave who will be present." This wasn't a request, it was mandatory. Two hundred-eighty were present, including the President, his wife and daughter, Frank Land, Ray Denslow, William R. Denslow, and George Marquis and their wives, General and Mrs.

Ralph Truman, John Vivian Truman and his wife, Governor Forrest Smith of Missouri, General Harry Vaughan and two other generals.

William Denslow had taken his two children to the hotel, but couldn't find a sitter for them, so they were left in charge of each other. When the dinner was over a Secret Service man informed Denslow that his children had been "quite active." They had made several trips in the automatic elevator to the top floor where the President was.

"When I returned to the room I paddled two young bottoms with the palm of my hand," said Denslow, "but before the tears ceased, their grandfather arrived, saying that he was going to take them up to see President Truman. I remarked that they could certainly show him the way!

"When the children returned, half an hour later, they were all smiles, and both clutched a brand new dollar bill, which the President had pulled from his billfold and autographed for them. They still have them."

Immediately following this affair, the President traveled to Grandview to install the officers of his mother lodge. He apologized to the lodge for his inability to attend more often. He told the members he enjoyed his visits because of "the fact I can be myself." It was noted that the President was accompanied to the lodge, and throughout his visit, by a large number of policemen who were Masons, as well as the Secret Service.

Truman had returned to Independence for Christmas and this gave him the opportunity for his Masonic functions. He noted that on December 24 he "took a nice walk!" He also dedicated the new Grandview Baptist Church building to which he had made many contributions for its construction. He added in his diary: "I am hoping to buy the site of the old church and build a good looking structure for Grandview Lodge 618 A.F.& A.M. No 'modern nut' architect will have anything to do with that." He wasn't home long. His Secretary of State called on the 27th and he had to rush back to Washington.

General Matthew B. Ridgeway, a member of West Point Lodge No. 877, New York, since 1924, had stemmed the Red Chinese tide in Korea. For some reason this didn't set too well with General MacArthur, who was also a Mason. Truman took note of what he considered underhanded sniping by MacArthur in a diary entry on April 6, 1951:

"MacArthur shoots another political bomb through Joe Martin, leader of the Republican minority in the House. Looks like the last straw. Rank insubordination. Last summer he sent a long statement to the Vets of Foreign Wars—not through the high command back home, but directly! He sent copies to newspapers and magazines particularly hostile to me."

Truman noted he had traveled to Wake Island to meet MacArthur face to face to reach an understanding. But this did not appear to do the job.

On April 9 the President met with military and congressional leaders, then issued orders for MacArthur's recall. He turned the military command over to General Ridgeway. This information wasn't released to the press at that time, but someone leaked Truman's proposed action so he had to release his orders earlier than planned. On April 11, 1951, the President officially relieved MacArthur of his command.

"Quite an explosion," Truman wrote in his diary the next day. "Was expected but I had to act. Telegrams and letters of abuse by the dozens."

MacArthur came home to a hero's welcome. He was invited to address a joint session of Congress. Then he began to "fade away." Truman firmly believed the general had made a fool of himself and had become a "drug on the market" with the Senate Republicans.

Among only three items about Truman the librarian found in the House of the Temple of the Scottish Rite, Southern Jurisdiction, was a reprint from *The American Mercury* for May, 1951. Typed at the top of the cover page was: "Are these the earmarks of a good 33rd degree Mason? D.D. Gibson, Dade City, Fla." The reprint was: "IN THE MERCURY'S OPINION: Is Truman Honest?" The vicious article stated among other things, that the lawyer for the President's brother, Vivian Truman, said: "Harry Truman is a deadbeat and has been all his life. Vivian is a splendid citizen, honest and responsible; Harry is the bad apple in that barrel. He has escaped his responsibilities simply by slopping at the public trough where his salary wasn't garnishable."

On May 10, 1951, President Truman presented Congressional Medals of Honor in a White House ceremony. The receipients were: Lt. Carl Dodd, left, Sgt. John A. Pittman, on Truman's left, and M/Sgt. Ernest R. Kouma. General George C. Marshall is on the far right.

[National Park Service photo by Abbie Rowe/Truman Library]

The writer of the article mentioned several columnists and newspapers which had defended Truman against the slanderous attacks that had been made. But the *Mercury* wanted it understood it didn't believe any of the President's supporters. It evidently didn't want to be confused by facts.

It is difficult to determine exactly what the *Mercury* was referring to in calling the President a crook and other unsavory things. His political enemies had claimed the people in his administration were "grafters," "five-percenters," among the milder accusations. Harry Vaughan did accept some deep-freezers from a friend and did have one placed in the Truman home in Independence. He did it, evidently, because it was reported the Trumans received donated food to be distributed to those in need.

After the Republicans took over the government, they spent the first two years searching the records to find "proof" of Truman's "wrong-doing." Not one shred of evidence of anything underhanded was discovered after thousands of hours of wasted time at the expense of American taxpayers.

With the end of 1951 close and the last year of his term approaching, Truman considered what would happen to the country if the isolationists gained control of the White House. He wrote to Dwight D. Eisenhower, then the North Atlantic Treaty Organization (NATO) commander in Europe, asking for his political intentions. He told the general: "I have the utmost confidence in your judgement and your patriotism." Eisenhower told the President he had no political ambitions.

The following letter was written by the President to Harold L. Reader, Grand Secretary of the Grand Lodge of Missouri, on May 28, 1951:

> I have an opportunity to present my home town Lodge at Grandview with a building and I think I remember that Masonic Temples should be built and owned by the Grand Lodge of Missouri. I own the property where the building will be placed and some of my national friends are anxious to furnish the money. The land and the building will be turned over to the Grand Lodge. Then it can be rented by the Grand Lodge for whatever figure is fair and right to my little home town Lodge and the rental can go into the Masonic Home Fund. At least that is the way I have it in mind to arrange things.
>
> I wish you would find out just exactly what sort of an arrangement can be made along that line and let me know so I can take the matter up with the Internal Revenue Department and have arrangements made so the contributions can be classed as gifts to charity and can be deducted from their income tax returns. I think the arrangement which I have suggested would authorize just such a deduction the same as contributions to any other charitable organization.
>
> I propose to build an ideal "country" Masonic Building that will be a model for all the rest of the State when it is finished. As you know, I started that little Lodge in 1911 with twenty people. It now has a membership of over two hundred, is prosperous and is doing a lot of good work in that little neighborhood out there. I intend to place a Library and Museum on the farm just north of town which will contain all my official papers and documents; copies of all those of the other Presidents, and such other historical data as the Archives can duplicate and spare for that Library.
>
> I hope to make it a Research center for the various State Universities and Colleges and other Colleges in that neighborhood. It is only a short distance from the Missouri State University, University of Kansas, Agricultural College of Kansas, University of Oklahoma, University of Arkansas, University of Iowa at Iowa City and Agricul-

tural College at Ames, Iowa, University of Nebraska at Lincoln, University of Illinois at Urbana, as well as the State Teachers Colleges at Pittsburg, Kansas, Maryville, Kirksville and Warrensburg, Missouri, the Westminister College at Fulton, Missouri, Drury College at Springfield, St. Benedict's College and Mount Saint Scholasica's College both at Atchison, Kansas, as well as numerous other Colleges in that vicinity. It will be a nonsectarian project.

It seems to me that it would be a fine thing if we could arrange an educational center such as that, located as that one will be, accessible to all the Colleges and Universities in the neighborhood so that men who intend to write a thesis for a Ph.D or any other doctors degree could have easy access to information and documents only accessible in Washington.

As you know, there is a University in Kansas City and two in Saint Louis, Washington and Saint Louis Universities, and there are numerous other schools, which would have access to a place of this sort if it were conveniently located. Perhaps their students would not be able to go to Washington Library of Congress and the various Research Libraries east of the Appalachian Mountains.

I thought you would be interested in this because I want to make it a major educational project, and I also want to have in the same neighborhood this ideal "country" Masonic Lodge building for the edification of those Brethren who find it necessary to take a look at the Library. These two buildings will be about a half or three-quarters of a mile apart.

Wish you would consult Ray Bond, George Marquis, Ray Denslow and anyone else you care to and let me hear from you.

Reader told Truman it was a wonderful idea. "Both the Temple and the Library-Museum will be of incalculable benefit, and the good accomplished through the years will be beyond estimate." The Grand Secretary also informed the President that the Grand Lodge "never holds title to real estate unless a Charter is arrested or surrendered, in which case the property reverts to the Grand Lodge." Grandview Lodge would hold the title to whatever property it acquired through whatever means.

Arrangements were started in August, 1951, for the President, who was also the Master of the Missouri Lodge of Research, to visit the Jackson County Public Library to view the lodge's display. The visit took place on September 5.

The end of 1951 found the situation in Korea drastically improved. General Ridgeway, unlike MacArthur who had tried to manage the fighting from Japan, directed the action from the field and had turned the morale of his army around. The Presi-

President Truman beside the bronze bust of him done by Felix de Weldon. The bust was unveiled on June 6, 1951, in ceremonies at Alexandria—Washington Lodge No. 22, Virginia.

[Photographer unknown]

dent believed the North Koreans knew they were whipped, but refused to surrender because Truman would not order the North Koreans who had defected to the South returned to certain death. So, the fighting continued throughout 1952.

In his diary entry of February 20, 1952, Truman took note of the way he was protected: "The 'boss' [Mrs. Truman] and I had breakfast at 8:30 and about 8:50 I went to the White House office. Since the assault on the police and the secret service, I ride across the street in a car the roof of which will turn a grenade, the windows and sides turn a bullet and the floor will stop a land mine! Behind me in an open car ride six or seven men with automatics and machine guns. The uniformed police stop traffic in every direction—and I cross the street in state and wonder why anyone would want to live like that. When I take my morning walk at 7 A.M. a guard walks beside me and he's always a fine man and a congenial conversationalist. Behind me are three more good men, athletes and *good shots,* across the street is another good man and a half block behind me is a car with maybe five or six well equipped guards. It is a hell of a way to live. But after the assault on the Blair House I learned that the men who want to keep me alive are the ones who get hurt and not the President. . . . So now I conform to the rules without protest."

On March 27, 1952, the President noted in his diary: "The 'boss' and I were formally received at the Pennsylvania Ave. entrance to the renovated White House." He was presented with a gold key which he was assured "would *not* open any door on the place." He was impressed with the improvements. "I spent the evening going over the house," he wrote. "With all the trouble and worry it is worth it—but not $5^1/_2$ million dollars! If I could have had charge of the construction it would have been done for half the money and in half the time!"

In the days of operative masonry, workmen would carve their personal mark on the stones they placed in a building. This has been carried over to Speculative Masonry through the Mark Mason degree. Evidently, many Freemasons worked on the building of the original "President's Home," which would later be called the "White House."

After it was determined the White House was about to fall apart and required a complete overhaul, Harry Vaughan, Truman's personal aide, discovered several stones with Mason's marks on them. He conveyed this information to the President. Truman, ever the Freemason, determined these certainly had historical value and should be preserved. He took the proper steps to do this.

Late in 1952 the President informed the Grand Lodge of the District of Columbia about these stones. He said he had saved enough to give one to each of the forty-nine Grand Lodges in the country, and asked this Grand Lodge to take the responsibility of distributing them. This was done, accompanied with an appropriate letter from the President. The letter read:

> Through the good offices of an ambassador from the Grand Lodge of the District of Columbia, which is Masonically supreme in the Capital of the Nation, I place in your hands a stone taken from the walls of The White House during its just-completed rebuilding.
>
> A sufficent number of these stones, each with a Masonic symbol upon it, was discovered to give one to each Grand Lodge in the United States.
>
> These evidences of the number of members of the Craft who built the President's official residence so intimately aligns Freemasonry with the formation and the founding of our Government that I believe your Grand Lodge will cherish this link between the Fraternity and the Government of the Nation, of which The White House is a symbol.

Two lodges were also fortunate because the President presented them with one of these exclusive stones: Grandview, the lodge Truman founded, and Alexandria-Washington, the lodge which President Washington served as Master.

Dwight David Eisenhower, the man with no political ambitions, was nominated at the Republican convention to run for the Presidency. The Democrats nominated Adlai E. Stevenson, but only after Truman threw his support to him.

As a gesture of goodwill, and because he felt it important for the candidates to be informed of world affairs, Truman invited both to the White House for briefings. Eisenhower refused to go. The President wrote to him on August 16, 1952:

"Dear Ike: I am sorry if I caused you embarrassment. What I've always had in mind was and is a continuing foreign policy. You know that is a fact, because you had a part in outlining it. Partisan politics should stop at the boundaries of the United States. I am extremely sorry that you have allowed a bunch of screwballs to come between us. You have made a bad mistake and I'm hoping it won't injure this great Republic." He closed by saying: "May God guide you and give you light. From a man who has always been your friend and who always wanted to be!"

On December 6, 1952, Truman wrote in his diary: "Yesterday at 12:30 my mother-in-law passed away. She was a grand lady. When I hear those mother-in-law jokes I don't laugh. They are not funny to me, because I've had a good one. So has my brother. My mother was a good mother-in-law to Vivian's and my wife. It gives me a pain in the neck to read the awful jokes that the so-called humorists crack about mother-in-laws." He recorded how "the sabotage press" had condemned him in 1946 (should be 1947) when he "was on the same errand" to bury his mother. He knew this would happen again, but in his anguish he wrote: "To hell with them. When history is written they will be the sons of bitches—not I."

January 20, 1953, was a cold day, literally and figuratively. The Eisenhowers refused to have lunch with the Trumans.

After the inauguration was over, the Trumans went to the Acheson's house for a luncheon. There they said goodbye to the many friends who had stood by one another through eight hectic years.

At Union Station in Washington thousands of people were there to say goodbye. The train finally pulled away to the strains of "Auld Lang Syne."

Old Age

Remember now thy Creator in the days of thy youth, while the evil days come not, nor the years draw nigh, when thou shalt say, I have no pleasure in them;

While the sun, or the light, or the moon, or the stars, be not darkened, nor the clouds return after the rain:

In the day when the keepers of the house shall tremble, and the strong men shall bow themselves, and the grinders cease because they are few, and those that look out of the windows be darkened,

And the doors shall be shut in the streets, when the sound of the grinding is low, and he shall rise up at the voice of the bird, and all the daughters of musick shall be brought low;

Also when they shall be afraid of that which is high, and fears shall be in the way, and the almond tree shall flourish, and the grasshopper shall be a burden, and desire shall fail: because man goeth to his long home, and the mourners go about the streets:

Or ever the silver cord be loosed, or the golden bowl be broken, or the pitcher be broken at the fountain, or the wheel broken at the cistern.

Then shall the dust return to the earth as it was: and the spirit shall return unto God who gave it.

Ecclesiastes, 12: 1-7

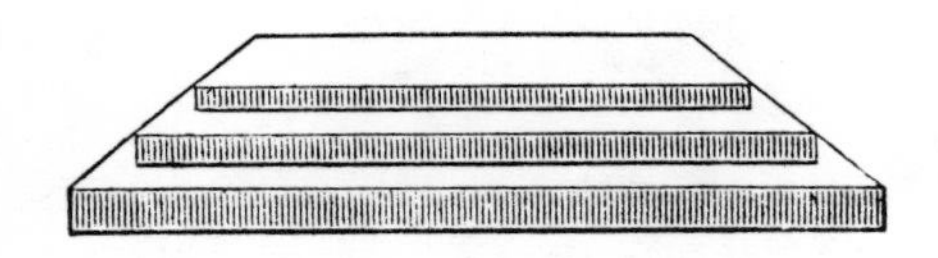

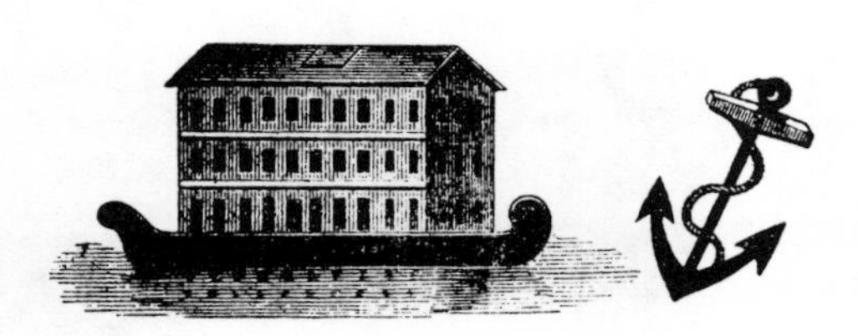

14. HOME

The remarkable send-off of "Citizen Truman" at Union Station in Washington was minor compared with his reception when his train pulled into Missouri on January 21, 1953. At the St. Louis station thousands greeted him, causing the Presidential train, the "Ferdinand Magellan," to be an hour late arriving in Independence.

More than ten thousand people were waiting for him in his small home town. And there were more than five thousand surrounding the Truman home when he arrived. "Mrs. T & I were overcome. It was the pay-off for thirty years of hell and hard work," he wrote.

Truman had to be pleased. All along the route thousands were at every station the train passed.

Many receptions followed, including a homecoming dinner for the former President and his family on February 5, 1953. At none of these functions was he surrounded by body guards. At Union Station in Washington his Secret Service men had shaken his hand for the last time and left him on his own.

Truman had never again expected to travel in a private railroad car, so he was agreeably surprised to be offered one by the Union Pacific Railroad. In it the Trumans began the first leg of their long-awaited trip to the Hawaiian Islands on March 19. Again crowds welcomed them everywhere they stopped. It was the same when they arrived at Honolulu.

Something of his philosophy was recorded in his diary on July 8, 1953: "I've always been a great admirer of three great men in government, Cincinnatus the old Roman Dictator, Cato the Younger who was the Republican Roman's greatest and most honorable administrator. And then George Washington our own first President.

"Cincinnatus knew when and how to lay down his great powers. After he had saved the Republic he went back to his plow and became the good private citizen of his country. Cato, in an age of grafters and demagogues, ran the great Roman Republic for the people. He audited and handled the finances of the

Roman Provinces and of Rome itself honestly—something unheard of in the declining Republic.

"Washington knew when and how to quit public office and lay down the immense power he wielded with the people, as did Cincinnatus. After he'd won the war to create this United States, presided over the Constitutional Convention, and set the country on the right road to greatness, he returned to his farm and became a model citizen of his country. He could have been king, president for life if he'd been ambitious for power."

Education was always a concern of Truman. In a note, evidently for his own consideration, he wrote that he was pleased with the results of the GI Bill of Rights. "It proved conclusively," he recorded, "that young men from 18 to 26 after some experience thirst for learning and that they are willing to work hard and at some disadvantage for an education." He was correct. Because of this bill which gave veterans an opportunity for higher education, thousands became productive citizens in fields they never before had dreamed possible.

"The old idea that grammar, rhetoric, logic, arithmetic, geometry, music and astronomy constitute the basis of an education is just as true now as it always has been," he continued, proving that he remembered his Masonic ritual well.

There were two primary goals Truman had in his "retirement": to write the history of the period during which he had served his country; and to build a library to house, not only his papers, but copies of the papers of all the Presidents of the United States. To achieve the latter goal he had to first complete the former goal and at the same time raise funds in other ways.

He was determined to write his own memoirs and not leave this for someone to distort after he was dead. He had told one of his assistants before he left office: "I don't want a pack of lying, so-called historians to do to Roosevelt and me what the New Englanders did to Jefferson and Jackson."

Actually, raising funds would have been no problem for the building of the library if the former President would have set aside the principles he had lived by all his life. He was offered all types of positions at vast sums of money with little or no work attached. Unlike public servants of later years, Truman refused all offers to trade his name and the prestige of his former position for financial security.

During the next three years, in his office in the Federal Reserve Bank Building in Kansas City, he dictated over a million and a half words. These were edited down to slightly over a half million and published in two volumes in 1955 and 1956. These became his *Memoirs*, and in spite of the many hands involved in the editing, the statements are clearly Truman's.

Former President Harry S. Truman shows his pleasure as he mingles freely once again with his Masonic brethren in September 1963 during the first annual communication of the Grand Lodge of Missouri after his return to private life.
[Arthur Z. Daily photo]

The Grand Marshal, Bruce H. Hunt, presented Past Grand Master Harry S. Truman of Missouri, and Past Grand Master Renah F. Camalier of the District of Columbia, to the Grand Lodge of Missouri on September 29, 1953. The *Proceedings* records, Camalier, "as a representative of former President Harry S. Truman and the Grand Lodge of the District of Columbia, presented to M.W. Brother Harry S. Truman, Past Grand Master of Missouri, a stone with Masonic markings thereon taken from the walls of the White House during its reconstruction. M.W. Brother Truman in turn presented the stone to Grand Master Rumer for the Grand Lodge of Missouri."

Frank Glenn, a book dealer in Kansas City, made a trip around the world early in 1954, and among the places he spent some time was Israel. The Grand Master of the new Grand Lodge of the State of Israel asked him to bring back a gavel to be presented to Past Grand Master Harry S. Truman. Bruce Newton, a Past Grand Master who lived in Kansas City, Kansas, was designated to make the presentation. George Marquis learned of this on June 21, 1954, while Truman was in a hospital recovering from a gall bladder operation.

Arrangements were made for the gavel to be presented to Truman during the annual communication of the Grand Lodge of Missouri in St. Louis on September 28. Truman had improved to the point where he was certain he could be present. But the fates intervened and Truman sent a letter to his friend Marquis.

"I am enclosing you copy of a letter which Dr. Wallace Graham wrote me when he found that I was contemplating a trip to St. Louis," Truman wrote. "I am going to ask if you will please receive the Gavel from Israel which they were intending to present to me and in my name present it to the Grand Lodge for their use and their museum if they decide to put it there.

"I don't know when I've ever been so thoroughly disappointed as I am in this instance but I don't see that there is anything I can do after I read this letter. I wish you would say to all of the people who have been expecting me and to the ones with whom I expected to room at the Hotel that this is one time when I can't do as I please, much to my regret." He added a postscript: "I hope you won't let them defeat Jim DeWitt—he is the fellow

By a twist of fate the stone saved by President Truman in the remodeling of the White House, and allocated for the Grand Lodge of Missouri, was presented to Past Grand Master Truman by Past Grand Master Renah F. Camalier of the District of Columbia during Missouri's session in September 1953.
[Arthur Z. Daily photo]

The White House stone which Truman had received was in turn presented by him to Grand Master Richard O. Rummer for the Grand Lodge of Missouri.
[Arthur Z. Daily photo]

we really want for Treasurer and I wish I could be there to work for him." DeWitt was elected.

The letter from Dr. Graham addressed to "Dear Mr. President" read: "I regret exceedingly to state that you must curtail your activities greatly. You must well understand that you are yet in the recuperative phase following a very serious illness with complications.

"It is my understanding that you are contemplating a trip to St. Louis which you have been looking forward to making for quite some time in behalf of the great body of Masons.

"It is imperative, at this time, that you follow my suggestion and defer this trip, as the last blood tests and evaluation of your complete physical condition does not warrant calling upon your reserve energy to fulfilling these obligations."

Within his address in presenting the Truman-Israel gavel, Bruce Newton of Kansas said: "In my address to the Grand Lodge of Kansas last February, I remarked that it is always a happy occasion when a new lodge is born into a large family like our own. It is equally so or even more enjoyable when a new Grand Lodge is born into the great family of Grand Lodges. There should be an especially happy and joyous feeling among the Masons of the world that a Grand Lodge has been formed at the legendary birthplace of all Freemasonry.

"Several weeks ago I received a letter from Mr. Glenn, a book dealer in Kansas City, who had recently returned from a trip around the world. He informed me that he had visited with Dr. Shaoni, Grand Master of Israel, who was desirous of showing his appreciation of Freemasonry in America by presenting a token of esteem to a distinguished American Mason.

"It is my great pleasure to make that presentation at this time to a man, who above all others in America, deserves the recognition. A man whose name will be revered among Masons along with that of Washington. A man whose fame as an emancipator will go down in history equal to or even surpass that of Lincoln. A man who has labored unceasingly and unswervingly through the heat of the day, against adverse criticism and personal animosity, amidst a world torn with war and strife, for the ultimate goal, 'That all peoples and all nations would realize and accept the fact that God is the father of us all and that we are all brothers.'

"I deem it a high honor and privilege to join with the Masons in another land across the sea in paying honor and homage to one to whom honor is due. So in the name of M.W. Brother Shaoni, Grand Master, and on behalf of the more than 8,000 Masons of Israel, I present this beautiful gavel to our own, and to your very own, M.W. Harry S. Truman, Past Grand Master of the M.W. Grand Lodge, A.F. & A.M., of Missouri and Ex-President of the United States of America, and wish for you, M.W. Sir, many long years of health, happiness and prosperity, and may you always continue to maintain your own self-respect, the esteem of your brethren, and the favor of God."

After the close of the Grand Lodge, J. Renick Jones carried the gavel to Kansas City and delivered it to Truman.

A young Mason worked at the Waldorf-Astoria Hotel in New York City in 1954 and he told Dr. Allan Boudreau, publisher of *The Masonic Philatelist*, about an experience he had that concerned Truman. The hotel manager received a request from the former President's room for a copy of the Bible. The manager sent for the young man, Bernard Topper, told him to take the Bible to the room, and suggested Topper ask for Truman's signature on his dues card. "I liked the idea," said Topper, "but remembered that I had Douglas MacArthur's autograph on the back of the card, but decided I'd take a chance."

William Hillman, author of *Mr. President*, answered the door and there were eight or ten men in the room. "I asked Mr. Hillman if Mr. Truman would sign the card, but made emphasis for him not to turn the card over," continued Topper. "Mr. Hillman approached the President and after a few words, I was motioned to enter. This I had not expected. As I approached, all I could feel were eight or ten pairs of piercing eyes. I was scared.

"The first thing Mr. Truman said was, 'Why can't I look on the other side of the card?' I sheepishly answered, 'You may not like what's written there, Sir.'

"With that, he turned the card over and upon seeing MacArthur's autograph, laughed and showed it to everyone. Scared as I was, I started to laugh. Mr. Truman remarked, 'Young man, we are brothers after all. I'll sign right under his name.' After signing, he wrote the initials, 'P.G.M. Mo.' He asked if I knew what it meant. I was kneeling next to Mr. Truman and proudly answered, 'Yes, sir, Past District Deputy of Missouri.' He then slapped me on the back and laughingly said I really demoted him and that it meant, 'Past Grand Master of Missouri.'

"We shook hands and I left. On my way back to work several thoughts went through my head and suddenly I realized that this was the greatest thrill of my life." A few months later Topper got what he considered a greater thrill—he was introduced to Mrs. Truman.

Talk about the proposed Truman library was prevalent, and among those who wanted to do something for its historical value was George E. Kern. According to Marquis, who told Truman, Kern was a "jewelry engraver" and "an ardent and active Mason of the East Gate Bodies." His company had made the trowel used for the laying of the cornerstone of the Eisenhower library in Kansas. He offered to do the same for the Grand Lodge of Missouri.

After a discussion with Truman, Marquis and Bruce Hunt, Kern offered to make, not only the trowel, but the vessels used in the ceremony. They determined these should be a silver vessel for oil; a silver vessel for wine; and a gold vessel for corn. The working tools would consist of the traditional square, level and plumb, and that all these should be retained and displayed in the library.

In his diary Truman wrote on February 2, 1955: "Had made arrangements to come to Dr. Harold Reader's 10th anniversary [as Grand Secretary] dinner at the Scottish Rite Temple on Lindell Blvd. . . . Arrived at Tower Grove Station and was met by one of my best friends, Roy W. Harper, Federal Judge, and by Judge Aronson of the St. Louis Circuit Court, a member of the Grand Lodge of Missouri, reporters, photographers, and members of the St. Louis Police Department, and driven to the Temple. Met dozens and dozens of Masons, signed cards, patents [Scottish Rite certificates] and just plain paper until dinner was announced."

Truman was pleased with the prayers by Rabbi Sam Thurmond, and said he didn't believe God was impressed by "pomp and circumstances, gold crowns, jeweled breast plates and ancestral background." Dr. Reader was presented with "a scroll that was covered with a beautiful sentiment and properly framed. They gave him some lovely roses for Mrs. Reader and then asked me to say a few words.

"I told them of my long acquaintance with Dr. Reader, our World War I association, our Masonic association and then launched into a world peace appeal on the basis of the Fatherhood of God and the Brotherhood of Man. They gave me an ovation and almost mobbed me after the meeting. I had to be rescued from the handshakers and the autograph hounds."

What did he think of the affair? "It was a most pleasant and profitable evening for me. Not profitable financially because I paid my transportation charges, tips and all. But profitable because I saw and talked to friends who are real. They know, like and approve of me and my actions, win lose or draw.

"A great Baptist preacher, a Jewish Rabbi who prayed for me when I most needed it, 800 men from all walks of life who are not sure what they believe or what they are for—well they decided, all of them, that they wanted world peace after I'd talk to them—and who doesn't?"

In a handwritten note at the bottom of a letter Truman told Marquis: "Reader's party was a grand success except for one speech by the former Grand Master of 1940-41. Your letter brought down the house, saw a lot of old friends and very nearly lost both arms—they tried to pull them off. There were 800 present."

Truman had envisioned his library, along with a new building for his mother lodge, on his farm property in Grandview. Lengthy discussions took place over the location and among those involved was Rufus Burrus, Truman's friend and attorney. "Independence was the place for the library," said Burrus. "When Harry was convinced of that we started looking for a site. It was agreed that Slover Park was the place for the Harry S. Truman Library, but there wasn't enough room for it, so the mayor led a drive to purchase a block of houses to make the room needed. It was a high point and an ideal location. The state came along with us and agreed to change the route for Highway 24 and put it above grade. it was within walking distance of his home, and he used to walk there often."

A Truman Library Association had been established to handle the fund raising, financing and building of the Truman Library. Early in the spring Burrus received a telephone call from an alarmed member of this Association. "He told me that Truman wanted to get started on the library, and he had told Truman he couldn't. I asked him why he had told him he couldn't. 'Because we have no plans, not enough money, no contractors, or anything,' he said. I told him there was no way we could stop Harry, even if we wanted to. He was the one who raised the money, and he was the one who was entrusted with everything.

"When we all met for lunch, Truman said that [the contractors] had agreed to build a library for one dollar. I said: 'Chief, let's shake hands on that. We can't get it done any cheaper.' He told me to go out and make it legal. I knew what he meant. I went out with a contract of a half page or so, and gave them one hundred thousand dollars, and told them I would give them more when they needed it."

Truman had his contractors and a contract. All that remained was a formal ground-breaking ceremony. This took place on May 8, 1955, Truman's seventy-first birthday, when, with a gold-plated shovel, the former President of the United States turned the first spadeful of dirt for his library.

The newspaper account read: "Gathered around him at ground-breaking ceremonies in Slover Park were many who had been closest to him in the days when the papers to be housed in the $1,750,000 structure were being written." The mayor of Independence, Robert Weatherford, was the master of ceremonies and "ran the show." Dr. Elmer Ellis, president of the University of Missouri, addressed the more than twenty-five hundred present for the occasion. But the principal figure was a smiling and joking Harry S. Truman.

Dr. Ellis, within his speech, said: "Here will be a collection of the arts, mementos of official and private life, replicas of a national shrine, the executive offices in Washington, all intimately connected with the destiny that brought the man from Independence to the position of leadership in the greatest crisis in the world's history.

"The man from Independence, his personality, his work and his fame will all be enshrined in an American institution combining a museum with a great research library."

With his "manual labor" over, Truman became a supervisor. Burrus tells the story: "Truman would be out there every morning. He knew them all. They weren't working for [the contractors], they were working for Harry Truman. Instead of working eight hours a day, they worked what was equal to ten or twelve. The library cost us $1,750,000, including the furnishings, but only because those contractors had the sub-contractors squeeze the profits out of what they did. Then they had the trades people do the same."

The first volume of Truman's *Memoirs* came off the press and he had a disagreement with Ken McCormack, editor-in-chief of the publisher, Doubleday and Company. McCormack proposed a limited edition of the volume be published, and that Truman be given five hundred copies to do with as he pleased. Truman told him on July 1, 1955: "I want five hundred copies of the edition to which you referred in your telegram, but I will not accept them as a gift. I want you to bill me for them at the publisher's price, and I will send you a check immediately."

About the limited edition: "I cannot possibly enter into a program which would look as if I were selling autographs instead of a book. I want the book sold on its merit. If it cannot be sold that way, then it's not worth having. I have a very strong feeling about any man, who has had the honor of being an occupant of the White House in the greatest job in the history of the world, who would exploit that position in any way, shape, or form. I hope you understand the situation."

He did carry out his agreement to autograph copies sold by the combined bookstores in Kansas City. They "set up shop" in the Meuhlebach hotel for this purpose, and with the advance sale being almost fifteen thousand copies, ten thousand were made available at the hotel to be autographed.

In May, 1956, after many delays, the Trumans left for England where he was to receive a long delayed honorary degree from Oxford. The first delay was caused by the writing of his *Memoirs*; the next, by his gall bladder operation; the latest delay was caused by the marriage of their daughter to Clifton T. Daniel on

April 21, 1956. But disaster struck; he fell on his steps while preparing for the trip, and tore some ligaments in his right ankle. His doctor bandaged the injured limb and he was able to hobble around.

Before leaving, however, Truman, along with his cousin, Major General Ralph Truman, drove to Kansas City, Kansas, where they dedicated a new armory.

Again Truman was amazed at the reception he received wherever he traveled in the United States. Schedules were difficult to maintain because of the crowds wanting to see and touch the former President. While in New York City Truman had the honor of presenting the Four Freedoms Award to his friend, Governor Averell Harriman.

The crowds continued to turn out all through Europe to greet the Trumans. He noted in a letter from Naples on May 23: "I'm not a good sightseer and I'd rather be home. Can't see what I want to for the reporters & photo men." He visited the home of Mozart, a Freemason who had composed several pieces of Masonic music, and Truman was invited to play one of Mozart's instruments.

When the Trumans finally arrived in England they had an opportunity to share old times with Winston Churchill and his family. They discussed Potsdam, "its agreements and Russian perfidy." Lord Beaverbrook told Truman that the former President had been the greatest ambassador of good will the United States had ever had.

Truman finally received the honorary degree from Oxford, and on June 28 they again boarded the *United States* for the return trip home.

Among the hundreds of items written by Truman and recorded in Robert H. Ferrell's *Off the Record* is one of December 17, 1958, addressed to "Mr. Pickwick" of the Pickwick Hotel in Kansas City:

> You have a clock over your bus depot that gives me a case of time-ophobia. I look at that clock every time I go to the Federal Reserve Building's privy, on floor 11.
>
> When my watch and all four of my clocks say it its 9:25 A.M. Central Standard Time, that damned clock of yours will say it is 6:40. I don't know whether it is afternoon or forenoon or just halfway between Eastern Daylight Time and no time at all.

> Just because you are named for Charles Dickens' Mr. Pickwick doesn't give you authority to mess up our local time.
>
> It is bad enough when these municipalities like New York, Chicago, St. Louis and some others ball up the Standard Time Zones. It took almost forty years to attain a sensible time zone set up for this round globe of ours and now we might just as well go back to meridian time of the 1820's.
>
> You shouldn't contribute to that confusion.

In fairness to "Mr. Pickwick," Ferrell said the hotel was next to the bus station "and on top of the bus station was a clock," evidently the one whose accuracy Truman questioned.

On January 26, 1957, Frank S. Land was honored for his contributions to Freemasonry and the Order of DeMolay. Harry Truman, Honorary Grand Master of DeMolay, supported this project from the beginning, and he was present for the ceremonies. Truman had been a long-time advocate of the need for the Order of DeMolay, which he continued to serve as Honorary Grand Master, and had been closely associated with Land.

Truman's "retirement" was expensive, mainly because he had served as President of the United States. He received no subsidies from the federal government. The days of Secret Service protection for former presidents and their families had not arrived. He had no paid government servants, expense money, paid secretarial assistants, nor anything else. When he traveled he was on his own. Chances for him to "sell" his name and reputation were numerous, but although he needed the money he turned down all such offers. He hoped to earn what money he needed through his writing and lecture fees. As President he had helped Eisenhower receive a tax break for his writing, but no one interceded for Truman when he received payment for his *Memoirs.* About sixty-five percent of what he received was collected by the Internal Revenue Service over a five-year period.

Congress had taken note of the extraordinary expenses of former Presidents and was considering doing something about this. Truman wrote to John W. McCormack, at the Representative's request, on January 10, 1957, outlining some of the problems he had encountered in addition to the loss of revenue from the sale of his two volumes.

"In order to be able to transact the business of writing the Memoirs, and to meet the tremendous burden of handling the largest volume of mail in the State, I had to rent an office in Kansas City and the total overhead for the period from February 1953 until about November of last year, 1956, amounted to a sum over $153,000.00. Had it not been for the fact that I was able to sell some property that my brother, sister and I inherited from our mother I would practically be on relief but with the sale of that property I am not financially embarrassed. However, it does seem to me in all fairness that part of the overhead should be met. I would say 70% of the $153,000.00 that I have been out for office help, rent, postage, telephones and everything else that goes with the expense of an office for a former President should be paid.

"I don't want a pension and do not expect one but I do think 70% of the expenses or overhead should be paid by the Government—the 30% is what I would ordinarily have been out on my own book if I hadn't tried to meet the responsibilities of being a former President.

"As you know, we passed a Bill which gave all five-star Generals and Admirals three clerks, and all the emoluments that went with their office when they retired.

"It seems rather peculiar that a fellow who spent eighteen years in government service and succeeded in getting all these things done for the people he commanded should have to go broke in order to tell the people the truth about what really happened. It seems to me in all justice a part of this tremendous overhead should be met by the public.

"I don't want any pension and never have wanted any because I'll manage to get along but I am just giving you the difference in the approach between the great general and myself on the Memoirs. My net return will be about $37,000.00 total over a five-year period! It was a package deal. I receive no royalties.

"I would never have given you this information if you hadn't asked for it."

According to Ferrell, Eisenhower received $635,000 for his *Crusade in Europe* and paid a tax of twenty-five percent; Truman paid sixty-seven percent, plus the cost of researchers, writers, and hundreds of copies he gave away.

What a difference between then and now! All former Congressmen, as well as former Presidents, receive generous retirement benefits.

Work on the Harry S. Truman Library progressed nicely, and the day for its dedication approached. "Truman wanted to have the Library dedicated on July 4th," said Burrus, "but there were too many things that interfered. But he made sure there would be a celebration at the Library on the 4th from then on." The day set was Sunday, July 6, 1957, and dignitaries from all over the country were notified and invited.

On April 9, 1957, Truman answered Ray Denslow's invitation to be present for "Trenton's centennial celebration" the week of June 16: "There will hardly be time enough for me to do everything that has to be done in preparation for the library dedication on July 6th. Of course, if there is any way for me to visit Trenton during that week, I will let you know. At the moment it looks very unlikely.

"I am counting on your presence on July 6th, for I want the Masonic cornerstone laying to be a grand success. The Chief Justice of the United States will make the dedication address in the afternoon, and I want my Masonic friends to meet him. He is the salt of the earth. There is one thing wrong with him. He's a Republican, just as you are, and can't help it."

It is highly unusual for Freemasons to lay the cornerstone in a building that is completed and ready for dedication, but that is exactly what happened at the Truman Library. At 9:00 a.m. on July 6, 1957, Grand Master Harold M. Jayne opened the Grand Lodge of Missouri at the Masonic Temple on Pleasant Street. Past Grand Master Harry S. Truman, and Past Grand Master Earl Warren of California, Chief Justice of the United States Supreme Court, were among the many Masonic dignitaries present. From the Masonic Temple they marched to Delaware Street to form the line of march in front of the Truman home. Over a thousand Freemasons joined those who had been present in the temple.

The American Legion band headed the procession, followed by the Knight Templar with their drill teams. The William Chrisman High School band was also a part of the procession which marched from Delaware Street to the Library. There the Ararat

Shrine Chanters joined them and during the ceremony sang "The Lord's Prayer."

Promptly at 10:30 a.m. they arrived at the site and the time-honored ceremony for the laying of a cornerstone by Freemasons was performed. When this was completed the Masonic leadership joined the other dignitaries for lunch at the Laurel Club in Independence.

The steps of the Library served as a platform for the dignitaries and at 2:00 p.m. Truman, smiling broadly, introduced each of them to the several thousand who had joined him in his triumph.

Former President Herbert Hoover was there, as were Mrs. Eleanor Roosevelt, United States Senators and Representatives, the Governor of Missouri and governors from six other states, representatives from many universities, and contributors to the Library fund. The Chief Justice then gave the dedication speech which was carried by radio and television.

"This is an important event in the life of the nation and I am happy to participate in it," said Warren. "The library which we dedicate is destined to become a midwestern center of study and research, not only for the period of Mr. Truman's Presidency, but also for the whole complex picture of events surrounding it. The impetus it provides for extending the research resources of this great section which has meant so much to the development of the nation as a whole, represents a milestone in American history."

Warren continued with the history of Independence and stressed its value as an early outpost of civilization. "Mr. Truman's grandfather owned one of these outfitting stores," added Warren, [and] "eventually himself succumbed to the gold fever."

He went on: "Mr. Truman's Presidency naturally reflected this daring spirit of pioneer days as well as his own character as a man of action: tireless, fearless and decisive. . . . The Truman era is already recognized as one of the most momentous periods in the history of our country and of the world. . . . The best evidence of the magnitude of the office he held, of the considerations basic to his decisions, of the methods he adopted to meet new and pressing problems, will be found in the Truman papers housed in this library. Without them, the world would never fully understand his courage and stamina in responding in the vigorous and effective way he did to crises such as few other executives have had to face."

The Chief Justice took note of the crises Truman had contended with throughout his Presidency, and how, because of Truman, "Arrogance was frustrated as had previously been done in Europe with the Berlin Air-lift." He stressed how Truman had carried the nation from isolationism to that of a world leader offering aid to the distressed and oppressed.

He spoke of the many benefits produced by the G.I. Bill of Rights and how the country became the beneficiary of this act. "It is fortunate that the Truman Library is to become a part of our vast and growing educational system—that it can be a major influence in the process of training an ever growing number of research students," he added.

"People from the universities and colleges of this country and from foreign countries will beat paths leading to and from Independence, reminding us of those of the nineteenth century," said Warren. "These new trails will be kept open because there will be sustained use of the Truman papers by future generations of writers, biographers, historians, political scientists and others. The traveler following these new trails will explore the background which the Truman Library will provide for a more complete understanding of the contributions made by his administration. Independence will become even more distinguished as a center for the cultural development of our country than it was for its geographical expansion." This prophecy has been more than fulfilled over the years.

"Mr. Truman, the private citizen, now back at home, continues to dedicate his life to the public good," Warren continued, "to make certain that the years of his administration will not be such a dark age. Today he performs a characteristic service in giving both his time and his substance to do that which in this instance only he can do. He is providing the people of America and the people of the world with the means to form their own estimate of his public service. Mr. Truman, who has an abiding interest in our national history, has arranged for the preservation of his papers in this library in such manner that his administration will be one of the clearest ages of history. It is in compliance with his public-spirited generosity that I dedicate this building as a museum and a library to safeguard, exhibit, and facilitate the use of its valuable resources that the American people, and, all the peoples of this earth, may gain by their wide and wise use understanding of ourselves and our times, and wisdom to choose the right paths in the years that lie ahead.

"In doing so I share with all Americans the hope that Mr. Truman will live long to see the results of his work and to be accorded recognition that the future of mankind will be richer because of his having passed this way."

Harry Truman told those present, as he had many times previously: "This library will belong to the people of the United States. My papers will be the property of the people and be accessible to them. And this is as it should be. The papers of the Presidents are among the most valuable source materials for history. They ought to be preserved and they ought to be used."

The president of the Truman Library Association, Basil O'Connor, representative of the seventeen thousand-plus individuals and organizations who financed the Library, presented the deed to the property to Franklin G. Floete, General Service Administrator of the United States government. The former President turned over his papers, consisting of more than three and a half million documents, to Dr. Wayne C. Grover, Archivist of the United States. Truman then gave the government his collection of books numbering over ten thousand. This was followed by the presentation of gifts and mementos the President had received during his term of office.

Among the gifts were a rare Persian rug given to Truman by the Shah of Iran, the original table on which the United Nations Charter was signed, and hundreds of other items, many of them priceless.

The Harry S. Truman Library was built by Truman and his friends without any government funds. Money that Truman earned for writing and lectures and which could have been used, without criticism, for his personal needs, was turned over to his Library Association. He had worked tirelessly to fulfill his dream for the people of America and the world. Even the Library plans were basically Truman's.

Independence's most famous citizen had brought honor and recognition to his home town and home folks.

15. THE STATESMAN

No longer did Harry Truman have to travel all the way to an office in Kansas City: he now had what he had long wanted in Independence. Nor did he have to contend with crowds at the Pickwick Hotel coffee shop wanting his autograph or to shake his hand while he tried to eat lunch. That had sent him, reluctantly, to the Kansas City Club, composed predominately of conservative Republicans. He was agreeably surprised to be heartily welcomed and soon became "one of the boys." He had also become a recognized statesman, one who would be welcome in any group any where.

Along with his spacious suite of offices in the Library went the privilege of walking or driving the short distance to his home to enjoy lunch with his wife. He also had an attractive place to entertain the many visitors who constantly called on him. There was ample room for his secretaries, and all this was next to the replica of the Oval Office of his White House days. This would become one the most sought-after attractions in the museum.

The auditorium that would seat two hundred-fifty people became one of his favorite places in the library. Frequently he would welcome visitors, especially students. He welcomed their questions and gave them truthful answers.

Harry Gershenson, another of Truman's long-time Masonic friends, often visited the former President at his Library. "It was a joy to watch him greet the school children when they came to the Library," Gershenson said. "He would speak to them from the stage of his fine auditorium, telling them about our country, the Constitution and what it's all about. Then he would frequently take them on a personal tour of the Library and Museum. He explained the meaning of the mementos and everything else. I really enjoyed trailing along with them and listening to Brother Truman describe what they saw and answer their questions."

The auditorium was the site for many historical moments, including a Kennedy press conference in 1960 when he became the nominee of the Democratic Party, and for the signing of the Medicare Act by President Lyndon B. Johnson.

The Harry S. Truman Library, Independence, Missouri

[Truman Library]

The Masonic display in the museum in the early days was good, according to Rufus Burrus, who added: "There were many things on display, then several things were stolen, including some priceless coins, while Truman was alive. And someone stole priceless swords that Arabs and others had given him. They were worth millions of dollars because of the jewels they had. Later those folks from Washington came here and changed everything. I wanted to kick someone on the shin and make them put those things back. But I can't get anything done."

One Masonic item that does have a place of honor in the Museum is the Greta Kempton portrait of the President in his Masonic regalia. Truman was always proud of that portrait and received many requests for copies. Some prints did arrive and on October 9, 1957, he wrote to Edward K. Thompson, evidently a photographer: "You don't know how very much I appreciated your going to all the trouble to make those 200 proofs of the color picture of me in my Masonic regalia. I have been trying my level best as the people, in the time of Mark Twain, would say out West, not to be in a position of asking favors for no good reason, except the reason that I was in the White House, so I am going to take you at your word and enclose you a check for $200.00 on the Riggs National Bank of Washington.

"If there is anything in the world that I dislike, it is a man who is always mooching things, based on some service he may have rendered publicly."

A list of the books Truman believed were important was sent to Governor Orville Freeman of Minnesota. Freeman had been impressed with Truman's interview with Edward R. Morrow which had been on television, and believed the former President could give him good advice as well as titles of books to read. Among the books Truman suggested was Representative Sol Bloom's "accumulation of George Washington's papers which were published by the government." These were published in 1932 for the two hundredth anniversary of the birth of Washington. Among the several volumes was valuable information about the Masonic life of the first President. Much of this information was recorded in *G. Washington: Master Mason.*

In the same letter Truman said: "The simplest conclusion I reached was that the lazy men caused all the trouble and those who worked had the job of rectifying their mistakes."

Truman's friend, Harry Gershenson, was President of the Bar Association in Missouri and he asked Truman to address the Supreme Court and newly enrolled lawyers in Jefferson City, Missouri. "He was not a lawyer," said Gershenson, "but he did attend law school for two years. It was amazing how he held those lawyers spell-bound for over forty minutes. He had a great grasp of the Constitutional principles of our country. Most people don't know that he had a real grasp of the Constitution, more so than most lawyers. Even before he went into the White House he was a student; he had always been a student of the history of our country."

Again Truman took note of the anti-Masonic period in response to an article by a political writer: "I read with interest Richard Rovere's article about Joe McCarthy. . . . Mr. Rovere has written a telling piece, and I wish he would do one or two or three others on the country's great demagogues—Huey Long, Tom Heflin and Pitchfork Tillman.

"Then there was that period in the history of the United States, between 1824 and the late '30s, when the anti-Masonic affair came forward. Its proponents even got seven votes in the Electoral College. Shortly afterward, the same people began burning Catholic churches in the northeast part of the United States and tarring and feathering Catholic priests.

"Cotton Mather, with his fight against witchcraft in Salem, was, of course, our first really gifted demagogue. New England historians always try to put a muffler on that, and I would like to see Mr. Rovere do something on all of our periods of hysteria."

On January 16, 1959, he wrote in his diary: "Last evening I went to a little town in eastern Kansas called Louisburg for the purpose of giving a fifty-year Masonic button to Mr. Hugh Lee. It was a grand meeting. Was there because my nephew Harry wanted me to be. Of course his brother Gilbert and my brother Vivian were all interested, too. More than 300 were present for dinner and a thirty-minute meeting.

"I have been refusing invitations from every state in the Union for every sort of meeting from cat shows to State money dinners.

"There are three four-drawer files full of refusals and enough acceptances to fill another one and a mulberry coffin too. When a notorious person is buried in a mulberry coffin he goes through 'Hell a poppin'.' It is the wood our forefathers avoided for fireplace use because it threw coals of fire all over the room."

Ivanhoe Masonic Temple was the site of one of the greatest Masonic meetings ever held in Missouri. The date was May 18, 1959; the occasion was the presentation of a fifty-year award to the only President of the United States to reach that golden age in Freemasonry.

Andrew Jackson had been the only President other than Harry S. Truman to serve as a Grand Master, but Jackson died before he reached that fifty-year milestone.

Grandview Lodge No. 618 knew its quarters could never hold the number of Masons who would want to honor the former President, so it asked for and received a dispensation to meet in Kansas City. Even so, only four hundred could be seated for dinner while hundreds more waited in the lodge room.

Truman was presented with an honorary membership certificate from the Grand Lodge of Israel by Grand Master Jonas Ron of Israel. A life membership from the *Gran Loge de France* was presented by Past Grand Master Ray V. Denslow, and a life membership certificate of the National Sojourners was also awarded. Past Grand Master Harry S. Truman was then presented with a framed copy of his original lodge petition by Belton Lodge. Finally the fifty-year pin was presented by Grand Master Robert L. Aronson, who recapped the Masonic life of Truman.

Truman said it was one of the most moving experiences of his life, and the fifty-year pin was something "I think I have earned."

He felt many of the honors he had received previously had been given to him because of his official position. To receive the fifty-year award one simply had to live long enough.

Burrus remembered that occasion: "Grandview Lodge got a dispensation to hold the fiftieth anniversary of Truman's Masonic affiliation in Ivanhoe Temple in Kansas City. And they had folks from all over the country—Past Grand Masters, and all. They had over five thousand people and couldn't seat them all. Truman told me, 'Ruff, I don't think I've ever had anything touch me as that did.' I'll never forget how he said it. Judge Aronson gave an excellent address and it wasn't written down. We made him go back and write it out, and he did, that same night while it was fresh in his mind."

The correspondence Truman received, answered and initiated was indeed varied. So were the people who wrote to him on every subject imaginable. Whether they were young or old made no difference, and it didn't matter whether or not they agreed with him—he answered everything he received. He felt that because the people had honored him by electing him President of the United States he should continue to serve everyone.

He discussed music with Sammy Kaye and Guy Lombardo, telling the latter that the "Missouri Waltz" was not a proper state song. The National Anthem he condemned because "we both know it takes a tenor, a baritone and a bass to sing the Star Spangled Banner. I never understood why it was not set to music that every single soldier in the Army could sing." He made it clear, though, that he always stood at attention for both songs.

A gradeschool student wanted to know what he should study. Truman told him. And Truman wasn't happy with the chairman of the Democratic Party and didn't care who knew it. But he continued to work for his party and told a friend, "I'm going to paste them hip and thigh in this '58 go-around and then try to smash them in 1960—if we can get a candidate to do it with."

On December 10, 1959, Truman wrote to an historian, Dr. James I. Robertson, Jr., who would become a well-known book reviewer, particularly books about the American Civil War. "Seems to me," he told him, "its proper name is the War Between the States, because it was a war to decide that the Government of the United States is a permanent entity and cannot be dismembered at the whim of anyone."

Within a letter he wrote but did not send to Dean Acheson, Truman recorded his feelings about John Kennedy's *Profiles in Courage.* "I'm afraid that this immature boy who was responsible for picking out five great Senators may not know any more about the Presidency that he will occupy than he did about the great Senators. Only one, Henry Clay [a Mason], belonged in the list. I sent him a list of a dozen or so but it wasn't used. So, what the hell, you and I will take it and not like it but hope for the future."

The former President refused to go the Democratic Convention in Los Angeles because he felt the Kennedy Machine had the nomination locked up. But once Kennedy was nominated Truman worked for him. After the inauguration Truman wrote Kennedy: "You'll never know how very much I appreciated all the courtesies you extended to me at inauguration time. I was invited into the White House for the first time in eight years."

Truman did not forget his plans for his mother lodge. He still wanted a model "country lodge temple" built on the site of the old Baptist church he had purchased. He drew a sketch of the building he wanted to see erected, then had an architect make drawings of the floor plan. He offered Grandview Lodge the plot of land and said he would help the members raise funds to build it.

The members took Truman's offer under advisement and sent out an appeal for funds along with a sketch of the finished temple. The appeal went on for some time without much success. The discussions, at times rather heated, also went on in the lodge over the pros and cons of whether or not to build, and particularly where to build.

According to Harold Thornton, who was Master of Grandview Lodge in 1961, Truman's offer of a gift of the property had strings attached. He wanted the temple built exactly as he had planned and with the East in the lodge at the east of the lot. This would have put the entrance in the East of the lodge, and most of the members objected to this. The lot fronted on a side street and the members offered to purchase fifty feet more than Truman had offered fronting on Main Street. This would enable the entrance to be changed, but Truman would not agree to sell the

Truman's concept of the lodge building he wanted built by Grandview Lodge No. 615, Missouri, on land he wanted to donate to his lodge.

[Artist's drawing]

lodge the property, because he had a tentative offer from the government to purchase that property for a post office.

On April 26, 1961, Truman sent the lodge a letter which read: "I am very much interested in the effort that is being made to build a Masonic Temple in Grandview. I sincerely hope it will be successful. . . . I am also hoping that it will be possible for me to present the site to the Lodge when the details with regard to it have been worked out."

A few days later the lodge held a dinner with Truman as the guest of honor to celebrate his seventy-seventh birthday. "A short time later," Thornton said, "I had the dubious honor of returning the deed Brother Truman had presented the lodge. The members had decided we couldn't raise the funds to build the marble temple he insisted be built, and the lot wouldn't accommodate it, anyway. And he wouldn't sell us the additional space we needed."

"He was heartbroken," said Burrus, "when his lodge refused to take that plot and build on it. He told me, 'I don't know what to do. I want them to have it.' They were young people who didn't know really what to do. They went out there on Highway 71 and built. After they turned down Harry's offer, he gave them $5,000 for their building fund."

A post office was built on the property Truman had reserved for it; the lot he wanted to give his lodge is used to park its vehicles.

Walter P. Reuther, president of the United Automobile Workers, invited Truman to help him celebrate the twenty-fifth anniversary of a sit-down strike. Truman wrote to him on January 24, 1962: "I am sorry to say that it will not be possible for me to be with you on February 4th anyway, but, between you and me and the gatepost, I don't think you would want me there because I would tell them exactly what I think about sit-down strikes. I am for Labor and the right to strike but when you destroy a man's business, especially a little man, it just isn't right and you know it as well as I do."

What will history say about the Truman Presidency? It is difficult to say. But more and more intelligent people have come to believe he did far more good than was once realized. Joseph Alsop, the columnist who was a frequent critic of President Truman, changed his opinion in 1965. He freely admitted he had underestimated Truman's leadership. And he offered to make a public apology. Truman wanted no part of that. He wrote Alsop: "There is something in my make-up that rebels at the thought of exacting an apology from anyone who has publicly disapproved of me—and I surely would not expect to receive one from so talented an observer as yourself.

"But I warmly welcome your reassessment of 'the period' and dare hope that it might be sustained by the ultimate judgement."

How did he feel about memorials to him? It was proposed that a memorial hospital be built in his name in South Korea. Truman wrote to Father Paul White who had asked permission to use Truman's name: "It has been, and is, my personal preference not to encourage the building of any memorials or monuments to me. I consider that whatever useful acts may have been performed during my administration were in fact the acts of the American people."

The Grand Master of Masons in Greece wanted to have a monument erected to memorialize the former President. Truman answered him on June 6, 1963: "I have a very peculiar complex in that I am not very much in favor of erecting monuments to people who are still walking around, because they might do something before they died which will cause you to want to tear the statue down. I hope that will never happen in my case, however."

Grandview Lodge had urged him to let the name be changed to Truman Lodge. He absolutely refused. But he had no control over lodges in other jurisdictions which adopted his name.

To celebrate his eighty-third birthday on May 8, 1967, Eva Beaver wrote a poem entitled "Harry Truman—Mr. Mason." Truman appreciated her sentiments and told her so.

"While sitting in his office one day," Burrus recalled, "he said, 'Ruff, I want to have my last resting place at a point halfway between where I sit and where the grove is for the Oval Room.' I said, 'Yes, Sir! I'll see that I get that done for you.' And he said, 'The next thing I want is for you to see that I have a Masonic service as a part of my last resting place.' As time went on I knew there would be an official recognition of his death when the time came, and it would be the army's duty to carry that out for the President. So I got in contact with the commander in this area. He was a Republican and he got to be a two-star general.

"From time to time army personnel would come to the library and look over the site. Truman looked them over through his window and told me he was going to outlive all of them.

"Mrs. Truman didn't warm up to the fact that he ought to have a Masonic funeral, but we finally were able to convince her. She was glad we did."

But the former captain of the Democratic Party wasn't about to leave the earthly scene. He continued to travel when asked by his party to go out "and bring back a few Republican scalps." This he thoroughly enjoyed doing. Whether or not he had a prepared speech made little difference. He had learned years before to speak "off the cuff" and that is when he was most effective.

Truman was at a loss for words, though, when President Kennedy was assassinated in Dallas, Texas, in 1963. He was so

Harry Truman—Mr. Mason

True to his principles and ideals
Regardless of what man thought,
From his determination to duty
Harry Truman couldn't be bought.

With courage of his conviction
Prudence and fortitude for peace,
He challenged the forces of power
And caused the war to cease.

For his belief he fought hard
From truth he did not hide,
Developing the virtues in man
Was his aim and greatest pride.

No man is more entitled
To wear the compass and the square
No servant in public office
Has been more just and fair.

He should be called MR. MASON
Who added Brotherhood to history,
Traveling by virtue to the East
To claim the thirty-third degree.

No earthly honor is greater
Than the love that he has shown,
To be reaped in tomorrow's world
When true Brotherhood is known.

Eva Beaver

shocked he couldn't speak and walked away from reporters who were questioning him. It was at Kennedy's funeral that Truman and Eisenhower returned to "speaking terms." They traveled to the cathedral together, then returned to the Blair House where the Trumans were staying. There they had several drinks together and chatted as though there had never been any differences between them.

And he continued to support Freemasonry. Burrus noted: "Truman was an excellent ritualist. He knew the ritual letter-perfect, and did all his life. He knew how to give it to them with emphasis and in a way to make them understand. He enjoyed doing it. As he grew older I didn't want him going out to Grandview by himself, so I started taking him out. He was fifteen years older than I am."

Although Truman maintained a schedule that lesser men couldn't match, it finally began to break him. Old age didn't come to him gradually. When the break came it was rapid, but he never lost his sense of humor.

"When Truman got too feeble to go to the library," said Burrus, "I would go to his house frequently. The room that he and Bess used didn't have a telephone. I asked them to let us put one in the room, but he said they didn't want one there. If the phone rang and they wanted to answer it, they'd do it, if not they'd just let it ring. Their house was hot and uncomfortable, and they wouldn't let us put in an air conditioner for a long time. When we did, they would only let us put one in the bedroom.

"After he died, Bess wouldn't let us make any repairs to the house. We did finally fix a leak in the roof without asking her, but she wouldn't let us repair the falling plaster in the ceiling. She didn't want any workmen in the house. As time went on Bess became more feeble and reached the point where she spoke to no one. She didn't want to ever stay in a hospital; she wanted to be at home."

On December 26, 1972, at eighty-eight years of age, Harry S. Truman died.

The last rites took place on December 28, 1972, mainly from the stage of the auditorium in the Harry S. Truman Library. He did not have exactly the Masonic funeral he had long requested; the Masonic portion was limited to five minutes. And he was almost deprived of that. Grand Master W. Hugh McLaughlin was finally told he would be limited to five minutes for his presentation to a nation-wide television audience.

"The Grand Lodge of Ancient, Free and Accepted Masons of the State of Missouri shares the grief and sorrow of Mrs. Truman, Mrs. Daniel and her family, Miss Mary Jane Truman and other family members in the loss of our beloved and cherished native son," said McLaughlin. "This expression comes from the Grand Lodge officers and from more than 108,000 of his Masonic brothers in Missouri.

"We express our gratitude to the family, to Father Lembecke, and to all other participants for the privilege of sharing in this service. We join, humbly and reverently, in paying lasting tribute to a great American and a renowned world statesman.

"Masons are taught never to engage in any solemn, great or important undertaking without first invoking the aid and blessing of Diety. Shall we pray?

"We hail you, Supreme Architect of the Universe. We come to you with spirits bowed low and ask the bounty of Thy Grace and Mercy in our bereavement. May our deeds be such as to prepare us for entry into Your spiritual kingdom, that house not made with hands, eternal in the heavens. Amen.

"President Truman distinguished himself in many Masonic services, the most laudable of which was that of Grand Master of Masons of this state in 1940 and 1941. At that time he was also a member of the United States Senate. We express our gratitude to Mrs. Truman and Mrs. Daniel for sharing a portion of his exciting, magnificent life with us. He was our brother by adoption. He was our companion by choice.

"The tenets of a Mason's profession are Brotherly Love, Relief and Truth. There abide with us Faith, Hope and Charity. The greatest of these is Charity for it extends through the boundless realms of eternity. Our notable brother exemplified Charity in a universal way when he directed relief to be administered, on an unprecedented scale, to alleviate human degradation in the aftermath of World War II.

"The lambskin or white leathern apron is the badge of a Mason, more ancient than the Golden Fleece or Roman Eagle. It is white to admonish us to keep our personal lives pure. Our exalted brother wore it proudly and worthily.

"The beehive is an emblem of a Mason's industry. By it we are taught to be workers in the great hive of nature. Even in his later years our distinguished and beloved citizen practiced that teaching. No more striking example than this great edifice, named for him, in which he performed his last labors, could conceivably be demonstrated to us today.

"It is, therefore, fitting that we should assemble here to pay this deserved tribute. We, as Masons, extol his many virtues, not the least of which was his recognition of the high level of individual dignity. May we emulate him in his simple, sincere, sturdy and forthright conduct. May all our good intentions be crowned with success. May Brotherly Love prevail in all the earth and every moral and social virtue cement us."

McLaughlin did an excellent job with the time alloted and under the pressures he had to contend with. Many of the important points covered in the last rites of the Masonic Fraternity were nicely woven into his address. The former Grand Master and President would have been pleased.

The body of the former President was laid to rest in the spot he had selected. Ten years later, the "girl with the golden curls" he had loved all his life joined him. The beautiful section is lined with flowers and flags of the fifty united states of America.

The Last Whistle Stop

16. POSTSCRIPT

In recent years Harry S. Truman has climbed toward the top of the list of great Presidents who have served the United States of America. It is interesting to note how often he is quoted, not particularly by members of the party he once headed, but by the party he fought with a passion. During the 1984 Presidential campaign, for instance, Republicans extolled Truman's virtues; the Democrats ignored him.

And political campaigns were one of the many things that concerned Truman. The convention system had its faults, he noted, but he could think of no "better method for choosing a presidential nominee." He did suggest: "The ideal situation would be for all the candidates—local, state, and national—to be heard on a fair basis by all the people of the country over the communication facilities of the nation." But this had to be on an equitable basis so that wealth wouldn't be influential.

"Actually," Truman wrote in his *Memoirs*, "there are two big evils which have to be overcome if the operation of our election system is not to be hampered or endangered. The old 'boss' system was a vicious arrangement in both parties. Men like Mark Hanna of Cleveland, George Cox of Cincinnati, Bill Thompson of Chicago, Tom Pendergast of Kansas City, Ed Crump of Memphis, and dozens of others, exercised undue influence over the selection of candidates. But none of them was more wonderful than the present-day advertising-press approach to politics."

That Truman loved the "art" of politics there can be no question, but partisanship was set aside by him on all matters concerning the welfare of the United States in foreign matters. Here he firmly believed there should be no Republicans or Democrats, simply Americans. This he made clear to Dwight Eisenhower during the transition of their administrations.

Throughout his life Truman considered the interests of the United States and its people more important than politics or himself. This was evident in the hundreds of decisions he had to make throughout his career. Many of these decisions were and still are scoffed at by his opponents and critics. Yet, dozens of suggestions he made that were not adopted while he was in office were later enacted into practice.

Of all the decisions Truman made, none has had a greater impact on the world and public opinion than his order to drop the atom bomb in an attempt to end the war the Empire of Japan started. During the fortieth anniversary of this decision no topic in the news media was more prevalent.

A small group of "historians," particularly throughout August, 1984, condemned the dropping of the A-bomb on Hiroshima, Japan, as "unnecessary." In an ABC newscast on August 3, 1984, one of these historians, too young to have served in World War II, claimed there were documents to prove "only" forty thousand lives were saved because of Truman's decision to drop the A-bomb. He didn't say where these documents are, nor how many documents he examined.

This same historian claimed Admiral Leahy was against dropping that bomb. Actually, William D. Leahy claimed the bomb would not explode, and that was the reason he was the only advisor to the President who preferred an air bombardment and blockade. General Marshall, along with the others, pointed out how saturation bombing had not worked to bring Germany to surrender—land forces had to do that.

Most of the present day "experts" appear to overlook several important facts: The President was as concerned with saving *Japanese* lives as he was those of Americans. The best estimates of casualties if the war continued were placed at one million American and five to ten times that many Japanese.

Another point these experts overlook is that the President warned the Japanese of dire consequences if the Empire did not surrender before the first A-bomb was dropped. This was ignored. So was the warning before the second one became necessary. The critics claim Japan was on its "knees" and had offered to surrender. That message was received on August 10, after the second bomb had been loaded. And there was no assurance it was sent by the controlling war lords of the Empire, or that the militarist fanatics would ever permit Japan to surrender.

How many lives were saved? No one on this earth can say. But if one really analyses the battles in the Pacific, and how much more fanatical the fighting would be for the Japanese homeland, the estimate of millions is not unreasonable. Then, too, one never hears these critics mention who provoked the bloodshed by an unwarranted and unwarned attack on American servicemen and women. They conveniently forget the dead and wounded at Pearl Harbor, Hawaii.

Even before Pearl Harbor, Japan had invaded China, and savagely slaughtered hundreds of thousands of innocent people. It had conquered Southeast Asia, and the brutality of Japanese troops made Hitler's atrocities tame by comparison. These Japanese troops raped the Philippines, doused hospital patients with flammable liquids and set them afire. They used prisoners of war for atrocious experiments, and how can the critics forget the Bataan Death March?

On the same ABC broadcast from the Truman Library, a newscaster said Truman never had second thoughts concerning his decision to drop the atom bomb—publicly. Then with sarcasm in his voice he claimed: "But in his own library is a well-thumbed copy of Shakespeare's *Hamlet* with these words underlined in his own hand," and he quoted about "carnal, bloody and unnatural acts." This newscaster inferred the copy marked in Truman's "own hand" indicated "second thoughts." But where did he, and others who have purported to have seen this underlined copy of *Hamlet*, find it? According to C. Warren Ohrvall, Archivist for the Harry S. Truman Library, "no copy of this book has been found!"

The syndicated columnist Jeffrey Hart said in his column for August 5, 1985: "Truman really ought to be a Japanese hero. Not only did he end the war, but he also established Douglas MacArthur as a proconsul in Tokyo. The outmoded military rule was scrapped, the Samurai code put in a museum, and Japan put on the reasonable course of making Toyotas. Everyone won."

Hart then reported on the relief of the servicemen in the European theater. Thousands of them were scheduled to invade Honshu, Japan, in March 1946 for the main invasion. Men then in the Pacific and camps in the United States were scheduled to make the initial invasion in November 1945. The dropping of the A-bomb had brought cheers from men on all the fronts. Hart also noted that the estimate of lives that would have been lost ran into the millions.

The last paragraph of Hart's column proclaimed what most of us felt who were "where the action was" during that fateful August of 1945: "Yes, on this anniversary of Hiroshima and Nagasaki, both Americans and Japanese should pause to remember Harry Truman, the 'little man' from Missouri, who had a clear view of what needed to be done—and did it. I wish the same could be said of some of his successors."

ABC *Nightline* on August 6, 1985, carried a "what if" program which graphically depicted what would have happened had an invasion of the Japanese Islands been necessary. It was an horrendously accurate account. Among the items learned was that Japanese schools teach nothing about what brought about the dropping of the atom bomb. The Japanese have been led to believe the atrocities were all American.

Three dignitaries were interviewed on this *Nightline* program. Norman Cousins, an apologist for the Hiroshima episode, continuously claimed the bomb was unnecessary and "only" thirty to forty thousand lives were saved; that it was used merely to keep the Russians from sharing in the surrender of Japan. Alvin Coox, an historian, believed the bomb was not necessary, but in answer to a direct question, noted: "From the American point of view, regrettably, I'm a reluctant hawk." Dean Rusk, who in 1945 was a colonel in the War Department, defended Truman's decision throughout the arguments by the others.

With the exception of a handful of critics, the prestige and stature of the thirty-third President of the United States has increased. This is so, not only throughout the free world, but within Freemasonry.

With the approach of Truman's one hundredth birthday, Grand Lodges, lodges and Masonic organizations began asking for information about Harry S. Truman, the Freemason. So, The Masonic Service Association compiled as much information on the former President as possible. For two years it urged Masons throughout the country to hold special meetings in honor of this man who had spent sixty-three years working for the Craft.

The year 1984 found many Grand Lodges celebrating Truman's one hundredth anniversary in many imaginative ways. Everything from musicals to degree work carried his name.

Thousands who never knew the man learned of his interest in and work for Freemasonry.

C. Warren Ohrvall searched the many files in the Harry S. Truman Library and compiled papers covering the Masonic life of Truman. He made these available to all groups for the asking. Many lodge and Grand Lodge programs were built around segments of these accounts.

The Ancient Arabic Order Nobles of the Mystic Shrine asked the leaders of their Temples to hold special classes in memory of Truman. Many of them did and presented their new members with special certificates, coins and other mementos.

Royal Arch Masons, Knight Templars, some Scottish Rite Valleys, all groups Truman had supported throughout his lifetime, held special events. It was a year of unprecedented Masonic activity in the name of Harry S. Truman.

A Truman Centennial Committee was formed on the national scene with which the MSA worked closely to provide information for Masonry. This committee was headed by Clark Clifford, and its members included several Freemasons including former President Gerald R. Ford, General Donald S. Dawson, and Senator Robert C. Byrd.

Many Masonic publications, including *The Philalethes*, carried special editions on Truman, the Mason.

Other organizations he had worked with and for remembered him. *The Officer*, a publication of the Reserve Officers Association of the United States, featured Truman in its May, 1984, edition. Its cover carried fourteen stamps associated with Truman, one of the founders of the Association. Its editor, Colonel Norman S. Burzynski, said he was disappointed not to find more stamps from the NATO countries for whom Truman had done so much while he was President.

Articles in *The Officer* covered many of the important decisions Truman had made while President. The president of the Association, Colonel Walter G. Vartan, said: "ROA is proud to have been a part of this great patriot's life, and we are grateful benefactors of his personal commitment to our Association and the Reserve Forces of our nation."

The Blair House was President Truman's home for much of his second term as President because he had the White House completely renovated. Next to the Blair House stands the Lee House, which also became a part of Truman's residence. In 1924 this became the first headquarters of the Reserve Officers Association. The ROA placed a plaque on the Lee House noting this, and that President Truman signed the law giving the ROA its Congressional charter in 1950.

This organization also dedicated the fourth floor of its Minute Man Memorial Building to Truman's memory.

Another building was erected and named in memory of President Truman, the man who declined memorials to himself while he was alive. It was a state office building in Jefferson City, Missouri, officially named the Truman Office Building. The Freemasons of Missouri were present in large numbers for the cornerstone ceremonies on May 19, 1983. They heard Grand Master Earl K. Dille conduct the ceremony and extoll some of the virtues of the thirty-third President of the United States.

In large letters the wording on the stone reads: "THIS CORNER STONE WAS LAID BY THE GRAND LODGE OF MISSOURI A.F. and A.M., MAY 19, 1983. HARRY S. TRUMAN, GRAND MASTER 1940-1941."

In New York during 1984 a new Masonic Lodge was organized and proudly selected the name "Harry S. Truman."

Earlier the Grand Lodge of Missouri decided to adopt a distinguished service medal. It is named in honor of its most illustrious Past Grand Master, Harry S. Truman. The first recipient was a friend of Truman and a long-time Masonic writer, John Black Vrooman, one of the "little" Masons Truman admired.

Eugene M. Zukert, Secretary of the Air Force, 1961-65, praised former President Truman highly in an account in *The Officer*. In his opening he said: "As Commander-in-Chief he made momentous decisions in peace and in war." He enumerated some of them: the use of the A-bomb; civilian control of atomic energy; saving Turkey and Greece from communism; the National Security Act of 1947; the Marshall Plan which saved and helped rebuild western Europe; the Berlin Airlift; Korea.

"On the domestic side," continued Zukert, "he was a strong advocate of steps toward civil rights, and his decisions in the coal, steel and railroad strikes, while they may not have been popular, were certainly those of a decisive leader.

"The Truman record becomes even more impressive when you consider his background and the preparation that he had for the Presidency. I find it fascinating, even a miracle, that this plain-spoken, unpretentious man could have been projected on to the stage of world events and quickly established himself as a leader of stature. Perhaps the most surprising fact of all was that the power of our high office did not change him, neither his virtues nor his shortcomings."

Zukert made the same observation most of Truman's biographers have made about the President's background. They appear surprised to find that a man with little or no post-high school education could, and did, guide the country through one of the most difficult periods in its history. They all overlook, because they have no way of understanding, the full educational background of Harry S. Truman.

First, he was an enthusiastic reader, particularly of history and biographies. Second, he was a Freemason, not merely in name but in fact. What these biographers do not know is that a devoted Freemason obtains one of the most liberal educations it is possible to obtain. Few members of the organization, and none outside, realize this: but those who do become much better men than they would be otherwise.

Until fairly modern times the best educated of men were in the clergy and the trades. Each of these groups learned the liberal arts and sciences: Grammar, Logic, Rhetoric, Arithmetic, Geometry, Music, and Astronomy. The Freemason today still must learn something about these, but the interested Mason learns more than a mere "something." Truman was one of these. As he told Bess in one of his letters, he could recite the ritual for hours without stopping. What he didn't tell her was he had learned what that ritual really means.

As a Freemason, Truman also learned the meaning of Brotherly Love, Relief and Truth. He put the first two into practice continually; Truth he continued to seek, which is a never-ending quest. He learned that time, patience and perseverance could accomplish almost anything. His understanding of Masonry's Cardinal Virtues—Temperance, Fortitude, Prudence and Justice—shows up throughout his life.

Truman's knowledge of the fundamental purposes of Freemasonry, its history, symbolism, benevolence, its leadership qualities and its quest for Truth, gave him an educational background few of the leaders of the nation or industry could match at any price. And he had this background long before he was elected Grand Master of Masons in Missouri. He did not have a college degree: but a degree without the attributes Truman did have, is of little moral value.

The unbiased historian or reporter will find all these Masonic attributes prevalent in every decision, every suggestion, every plea Harry S. Truman made during his public life. By using these virtues in his private life he was able to influence many individuals to become better citizens, far better than they might otherwise be.

Thousands of school children, as well as adults, heard him speak of his philosophy from the stage of the auditorium of his Library. Millions heard him in radio addresses, and, to a limited extend, on television. Thousands of others were influenced by him through lectures in all types of settings throughout the country.

Zukert mentioned more of Truman's philosophy: "The cornerstone of his decision-making process, I think, was honesty. He tried to do what he thought was best for the country. The swing factor in these big decisions was not what would make him popular, what would get him re-elected, but what was best for the United States. He had a deep sense of the fitness of things. He was able to receive advice and fit it into his pattern of how things should be. One of the paradoxes of President Truman was that he was truly a statesman and yet he recognized the essential role of politics. He was a politician, and he was proud of it. But he had a sense which told him where politics should stop."

That is one of the keys to understanding Truman; he knew where politics should stop.

Politics stop without the doors of a Masonic Temple. This is as it should be and Truman recognized this from his earliest days within the Craft. He could have used Freemasonry advantageously throughout his political career, but he would not. He could have used the friendships he gained through Masonry, but instead he gave much more than he received. He continuously gave of himself.

He gave of himself, not only to his Brethren in Freemasonry but to every citizen of the United States and the world. His actions immediately after the end of the war in Europe prove this conclusively.

As a private citizen he continued to give of himself. He could have become rich in coin of the realm: instead he refused to prostitute his name or the office of the Presidency of the United States. Even so, he could have lived comfortably on the fees he received legitimately for lectures and writing. This money, however, he turned over to the Truman Library Association so a Library could be built for all the people to use.

Inscribed on the front of Truman's Library is a statement he made several times: **"This Library will belong to the people of the United States. My papers will be the property of the people and be accessible to them. And this is as it should be. The papers of the Presidents are among the most valuable sources of material for history. They ought to be preserved and they ought to be used."**

How much of an influence did Freemasonry have on the life of Harry S. Truman? He answered this on many occasions, even after his election as President of the United States:

"The greatest honor that has ever come to me, and that can ever come to me in my life, is to be Grand Master of Masons in Missouri."

—So Mote It Be—

Glossary

GLOSSARY OF MASONIC TERMS

A.A.O.N.M.S.: Ancient Arabic Order Nobles of the Mystic Shrine. Although its members must be Knight Templars or 32nd degree Scottish Rite Masons, it is not considered a Masonic association.

A.A.S.R., NMJ, or SJ: Ancient and Accepted Scottish Rite, Northern Masonic Jurisdiction or Southern Jurisdiction. It confers degrees four though 32 on members of Masonic Lodges who are Master Masons. It has a 33rd degree which is honorary.

A.F.& A.M.: Ancient, Free and Accepted Masons. The term used by several Grand Lodges, and their subordinate lodges use these initials after the name and number of the lodge. All lodges have numbers, except those in Massachusetts.

A.F.M.: Ancient Free Masons. Term used by the Grand Lodge of South Carolina

A.L.: Term for "year of light" which is determined by adding 4,000 to the current year. ie: 5985 for 1985.

Altar: The focus of Masonic Light in a lodge; symbol of faith.

Amaranth, Order of: Somewhat similar to the Order of the Eastern Star.

AMD: Allied Masonic Degrees controlled by the Grand Council of the Allied Masonic Degrees of the United States. Individual Councils are limited to 27 members, and members are selected by invitation only.

Amen: Response to the ending of a prayer (see also So Mote It Be)

Ancient Craft Masonry: Symbolic Freemasonry; Masonry since the Grand Lodge era (1717); consists of three degrees: Entered Apprentice, Fellowcraft, and Master Mason.

Anti-Masonry: Any movement designed to destroy or oppose Freemasonry.

Appendant body: Organization requiring its members to hold membership in a Masonic Lodge.

Apron: The "badge" of a Freemason worn in Masonic Lodges and official Masonic occasions, such as Masonic funerals and the laying of cornerstones. It is considered an emblem of honor and purity.

Architecture: A symbol of the need of knowledge and building.

Cardinal Virtues: Temperance, Fortitude, Prudence and Justice.

Charter member: One who was elected to membership prior to a charter being awarded.

Chief Justices who were Freemasons: Oliver Ellsworth, John Marshall, William H. Taft, Fred M. Vinson, Earl Warren (Marshall and Warren were also Grand Masters).

Communication: A name given to a Masonic meeting.

Compasses: One of the Great Lights in Freemasonry; a symbol of restraint; a two-legged instrument for drawing circles or measuring distances; six Grand Lodges use "compass" (a nautical instrument) evidently believing this is the singular of "compasses."

Conclave: A meeting of Knight Templars and some other bodies.

Convention: A formal, state, or national meeting; seldom, if ever, used as a term in Freemasonry.

Cornerstone: Usually laid, Masonically, in the Northeast corner of public buildings in keeping with ancient times; usually contains items of interest to future generations.

DDGM: District Deputy Grand Master. He is a Grand Lodge official responsible for a certain number of lodges in his jurisdiction.

Demit: (often misspelled "dimit") Permission given to a member to terminate his membership.

DeMolay, Order of: A youth organization for young men sponsored by Masonic Lodges or appendant bodies.

DGM: Deputy Grand Master; second only to the Grand Master; he presides or governs in the latter's absence.

Dispensation: Permission to set aside a particular law; authority to form a new Lodge or body.

EA: Entered Apprentice. The first degree in Freemasonry.

East: The position in a Lodge or Grand Lodge where the presiding officer sits; symbolic of the placing of the Tabernacle in the wilderness.

Eastern Star, Order of the: An organization of Freemasons and their female relatives; not a Masonic body. Local bodies are called Chapters and are governed by a Grand Chapter. However, as with all organizations connected with Freemasonry, the ultimate control is with the Grand Lodge of the jurisdiction.

Fellowcraft: The second degree in Freemasonry.

Freemason: A man who has received the Master Mason degree in a Lodge chartered by the Grand Lodge in its state or territory. He is often called a "Mason" or "Master Mason."

G: Symbol of God; of geometry; often combined with the Square and Compasses in this country in Masonic jewelry; the combination is the symbol of Symbolic Masonry.

GAOTU: Grand (or Great) Architect of the Universe. A title of respect given to Diety because Freemasonry is non-sectarian; its members must believe in one God, but what they believe about Him is determined by a man's own conscience, therefore, men of every religious persuasion can meet in Masonic functions without the age-old disagreements about religion.

Gavel: An emblem of the presiding officer's authority.

Gloves: A symbol of innocence or fidelity.

Grand Chapter, Royal Arch Masons: An appendant body of Freemasonry which confers four degrees, except in Virginia and West Virginia where two addition Council degrees are included. Local bodies are called Chapters.

Grand Commander: The presiding officer of each of the two Scottish Rite bodies.

Grand Council, Royal and Select Masters: An appendant Masonic body that confers two additional degrees (some add another); it is closely allied with the Royal Arch. This body has been merged with the Royal Arch in Virginia and West Virginia.

Grand High Priest: The presiding officer of a Grand Chapter of Royal Arch Masons.

Grand Lecturer: Teaches and controls the Masonic ritual as prescribed by his Grand Lodge. He is usually supported by District Lecturers.

Grand Lodge: The governing body of all Freemasonry in its state; each state has its own Grand Lodge, with the exception of Hawaii which is controlled by California. The District of Columbia has its own Grand Lodge. It governs all appendant bodies composed of Master Masons in its state, and there is no Masonic power that is higher.

Grand Master: The presiding officer of a Grand Lodge; he has the power to administer the laws of Freemasonry and the Masons residing in his jurisdiction when the Grand Lodge is not in session.

Grand Secretary: The continuing administrative officer of a Grand Lodge.

Honorary member: Title conferred by Lodge or Grand Lodge, usually for outstanding service to Freemasonry; usually carries all privileges of regular membership.

Installation: Formal induction into Masonic office.

Jobs Daughters, International Order of: A youth organization for young ladies who are relatives of Master Masons; sponsored usually by the Order of the Eastern Star.

Jurisdiction: The area a Grand Lodge controls, which is usually its state; power of a Grand Master who controls all the Freemasons in his state; area a Lodge controls.

Knight Templar (KT): members of the Knights Templar which is controlled by a Grand Commandery, which is controlled by the Grand Encampment, a national body and the only national controlling body connected in any way with Freemasonry. It is an appendant body, predominately Christian, whose members must be Royal Arch Masons. It confers three degrees, called Orders.

Landmark: In Freemasonry it means something of ancient usage, custom, practice, or belief, without which Freemasonry would become something other than what it is.

Lodge: A group of Freemasons who are banded together under a charter granted by the Grand Lodge holding jurisdiction over their state or territory. Also the building in which they meet, often called a Temple.

Lecture: Part of a degree; a recitation; an explanation.

Liberal Arts and Sciences: Free from narrowness; learning that contributes to a well-rounded education; an effective education.

Light: Knowledge, temporal and spiritual; Truth.

Made; Make: The conferral of the final degree in Symbolic Masonry; creating (or Raising) a Master Mason.

Mason at Sight: The conferral of all three degrees at one period on a selected man under the direct authority of the Grand Master. This is prohibited in a number of jurisdictions.

Masonic Service Association, The: An association of Grand Lodges of the United States which volunteer to join; a service organization for all Freemasonry.

Master: The presiding officer of a Masonic Lodge. He is often called "Worshipful Master," which is erroneous except when addressed in a Masonic Lodge, and then it is a term of respect similar to that of "Mister Chairman" or "Madam President."

Master Mason: This is the third degree conferred in Freemasonry and is the highest degree a Mason can receive, although other degrees with higher numbers can be obtained. No Mason who demits (resigns) from a Masonic Lodge and does not affiliate with another in a short period can retain his membership in any appendant body connected with Freemasonry.

Monitor: Book containing the portions of the ritual permitted by a particular Grand Lodge. It varies widely among jurisdictions.

Most Worshipful: A term denoting a Grand Master, which should only be used during a Masonic function; in Pennsylvania "Most" is never used, instead the term is "Right Worshipful."

M.O.V.P.E.R.: Mystic Order of Veiled Prophets of the Enchanted Realm (Grotto), an organization somewhat similar to that of the Shrine. Its state councils are governed by a Supreme Council. The presiding officers are Grand Monarchs.

Mystic Tie: Symbolically a bond of brotherhood.

Parliamentary Law: Governs most assemblies, but not employed in Freemasonry where the Master has full control of debate, work, and acts.

Past: A term used before another title, such as "Past Grand Master," which means the person has served in the office noted.

Patent: A certificate or diploma in the Scottish Rite.

Penalties: The only "penalties" known in Freemasonry are reprimand, suspension, or expulsion from membership.

Philalethes Society, The: An international research society whose membership is open to all Master Masons. It publishes an outstanding magazine bimonthly and holds annual meetings and workshops in Washington, D.C. each February, and otherwise meets at the call of the president.

Politics: Prohibited in a Masonic Lodge; Masonic meetings must be harmonious, the discussion of politics and religion can destroy this harmony.

Prince Hall Masonry: An organization of Black Freemasonry dating from the Revolutionary War period; considered "irregular" by some Caucasian Masons but its aims and goals are approved by others; it does have the legitimacy of time on its side, while other so-called Black organizations calling themselves "Masonic" do not.

Profane: A term used to mean "one outside the temple"; but it has a degrading meaning today and should never be used to describe a non-Mason.

Rainbow for Girls, Order of: A young ladies organization sponsored by Masonic groups. Unlike the Jobs Daughters, a young lady does not have to be a relative of a Master Mason to join, but must be sponsored by a Mason.

Recognition: The recognizing of another Masonic body or Grand Lodge as "legitimate"; determines where a Freemason may legitimately visit as a Mason.

Red Cross of Constantine: A small appendant invitational body requiring membership in the York Rite, and in some jurisdictions, the Shrine also; meets in Conclaves.

Regius Poem or Manuscript: Oldest Masonic document dating from about 1390 A.D. which places the date of Freemasonry, of some type, between the years 926 and 933 A.D., during the reign of King Athelstan, when he called the Masons to meet at York, England.

Right Worshipful: A title reserved for Grand Lodge officers, which include district officers. For example: Harry S. Truman became a "Brother" when he became a Master Mason, a title a Mason carries throughout his life; he was "Worshipful" when appointed charter Master of his Lodge; when he was appointed a District Deputy Grand Master this title was elevated to "Right Worshipful"; the day he was elected Grand Master he achieved the highest title a Mason can obtain, that of "Most Worshipful." Although these, and other titles, are often used in public, they should be reserved for Masonic functions only.

Rite: A ceremonious act or observance; a system, such as "York Rite"; "Scottish Rite."

Ritual: A means of conveying facts, or lessons, in an impressive manner that will leave an indelible imprint on the mind.

Royal Arch Masonry: See Grand Chapter, Royal Arch Masons. There is a General Grand Chapter of Royal Arch Masons, International, to which State Grand Chapters may belong on a voluntary basis; it is a service organization. It has officers with the title of "General Grand."

Royal and Select Masters: See Grand Council, Royal and Select Masters. It has a General Grand Council and operates similar to the General Grand Chapter. Now called Cryptic Masons in some jurisdictions.

Royal Order of Jesters: An invitational group connected with the Shrine; its organizational groups are called "courts."

Scottish Rite: See A.A.S.R.

Secret Society: Which Freemasonry IS NOT; it does, however, have a few secrets; a secret society is one about which the world knows little or nothing; Masonic buildings are clearly marked; its membership is published; its members openly wear its insignia.

So Mote It Be: So "May" or "Might" it be; an Old Saxon word adopted by Symbolic Masonry as another term for "Amen," although both are used within Freemasonry.

Speculative: The opposite of "operative" as used in Freemasonry; ie: Speculative Masonry is descended from operative masonry; a concept; a moral philosophy; one who searches for Truth.

Square and Compasses: Masonically these go together, because without compasses an accurate square cannot be made; without a square a building cannot be erected; the universal symbol of a Freemason.

S.R.I.C.F.: Societas Rosicrucians In Civitatibus Feoederatis is an invitational research body whose members are chosen in most jurisdictions from Master Masons. It should never be confused with the Rosicrucians who are not Freemasons and who believe in the study of all types of things many people consider strange.

Trowel: Symbol of a generous heart which spreads the cement of Brotherly Love; has many symbolic meanings in Masonic degrees; always used to lay cornerstones with Masonic ritual.

Truth: The ultimate foundation of everything that is good; Masonically, "the foundation of every virtue."

Valley: Term for a local Scottish Rite jurisdiction.

Work: Term for ritual conducted in a Masonic Lodge.

Worshipful: A term of respect which should be used only when addressing the presiding officer (Master) during a Masonic function.

York Legend: See Regius Poem.

[**Note:** This glossary barely touches on the countless number of Masonic terms and organizations.]

Ray V. Denslow, who figured prominently in the life of Harry S. Truman, wrote: "A few years ago we had only lodge, chapter, council and commandery, today we have an auxiliary built upon the foundation of each—and not content with these, our brethren rush about in an ambitious desire to learn more about co-masonry, adoptive masonry, and the like."

APPENDIXES

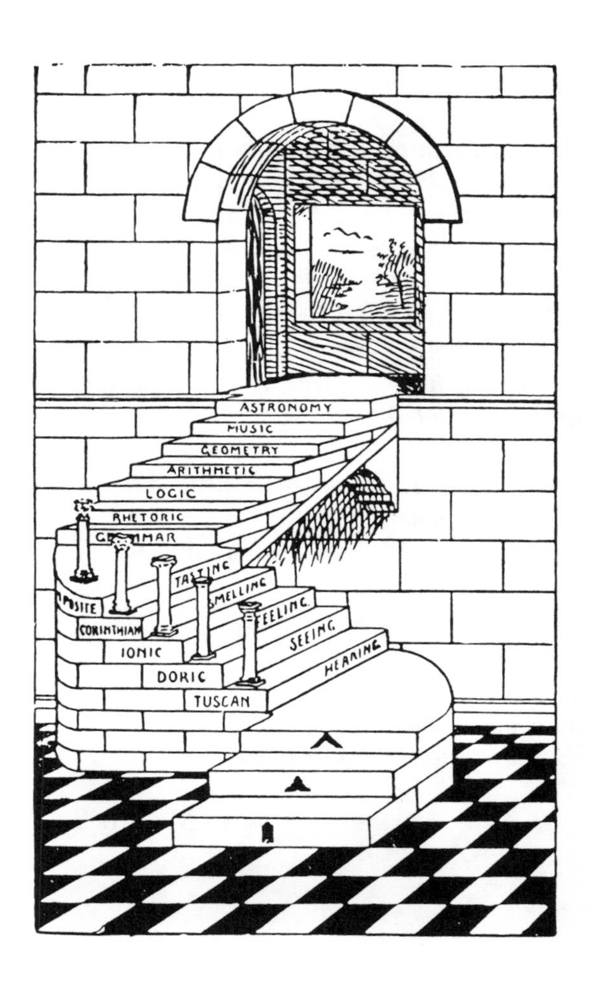
ASTRONOMY
MUSIC
GEOMETRY
ARITHMETIC
LOGIC
RHETORIC
SMELLING
FEELING
SEEING
HEARING
CORINTHIAN
IONIC
DORIC
TUSCAN

PRAYER AT THE RAISING (CREATING) OF A MASTER MASON
(Based on Job: Chapter 14)

Thou, O God! knowest our downsitting and our uprising, and understandest our thoughts afar off.

Shield and defend us from the evil intentions of our enemies, and support us under the trials and afflictions we are destined to endure while traveling through this vale of tears.

Man that is born of a woman is of few days, and full of trouble.

He cometh forth like a flower, and is cut down: he fleeth also as a shadow, and continueth not.

Seeing his days are determined, the number of months are with thee, thou hast appointed his bounds that he cannot pass:

Turn from him, that he may rest, till he shall accomplish, as an hireling, his day.

For there is hope of a tree, if it be cut down, that it will sprout again, and that the tender branch thereof will not cease.

But man dieth, and wasteth away: yea man giveth up the ghost, and where is he?

As the waters fail from the sea, and the flood decayeth and drieth up:

So man lieth down, and riseth not: till the heavens be no more.

Yet, O Lord! have compassion on the children of Thy creation, administer them comfort in the time of trouble, and save them with an everlasting salvation.

—So Mote It Be— Amen.

A. THE MASONIC RECORD OF HARRY S. TRUMAN

Symbolic Masonry

Belton Lodge No. 450, AF&AM, Belton, Missouri
Entered Apprentice, February 9, 1909
Fellowcraft, March 9, 1909
Master Mason, March 18, 1909
Junior Warden, 1910
Grandview Lodge No. 615, AF&AM, Grandview, Missouri
Organized lodge in 1911
Appointed Worshipful Master; Charter (first) Master;
Secretary for five years; Master (again) in 1917
Grand Lodge of Missouri
District Deputy Grand Master, 1925-30
District Lecturer, 1925-30
Appointed to Grand Lodge line, 1930
Grand Master, 1940-41
Missouri Lodge of Research
Signed dispensation for formation and signed Charter in 1941
Instituted the Lodge and installed the officers in 1941
Served through the line while U.S. Senator, Vice President and President; Master, 1950-51, while President of the United States
Honorary member of several Masonic Lodges
Honorary Past Grand Master of several Grand Lodges

York Rite

Orient Chapter No. 102, Royal Arch Masons, Kansas City, Missouri
Degrees conferred November 11 and 15, 1919
Shekinah Council No. 24, Royal and Select Masters, Kansas City, Missouri
Degrees conferred December 18, 1919

Palestine Commandery No. 17, Knight Templars, Independence, Missouri

Orders conferred June 7 and 15, 1923

Scottish Rite

The Valley of Kansas City, Orient of Missouri

Lodge of Perfection, January 24, 1912
Chapter Rose Croix, March 27, 1917
Council Knights Kadosh, March 29, 1917
Consistory (32nd degree), March 31, 1917
Coroneted 33rd degree, Honorary, October 19, 1945
(the first President of the United States to receive this degree)

Shrine

Ararat Temple, Kansas City, Missouri

Created a Noble, April 2, 1917
Orator, 1932; Marshal, 1933; Second Ceremonial Master, 1934; resigned office in 1934 on election to U.S. Senate

Masonic-related Bodies

Kilwining Council No. 19, Allied Masonic Degrees, Columbia, Missouri
Mary Conclave No. 5, Red Cross of Constantine, Kansas City, Missouri
Kansas City Chapter No. 63, National Sojourners
Kallipolia Grotto, M.O.V.P.E.R.
Kansas City Court No. 54, Royal Order of Jesters, Missouri
Grandview Chapter, Order of the Eastern Star, Charter Worthy Patron

Mary Jane Truman was Worthy Grand Matron, 1950-51 and installed by her brother, President Harry S. Truman

Honorary Member of several Masonic Lodges, Grand Lodges, and Appendant Bodies

B. GEORGE WASHINGTON, THE MASON

(Grand Master Harry S. Truman addressed a nation-wide radio audience over the Columbia Broadcasting System on Saturday, February 22, 1941. His topic was George Washington as a Master Mason. This was the first time a speech favorable to Freemasonry was broadcast nationally.)

Ladies and Gentlemen of the Radio Audience:

It is my privilege to discuss with you for a few minutes George Washington, the Man and the Freemason.

On the back of a picture at Mount Vernon is one of the greatest tributes ever paid to the Father of His Country. I shall quote a few sentences from that tribute:

> Washington, the defender of his country, the founder of liberty, the friend of man. History and tradition are explored in vain for a parallel to his character. In the annals of modern greatness he stands alone, and the noblest names of antiquity lose their luster in his presence. Born the benefactor of mankind, he united all the qualities necessary to an illustrious career. Nature made him great; he made himself virtuous. Called by his country to the defense of her liberties, he triumphantly vindicated the rights of humanity, and on the pillars of national independence laid the foundations of a great Republic. . . . Magnanimous in youth, glorious through life, great in death, his highest ambition, the happiness of mankind; his noblest victory, the conquest of himself; bequeathing to posterity the inheritance of his fame, and building his monument in the hearts of his countrymen, he lived, the ornament of the eighteenth century, and died, regretted by a mourning world.

This tribute is almost perfect, and it fits the character of one of the greatest men in history.

In 1840, Senator Ashur Robbins of Rhode Island, an 81-year-old Whig, made the statement that Washington made him think of Virgil's lines, "I verily believe, nor is my confidence unfounded, that he is of divine descent." This was a spontaneous tribute, paid to him at a banquet. The Senator from Rhode Island then expressed the hope that his countrymen would prove themselves to be worthy of Washington's fame.

Washington had more to do with the creation of this great Republic than anyone else in Revolutionary times. The fact that we are a great nation is due to a great extent to his foresight and leadership.

As Commander-in-Chief of the Continental Army, he took a ragged, ill-equipped force and made an Army of it, and as a military tactician won the praise of Frederick the Great, Napoleon Bonaparte, and the Duke of Wellington. His military campaigns compare favorably with those of the greatest leaders in history.

In 1776, contempt for the American Army had reached the point where the British Commander dispersed his troops in order to take advantage of billeting facilities, and neglected to throw up intrenchments. East of the Delaware, Hession commands were quartered in Trenton, Mount Holly, Black Horse, Burlington and Bordentown. Washington planned to attack all these troops in their winter quarters the morning after Christmas. Five bodies of Americans were to take part, and three columns were to cross the Delaware and converge on Trenton. Washington accompanied the column that had the longest march, after it crossed the river. Time pieces were set by Washington's watch, and a zero hour fixed in the modern way. The surface of the Delaware was a mass of floating ice, and two of the column commanders concluded it would be impossible to cross. The night was bitter cold, and a sleet storm assailed the troops. All division commanders failed except those who were with Washington; and one of these would have given up, if Washington had not been present. This commander sent word to Washington that the firearms of the men were wet. "Tell General Sullivan," said Washington, "to use the bayonet. I am resolved to take Trenton."

More than ten hours were consumed in crossing the river, and the troops had to march nine niles into the blinding storm. An aide of General Gates, with a message of explanation and excuse from his chief, found his way to Washington by following the bloody tracks of the soldiers.

The action was soon over. Twenty-two Hessions were killed. Washington reported "the number that submitted. . . . was twenty-three officers and eight hundred and eighty-six men. . . . Our own loss is very trifling indeed, only two officers and one or two privates wounded." Lieutenant James Monroe, later President of the United States, and Captain William Washington were the wounded officers. Later reports increased the number of prisoners to about one thousand.

Washington recrossed the Delaware with his prisoners. The British troops at Burlington and Bordentown abandoned their sick and their heavy baggage and retreated to Princeton. Cornwallis was sent from New York to retrieve the disaster. Washington's army again crossed the Delaware into New Jersey on December 31, 1776. To retain his troops in service, he and his officers pledged their personal funds. On the evening of January 2, 1777, with about 5,000 men, in a selected position on high ground outside of Trenton, he confronted Cornwallis, who had an equal or greater force. Washington's object was to strike quick blows at the British detachments and supplies, while avoiding battle with their main forces.

The situation was "most critical," as Washington himself said. Leaving his campfires burning, he slipped away to Princeton. About sunrise the next morning, Washington met a British detachment. In two sharp, quick actions, he defeated the enemy, and captured 230 prisoners.

Before the end of the month he had recovered all of New Jersey except three British posts at Paulus (Powles) Hook, Amboy, and New Brunswick. Trenton and Princeton marked an epoch in the American Revolution. They revealed to the British the spirit and genius of the man with whom they had to deal. On Christmas Day, the Revolution was apparently near its end; within less than two weeks, the British were concentrating and preparing to defend themselves in their winter quarters.

By his victories and the spirit which they infused into the despairing people, Washington saved the Revolution in its darkest hour. There were still many anxious days before the final triumph, but the tide of American disasters had passed its lowest ebb. Von Moltke, the great modern German strategist, says, "No finer movement was ever executed than the retreat across the Jerseys, the return across the Delaware a first time, and then a second, so as to draw out the enemy in a long, thin line." Horace Walpole pronounced Washington's march through the British lines "a prodigy of generalship." In London, the youthful Lafayette heard of Trenton and Princeton, and hastened his preparations to sail for America.

As a leader of men, Washington is without parallel in the history of our country.

As President of the Constitutional Convention, he had much to do with the creation and adoption of the Constitution of the United States. He went to the Convention under protest, but deemed it his public duty to go. He wrote Governor Randolph, of Virginia:

> I apprehend too much cause to arraign my conduct with inconsistency in again appearing on a public theatre, after a public declaration to the contrary, and because it will, I fear, have a tendency to sweep me back into the tide of public affairs, when retirement and ease are so essentially necessary for and is so much desired by me. However, as my friends, with a degree of solicitude which is unusual, seem to wish for my attendance on this occasion, I have come to a resolution to go, if my health will permit.

Again, he wrote James Madison as follows:

> It gives me great pleasure to hear, that there is a probability of a full representation of the States in convention; but if the delegates come to it under fetters, the salutary ends proposed will in my opinion be greatly embarrassed and retarded, if not altogether defeated. I am desirous of knowing how this matter is, as my wish is that the convention may adopt no temporizing expedients, but probe the defects of the constitution to the bottom, and provide a radical cure, whether they are agreed to or not. A conduct of this kind will stamp wisdom and dignity on their proceedings, and hold up a light which sooner or later will have its influence.

[Washington was chosen President of the Constitutional Convention and throughout all its sessions its deliberations were conducted in secret. No journal was maintained and it was years after the Convention before some of its debates and actions were revealed. These later revelations proved the wisdom in choosing Washington as its presiding officer.]

As the first Chief Executive of the United States of America, Washington established the Republic on a firm foundation upon which it has continued to endure to the present age.

During its first critical eight years of existence, the whole country turned to President Washington as the most sagacious, most experienced, and ablest man. His views on public questions and the methods of government which he favored quickly became a part of the history of the United States. During the eight years of his presidency no serious national question arose in which Washington's convictions and decisions were not essential. He was the center of all the great legislation during his two presidential terms. He had the opportunity to lay down principles on such vital questions as public revenue, public debt, the civil and criminal law of the federation, the admission of new states, the treatment of the Indians, the system of taxation, the protection of life and property. Though he vetoed but two bills as President, his influence was felt on every important act of the Congress.

Washington's first conquest was the conquest of himself. He set out certain rules of conduct by which he lived. Never in his military career, in his private life, or as President of the United States did he require of others that which he did not first require of himself. I am going to quote just a rule or two by which Washington lived.

"Undertake not what you cannot Perform but be Careful to keep your Promise. . . .

"Speak not Evil of the Absent for it is unjust. . . .

"When you speak of God or his Attributes, let it be Seriously & [with] Reverence. . . .

"Labour to keep alive in your Breast that Little Spark of Celestial Fire called Conscience."

These are four out of the 110 rules which he set out for himself under the label, "Rules of Civility and Decent Behaviour."

When Washington was twenty years old he became a Freemason and a member of Fredericksburg Lodge No. 4, at Fredericksburg, Virginia. Early in 1788 he was appointed Master of Alexandria Lodge No. 22 by Edmund Randolph, Governor of Virginia and Grand Master of Masons of that Great State. He was elected to the office of Master in the fall of 1788, and was Master of that Lodge when he was sworn in as President of the United States. He remained a member until his death, and was buried with Masonic honors.

Washington said in a letter: "So far as I am acquainted with the principles of Freemasonry, I conceive them to be founded on benevolence, and to be exercised only for the good of mankind."

Another quotation: "Being persuaded that a just application of the principles on which the Masonic fraternity is founded, must be promotive of private virtue and public prosperity, I shall be happy to advance the interest of the Society, and to be considered by them as a deserving Brother."

A large number of the signers of the Declaration of Independence [9] and the Constitution of the United States [13] were members of the fraternity. They were better men and better citizens because they believed in the principles for which Freemasonry stands. They put into the Constitution the principles in which they believed.

This great Republic is now facing a crisis unequalled in its history. Greed and thirst for power have created a situation in the world which has almost abolished liberty and peace in the Eastern Hemisphere.

One of the first things a dictator does is abolish freedom of speech, freedom of thought, freedom of religion. These are principles for which humanity has fought from the beginning of time, and for which it will continue to fight until the end. The first great President of the United States, the man to whom we are paying tribute today, was the embodiment of those principles.

In the Senate of the United States, on the Twenty-second of February every year, Washington's Farewell Address is read by some member of that body for the edification of the Senators. It would be a wonderful thing if everybody in the United States had an opportunity to listen to that Farewell Address at least once a year.

Washington was a great Freemason, and the greatest example of the principles for which Freemasonry stands. He was a leader, and he was a leader who would fight for his principles. He was a good citizen, and he stood for those things which make citizenship worthwhile. He was the Father of the greatest republic that the sun has ever shone upon.

As long as we follow the example and carry out the principles for which our first President stood, this Republic will always be safe, and will endure.

[Note: For a full account of George Washington, the Master Mason, see *G. Washington: Master Mason*.]

C. THE MASONIC SERVICE ASSOCIATION AND ITS MASONIC SERVICE CENTERS

A radio address of July 24, 1941 by
Senator Harry S. Truman, Grand Master of Masons in Missouri

At its annual meeting in Washington, D. C. in February of this year, The Masonic Service Association of the United States—an organization of the majority of the forty-nine Grand Lodges of Freemasons of the nation—heard General George C. Marshall, Chief of Staff of the Army, state that he hoped that the Freemasons of the United States would cooperate in the movement to foster it. Immediately thereafter, the delegates enthusiastically authorized the Executive Commission of the Association to engage in Masonic welfare work for the armed forces.

I now report to Freemasons, to the families of Freemasons, and to all who may be interested, as to what the Masonic Service Association has done to carry out that mandate, and what it expects to do.

The Executive Commission adopted plans which, under Major Charles S. Coulter U. S. A. Retired, Director of Welfare of the Association, had been years in the making and which have been approved by military authorities. These plans show the need for forty Masonic Centers in the various camps, cantonments and training areas. The estimated average cost was $5,000 per year per Center, with a twenty per cent allowance for overhead, supervision, traveling inspector service, and so forth, in addition, or a total amount of $250,000. This amount can be raised by a contribution equal to ten cents per member from all of the forty-nine Grand Jurisdictions of the United States.

In these days of big money, when even billions are a matter of course and a million is small change, I might be excused if I were apologetic for the small sum asked of the two and a half millions of Freemasons of the nation. But as a matter of fact I am proud that the small contribution requested can go so far and do so much. I am proud because I know why it can do so much; proud that so many devoted Masons are willing to give of their time and strength, sell their goods at cost, work for nothing or for a pittance, for the love of their fellow members of the oldest fraternal organization in the world.

The emotional appeal of Masonic relief is greatest in time of great disaster, such as devastating floods and earthquakes. This nation suffers now from neither flood nor earthquake, but the flood of fear for democratic institutions and the earthquake of world conflict has shaken the United States so hard that the greatest effort of man-power, money, and effort in all our history is being made.

Masons by the hundreds of thousands are being drafted, serving in the National Guard, or enlisting. That they need from their brethren all that brotherly service may supply them while giving up a year or more of their lives, while away from home and family, while serving their brethren, while serving the nation, is certain.

Masons responding to their country's needs average more than 50% of the officers, and over 10% of drafted and enlisted men. Masons' relatives constitute another 10 to 15% of the armed forces. A noted Masonic historian estimated that in the first World War, Masons and relatives formed approximately 24% of this country's armed forces.

At Camp Stewart, in Georgia, fifty-four members of one small Lodge are in the service. In a National Guard division in the far south, of nine thousand eighty-two men of all ranks, an investigation disclosed that more than five thousand are members of the Fraternity. Opened February first of this year, the Masonic Center at Columbia, South Carolina, during its first three months served Masons from twenty-three States, Hawaii and the Philippine Islands.

The Army has a well-planned welfare and morale program, which will function within the borders of camps, forts and training areas. But morale must be created and sustained outside such areas as well as inside. It is here that Freemasonry functions and here that the military authorities and the Masonic Grand Lodges want it to function.

Not all of it has come from Grand Lodges. Melvin M. Johnson, of Boston, Past Grand Master of the Grand Lodge of Massachusetts and Sovereign Grand Commander of the Northern Jurisdiction of the Scottish Rite of Freemasonry, sent five thousand dollars from his great organization. In strong contrast, both as to man and in amount, an ex-convict in the far west, pardoned and making good after a life time in prison, wrote: "I was never good enough to be a Mason but my father was, and I want to help—here's a dollar for ten Masons who cannot pay." From a woman unknown to any one in the Association came a check for a hundred and fifty dollars with a note saying: "To help comfort some other woman's sons." The little girls in their early teens of the Order of Rainbow will hold a nation-wide rally to gather funds "to send something to Daddy and brother in the camps." The National League of Masonic Clubs enthusiastically endorsed the program and is collecting money to add to the welfare fund. In the Grand Lodge of South Dakota a note was passed to a speaker who had just outlined the Masonic program for aid to the armed forces. The speaker read it aloud: "I have two sons subject to draft. Both will go when called. My personal check for fifty dollars to add to whatever money this Grand Lodge votes." It was signed by Sanford G. Donaldson, an active member of the Supreme Council of the Scottish Rite for the Southern Jurisdiction. These are but a few instances, chosen at random from the records.

The Center at Columbia, South Carolina, serves nearby Fort Jackson. The great concentration of soldiers at Camp Blanding, in Florida, is served by the Masonic Center in Jacksonville. The Masonic Field Agent at Anniston, Alabama, establishes Masonic contacts for and with the soldiers at Fort McClellan, where, among others, New York's 27th Division is training. In Louisiana, Camps Beauregard, Claiborne, Livingston and Polk are served from Alexandria. In my own State, Missouri, I am happy to note that the Masons in Rolla have generously contributed quarters in their fine Temple, where a Masonic Center now brings aid and comfort to Masons and Masons' sons, as well as their buddies, stationed at Fort Leonard Wood. Fort Sill, in Oklahoma, near the little town of Lawton, will have Masonic service in the very near future—just as soon as the Masons there can provide the necessary quarters for the Masonic Service Association to open its Center.

These Masonic Centers neither rival nor duplicate the excellent work being accomplished by social organizations. All are necessary and all should be encouraged. But for Masons and Masons' sons there are services which no other organization than their own can give, and it is primarily for this purpose that the Masons of the nation are contributing to help their brethren.

Masonic Centers provide a roster of Masons in the reservations. Masonic Field Agents visit patients in hospitals, taking small comforts and gifts, writing letters for the helpless; notifying families and home lodges of the sickness and its seriousness; obtaining assistance where needed.

Masonic Centers provide transportation for visiting families through the Center car. Visitors are conducted to hospitals or organizations and their calls made easy and comfortable. The same car takes visiting Masons to local Lodge meetings.

A bulletin board gives information about Masonic Lodges, with complete information about meeting places, dates and hours, names of secretaries. Assistance is given in drawing legal papers made necessary by affairs at home, through some local brother-lawyer, thus assuring the service men of sympathetic assistance. Temporary financial assistance is available in actual need through a rotating fund in the hands of Field Agents.

Home service is rendered Masons—obtaining requested information about home conditions of a brother, and financial needs. Officially a function of the Red Cross, through an arrangement with that organization, home service cases involving Masons are turned over to the Masonic Centers. Home service cases in the hands of the Craft are sympathetically and helpfully handled.

Masonic Centers aid Masons in temporary difficulties, through brotherly assistance by counsel or otherwise, whether the difficulties are military or civilian. It includes aid to Chaplains in Masonic cases, through the same system that handles home service. In all the military services the majority of Protestant chaplains are Master Masons.

In other words, Masonic Service Centers assume that brotherly relationship that members of the home lodges would assume if the Craftsmen were at home instead of far away in the armed services.

As fast as the Association can work and as money, voluntarily contributed, is received, this work will go forward. Surveys have been made in many areas where the service is needed. The Fraternity can well congratulate itself that it was first in the field, and that its quiet and unostentatious efforts for its brethren, their sons, their friends and fellow soldiers is being so rapidly established and extended.

With no fanfare or publicity, with no appeal for government money or public subscription, the Freemasons of the nation have made the cause of their fellow members their own; they transpose the words of Cain to read: "I am my brother's keeper!"

At a meeting in Washington attended by Congressmen who were Masons and addressed by Major Coulter, one Congressman rose and said "My Lodge has twelve hundred members. I herewith subscribe the necessary ten cents for each of them!" Twenty-five or more Senators and Representatives spoke in favor of the work, none opposed it, after which the resolution was adopted without a dissenting voice.

A quotation from a letter from a grateful father states: "The Masonic order is rendering a great service to our boys in camp. Members in Alexandria (La.) have called on our boy and invited him to meet with them. Some of the ladies of members have invited him to their homes. We thank you much; he is not lonely now."

The U.S.O. has a large program that will require much money to carry through. It deserves the support of all who have the welfare of the soldiers, sailors, marines and coast guardsmen at heart. It is especially important to those organizations and individuals who have no personal or fraternal outlet for their donations.

My Brother, can you spare a dime for these projects?

oOo

This talk was reprinted and sent to the Lodges throughout the country in September, 1941. With it these encouraging bulletins were added:

A new MASONIC SERVICE ASSOCIATION Service Center for men in the armed forces is now open at Rolla, Missouri, serving the soldiers at Ft. Leonard Wood. Brother Harry B. Sherman, in charge, reports much enthusiasm from the soldiers using it, and large crowds constantly thronging it.

Fortunately for Masonry, Masons have an excellent outlet of their own for their donations which is already in the field with a Center at Columbia, South Carolina, for Fort Jackson, and other Centers in the course of establishment at Jacksonville and Starke, Florida, for Camp Blanding; at Rolla, Missouri, for Fort Leonard Wood; and at Alexandria, Louisiana, for Camps Beauregard, Claiborne, Livingston and Polk. Others are planned. All Masons can contribute to this excellent work for brethren in the armed services through their respective Grand Lodges.

PRESIDENT OF THE UNITED STATES

D. UNVEILING OF THE GEORGE WASHINGTON STATUE GEORGE WASHINGTON MASONIC NATIONAL MEMORIAL

Shooters Hill, Alexandria, Virginia
February 22, 1950

(This address was made by President Harry S. Truman, Past Grand Master of Masons in Missouri, via radio at 3:00 p.m., E.S.T., on Wednesday, February 22, 1950 from the foot of the George Washington statue.)

It is a great privilege to dedicate this inspiring statue of George Washington.

This is the climax of many years of planning and effort. I congratulate particularly the Order of DeMolay, whose contributions have made this statue a reality. This heroic likeness of our first President makes even more impressive the entrance hall of this temple. It is altogether fitting that this work should stand in the community that Washington did so much to build, and so near his own home at Mount Vernon.

George Washington, like ourselves, lived in a period of great change—a period when new forces and new ideas were sweeping across the world. He was the leader of his people in a revolution against tyranny. He commanded an army in a long and bitter war. He was a major figure in the creation of a new kind of constitution. Finally, as the first President of our Nation, he translated that Constitution into a living government.

Washington's efforts for freedom were two-fold. He was concerned first with making the ideal of democratic government work. He was also concerned with the defense of that ideal against the forces opposed to it.

President Harry S. Truman at the podium dedicated the statue of George Washington, a gift from the DeMolays, at the George Washington Masonic National Memorial on February 22, 1950.

[Photographer unknown]

Washington was unwavering in his devotion to the democratic concept. He never yielded to those who urged him to assume extraordinary powers. Even in the darkest days of the Revolution, when his task as Commander-in-Chief of the American forces was rendered doubly difficult by the weakness of the Congress and the rivalries among the states, he always considered himself as a servant of the people. In all that he did, he strove to make democratic institutions more effective.

He knew, too, that they had to be defended—that there were times when the use of force to defend democracy could not be avoided. He not only led the armies in the revolution, but as President he was always alert to the necessity of a vigorous national defense.

The task of Americans today is fundamentally the same as it was in Washington's time. We, too, must make democracy work and we must defend it against its enemies.

But our task today is far greater in scope than it was in Washington's time. Not only are we concerned with increasing the freedom, welfare, and opportunity of our people, we are also concerned with the right of other peoples to choose their form of government, to improve their standards of living, and to decide what kind of life they want to live.

Since Washington's time the great principles for which the American Revolution was fought have become known throughout the world and have uplifted the hearts and hopes of generations of men. At the same time, through the progress of science, the nations of the world have been drawn together into a common destiny. Our security and progress are today more closely related than ever before to the advance of freedom and self-government to their greatest test.

At the same time, these ideals are under deadly attack from those who would destroy them. The most aggressive of these enemies today is communism. Communism seeks to induce men to surrender their freedom by false promises of a better life. But the great danger of communism does not lie in its false promises. It lies in the fact that it is an instrument of an armed imperialism which seeks to extend its influence by force.

Just as our thirteen original states found that survival and progress depended on closer association and common effort, so the free nations of the world today must seek their salvation in unity and concerted action. The real strength of the free nations is not to be found in any single country or any one weapon, but in the combined moral and material strength of the free world as a whole.

As members of the United Nations, the free nations are working for peace and international security in accordance with the principles set forth in the Charter. Within the context of that larger association, many of the free nations have joined together to strengthen the common defense of particular areas against aggression. That is the meaning of the North Atlantic Treaty and the Mutual Defense Assistance Program.

We shall continue to work with the other free nations associated with us in the common defense—for our defense is theirs, and their defense is ours. The united defense of these nations is a powerful deterrent to aggression, and it will become more powerful as time goes by.

In creating a common defense, we do not seek to impose a way of life on any nation. Freedom is not expanded by conquest. Democracy is not created by dictation. Freedom and democracy grow only by persuasion and example and through the actual experience of what they mean.

At the same time, freedom cannot grow and expand unless it is protected against the armed imperialism of those who would destroy it. The free nations, therefore, must maintain military force as a defensive measure.

While the free nations stand prepared to resist aggression, they are doing their utmost to find peaceful means for settling international disputes. They know that another great war could destroy victory and vanquished alike.

Consequently, we in the United States are doing and will continue to do all that lies within our power to prevent the horror of another war. We are working for the reduction of armaments and the control of weapons of mass destruction.

We are convinced of the necessity for an international agreement to limit the use of atomic energy to peaceful purpose, and for a workable international system to assure that such an agreement is effectively carried out. We believe that the United Nations is the proper forum in which to reach such an agreement. We firmly believe that all nations would gain by such an international agreement. We shall continue to work honestly and wholeheartedly toward that end. But we must remember that the outcome is not ours alone to determine. The actions of men in other countries will help to shape the ultimate decision.

We believe that the plan for controlling atomic energy which has been worked out in the United Nations and has been approved by the overwhelming majority of its members, would be effective. That plan, therefore, has our support. It has our support not because of its form or its words but because we believe it would achieve effective control. The stakes are too large to let us, or any nation, stand on pride of authorship. We ask only for a plan that provides an effective, workable system—anything less would be a sham agreement. Anything less would increase, not decrease, the dangers of the use of atomic energy for destructive purposes. We shall continue to examine every avenue, every possibility of reaching real agreement for effective control.

In the long run, however, our security and the world's hopes for peace lie not in measures of defense or in the control of weapons, but in the growth and expansion of freedom and self-government. As these ideals are accepted by more and more people, as they give greater meaning and richer content to the lives of millions, they become the greatest force in the world for peace.

The purpose of our participation in the United Nations and other international organizations is to strengthen this great force for peace. That is the purpose of the European Recovery Program and our Point Four Program to assist underdeveloped areas. That is the purpose of our foreign trade program and our other measures to help build world prosperity.

These programs are positive measures to increase the strength of freedom and self-government by helping meet the needs and fulfill the aspirations of their daily lives.

Today, in many countries of the world, the concepts of freedom and self-government are merely vague phrases. They express little to people who are engaged in a desperate struggle with ignorance and poverty. They mean little to men who must work from sun-up to sun-down merely to keep alive. They are not fully understood by men who cannot read or write.

On the continent of Asia and the islands of the Far East, in Africa and in the Near East, are millions of people who live in poverty and who have never known real freedom or democratic government. In their present condition, the immediate benefit of steel plowshares, or smallpox vaccinations, has more appeal than abstract ideas of democracy.

The communists are saying that they will bring food and clothing and health and a more secure life to these poverty-stricken peoples. We know that is not true. But it is not enough to tell such people that communism is a modern tyranny far worse than that of any ancient empire. It is not enough to tell them that communism leads only to oppression. People who have never known freedom and security themselves have little basis for judging how false are the claims of communism.

These people will turn to democracy only if it seems to them to be the best way to meet their urgent needs. The benefits of freedom and democracy must be demonstrated to them.

In many of these areas there are governments which are working to improve the conditions of their people. They know that the claims of the communists are not made in good faith. They do not want Soviet domination. If these governments are successful in raising living standards, and in building strong and stable democratic institutions based on popular support, their people will not go over to communism.

But these governments are struggling with titanic problems, as their people attempt to climb in a few years from economic misery to better standards of living. They need help. If these nations are to grow in freedom, they urgently need assistance in improving their health, their education, their productive capacity, their transportation and communication systems.

That is why I have requested the Congress to act as rapidly as possible on legislation to expand our programs for giving technical assistance to such countries as these, and to encourage American investment in those countries on a mutually beneficial basis. We are not trying to sell them automobiles and television sets. Our purpose is to help them to grow more food, to obtain better education, and to be more healthy. That is the way they can gain the physical and moral strength to be free and to maintain their own governments.

As these nations prove to themselves and to others the effectiveness of free institutions in meeting their people's needs, they will show as nothing else can the true value of democracy and the false claims of communism.

But the problem of making free institutions work is not confined to under-developed areas. The highly developed nations of Europe came out of the war with serious problems of their own. They were threatened with economic chaos. Their ability to maintain freedom and democracy was challenged.

The purpose of the European recovery program was to meet this challenge in the area of the world where the preservation of free governments was of supreme importance. The results which have been achieved so far under that program have amply demonstrated its wisdom.

With the aid we have provided, the nations of Europe have already made great advances in their production and have improved their trading relations with the rest of the world. Much more must be done before they reach the firm basis of economic self-support which is essential to the maintenance of free and democratic governments. Consequently, we must complete our program of assistance. It would be utter folly to lose sight of the importance of the European recovery program. It is essential to our hopes for peace.

The preservation and strengthening of free governments depends in large measure on the creation of firm economic conditions throughout the world and on an expanding world trade. Free nations can expand their trade only on the basis of mutual respect and fair dealing.

Our reciprocal trade agreements program and the International Trade Organization are the kind of international machinery which is necessary for increasing the trade of the world. We shall continue to use the procedures of the reciprocal trade agreements program to reduce trade barriers, but more than this is needed. That is why I have urged the Congress to act favorably on the creation of the International Trade Organization, through which the nations of the world can work together effectively to increase world trade.

This program and our other plans for international action are the practical way to move forward toward peace. They recognize that we must deal with the difficult world situation which actually exists. We must not be discouraged by difficulties and setbacks. We must not be misled by the vain hope of finding quick and easy solutions. We must move forward persistently and courageously along the hard path to a peace based on freedom and justice.

The progress we have made in this country since the days of George Washington is proof of the vitality and truth of the ideals he fought for. We must be no less firm, no less resolute, no less steadfast than he was. We move upon a greater stage than he did, but our problems are fundamentally the same problems that faced the first President of this Nation—to make democracy work and defend it from its enemies.

George Washington sought guidance from Almighty God as he faced these tasks in his time; let us be guided today by Divine Providence as we strive for lasting peace with freedom and justice for all mankind.

E. HARRY S. TRUMAN LIBRARY DEDICATION ADDRESS

Delivered by Chief Justice Earl Warren, Past Grand Master of Masons in California, at the Harry S. Truman Library, Independence, Missouri July 6, 1957

This is an important event in the life of the nation and I am happy to participate in it. The library which we dedicate is destined to become a midwestern center of study and research, not only for the period of Mr. Truman's Presidency, but also for the whole complex picture of events surrounding it. The impetus it provides for extending the research resources of this great section which has meant so much to the development of the nation as a whole, represents a milestone in American history.

The casual observer would have difficulty in appreciating the dynamic part this quiet home city of Independence has already played in the growth of our country. Used as the hunting grounds of the Indians before and after the arrival in America of Europeans, this area was once part of the colonial empire of France and Spain. It was acquired by the United States in the Louisiana Purchase of 1803. Independence soon became a frontier settlement, the jumping-off place for those hardy pioneers who gave forceful character to the midwest and the far west. It helped to impart to those great regions the spirit of the famous explorer Daniel Boone, whose son, Daniel Morgan Boone, is said to have been the first white man to visit this region. As more and more permanent settlers established themselves, Independence flourished as a trading post and outfitting point for the Oregon, Santa Fe, and California trails. The chain of events started in motion here in those days of the Argonauts, are among the most colorful and heroic of our entire history. The Mormons came here to make their home in 1831, but, after two turbulent years, they moved on. After long wandering and, at a site a thousand miles westward, they finally established their Zion and founded the great state of Utah. The growth of Independence was given a tremendous impetus by the 1849 gold rush which brought many prospectors to purchase supplies for their journey to California. They were a hardy and adventurous lot spurred on by the lure of gold. Thousands of them, in their prairie schooners or on horseback wended their way across plains, mountains and desert to the Pacific Coast. Of them it has been said that "The timid never started and the weak died on the way." Mr. Truman's grandfather owned one of these outfitting stores, and eventually himself succumbed to the gold fever. He made the trek to California and acquired a ranch at our capital city of Sacramento. Independence, now a typical American community, seems far removed from those days when it served as a western outpost.

Mr. Truman's Presidency naturally reflected this daring spirit of pioneer days as well as his own character as a man of action: tireless, fearless and decisive. Let me say that I personally came to appreciate his dynamic fighting qualities, perhaps earlier and more fully than some other people, in the fall of 1948, before he reached mid-point of his administration. The Truman era is already recognized as one of the most momentous periods in the history of our country and of the world. The demands then made upon the President were as diverse and breath-taking as they were ponderous. Complicated events crowded upon one another giving Mr. Truman little or no time to sit, ponder and mull over historical precedents. He was, like Grover Cleveland, confronted with conditions, not theories. Repeatedly he was called upon to act with promtitude and resolution. His response always was action; even split-second actions in matters of the gravest importance. The best evidence of the magnitude of the office he held, of the considerations basic to his decisions, of the methods he adopted to meet new and pressing problems will be found in the Truman papers housed in this library. Without them, the world would never fully understand his courage and stamina in responding in the vigorous and effective way he did to crises such as few other executives have had to face.

Toward the close of World War II, and within a few weeks after he assumed the Presidency, Mr. Truman was host to representatives of the peoples of the world who met in America to form a world organization dedicated to maintaining and enforcing peace. During his administration, the headquarters of the United Nations were established in this country, we are entitled to believe, largely by reason of his leadership, the hospitality extended by our people, and the manifest desire for universal order in the soul of every American. While the United Nations was as yet young and untried, and while we were engaged in making a profound adjustment to a peacetime economy—demobilizing our armies, putting the ships of our fleet in mothballs, dismantling aircraft, reestablishing a peace-time economy, and developing human relations in and out of this country—the whole process had to be reversed by the outbreak of hostilities in Korea. There, at the instance of Mr. Truman, troops of many nations, for the first time in history, fought solely to restore peace with freedom under an international banner. Aggression was repelled. The war was successfully contained. Arrogance was frustrated as had previously been done in Europe with the Berlin Air-lift.

Again, it was during Mr. Truman's administration, with the experience of the second World War behind us, that an end was put to any possibility that the United States could ever return to a policy of isolation and self-sufficiency. Out of that conflict had come the discovery of nuclear fission with implications for future good or evil and posing a grave challenge to the human family. Although we did not seek it, world-wide responsibility was thrust upon us. The obligation of this responsibility was accepted in an open-spirited way. We engaged to undergird the defenses of the free world. A daring new policy of international cooperation and assistance designed to reconstruct the world and to aid backward areas through economic and technical assistance was then promulgated and has since been continued.

Colleges and universities whose faculties and students will reap the greatest benefit from their use of the Truman Library were among the institutions that experienced conspicuous changes during the Truman administration. The United States government financed, in large part, the education of its veterans. The return to school of many thousands of serious and studious men,under the G.I. Bill of Rights Act, doubled the registration in institutions of higher learning. In this period, more than ever before, we recognized the need for college trained citizens and we began to wrestle boldly with our educational problems. It became national policy that our veterans, educationally speaking, must not become a lost generation. Since then, because of the war inflated birth rate, the size of elementary schools has doubled and now our high schools are feeling the effect of greatly increased enrollment. Shortly, the colleges and universities will have to double in size again. It is fortunate that the Truman Library is to become a part of our vast and growing educational system—that it can be a major influence in the process of training an ever growing number of research students.

Professor John D. Hicks of the University of California has aptly spoken of history as "an endless procession of human experience marching toward the present and the future. But the only way this procession can reach the current scene is through our recent past. The years just fading from our memories constitute, in a sense, the bridge over which the contributions of earlier ages must pass to make contact with the world of today and tomorrow."

The Truman papers will furnish substantial material "to keep this bridge in order." From them we are able to take inventory, to discover where we came from, how we got here, and, perhaps to chart our future route more intelligently. People from the universities and colleges of this country and from foreign countries will beat paths leading to and from Independence reminding us of those of the nineteenth century. These new trails will be kept open because there will be sustained use of the Truman papers by future generations of writers, biographers, historians, political scientists and others. The traveler following these new trails will explore the background which the Truman Library will provide for a more complete understanding of the contributions made by his administration. Independence will become even more distinguished as a center for the cultural development of our country than it was for its geographical expansion.

Again to quote the historian, the former preoccupation of that profession with the distant past had the effect "that the darkest age, historically speaking, was likely to be the age just gone by." Mr. Truman, the private citizen, now back at home, continues to dedicate his life to the public good—to make certain that the years of his administration will not be such a dark age. Today he performs a characteristic service in giving both his time and his substance to do that which in this instance only he can do. He is providing the people of America and the people of the world with the means to form their own estimate of his public service. Mr. Truman, who has an abiding interest in our national history, has arranged for the preservation of his papers in this library in such manner that his administration will be one of the "clearest ages" of history. It is in compliance with his public-spirited generosity that I dedicate this building as a museum and a library to safeguard, exhibit, and facilitate the use of its valuable resources that the American people, and, all the peoples of this earth, may gain by their wide and wise use understanding of ourselves and our times, and wisdom to choose the right paths in the years that lie ahead.

In doing so I share with all Americans the hope that Mr. Truman will live long to see the results of his work and to be accorded recognition that the future of mankind will be richer because of his having passed this way.

F. THE FLAG, SEAL AND COAT OF ARMS OF THE PRESIDENT OF THE UNITED STATES

(Based on a news release of October 25, 1945)

The flag of the President of the United States was revised by President Harry S. Truman in 1945 by Executive Order 9646.

Prior to 1916 the Army and Navy had separate flags for the Commander-in-Chief. In 1916 President Woodrow Wilson commissioned his Assistant Secretary of the Navy, Franklin D. Roosevelt, to design a Presidential flag suitable for use by both the Army and the Navy. That design was adopted by Executive Order on May 29, 1916.

There were several inconsistencies in the 1916 flag which President Roosevelt noted in 1945. The flag of the Commander-in-Chief had four stars; beginning in 1944 the flags of the Fleet Admirals and Generals of the Army had five stars. Roosevelt ordered it revised.

Commodore Byron McCandless had made a study of the history of various flags of the United States, so the job of revision was turned over to him. Roosevelt died before McCandless had completed several designs. It was June before President Truman could study them. When he did he proposed several changes.

Truman wanted the Presidential flag to have a circle of forty-eight stars, one for each state in the Union; additional stars to be added as new states were admitted to the Union. The eagle on the old flags that had been in existence since 1850 had the eagle facing left and toward arrows in its left talon. Truman believed the eagle should face to its right and toward the olive branches held in its right talon—away from the symbol of war and toward the symbol of peace.

The eagle in the older flags was white; Truman wanted the eagle in its natural color.

President Truman got what he wanted. So well has it been accepted there has been no change since 1945, except for the addition of two stars.

In bureaucratic language the Executive Order reads:

COAT OF ARMS, SEAL, AND FLAG OF THE PRESIDENT OF THE UNITED STATES.

By virtue of the authority vested in me as President of the United States, it is hereby ordered as follows:

The Coat of Arms of the President of the United States shall be of the following design:

SHIELD: Paloways of thirteen pieces argent and gulos, a chief azure; upon the breast of an American eagle displayed holding in his dexter talon an olive branch and in his sinister a bundle of thirteen arrows all proper, and in his beak a white scroll inscribed "E PLURIBUS UNUM" sable.

CREST: Behind and above the eagle a radiating glory or, on which appears an arc of thirteen cloud puffs proper, and a constellation of thirteen mullots argent.

The whole surrounded by white stars arranged in the form of an annulot with one point of each star outward on the imaginary radiating center lines, the number of stars conforming to the number in the union of the Flag of the United States as established by the act of Congress approved April 4, 1818, 3 Stat. 415.

The Seal of the President of the United States shall consist of the Coat of Arms encircled by the words "Seal of the President of the United States."

The Color and Flag of the President of the United States shall consist of a dark blue rectangular background of sizes and proportions to conform to the military and naval custom, on which shall appear the Coat of Arms of the President in proper colors. The proportions of the elements of the Coat of Arms shall be in direct relation to the hoist, and the fly shall vary according to the customs of the military and naval services.

The old Executive Order was recinded, and the Coat of Arms, Seal and Presidential flag as outlined above were offically adopted.

BIBLIOGRAPHY

Bray, William J., *Recollections of the 1948 Campaign,* an Oral History, Harry S. Truman Library, MO.

Cochran, Bert, *Harry Truman and the Crisis Presidency,* Funk & Wagnalls, NY, 1973

Denslow, William R., *10,000 Famous Freemasons,* Missouri Lodge of Research, 1959-1962

Ferrell, Robert H., Editor, *Dear Bess:* The Letters from Harry to Bess Truman, 1910-1959, W.W. Norton & Co., NY, 1983

———, Editor, *The Autobiography of Harry S. Truman,* CO Associated U. Press, 1980

———, *Off the Record,* Harper and Row, NY, 1980

———, *Harry S. Truman and the Modern Presidency,* Little, Brown and Co., Boston, 1983

Ford, Gerald, *A Time To Heal,* Harper & Row, NY, 1979

Freemason, The, Grand Lodge of Missouri, A.F. & A.M., Spring, 1973

Gies, Joseph, *Harry S Truman: A Pictorial Biography,* Doubleday & Co., NY, 1968

Gosnell, Harold F., *Truman's Crises:* A Political Biography of Harry S. Truman, Greenwood Press, CT, 1980

Harry S. Truman Library, Thousands of papers, pictures, and other items, Independence, MO.

Hunt, Bruce H., "A Masonic Review" and other items about Harry S. Truman, the Mason, Grand Lodge of Missouri

Indiana Freemason, The, Grand Lodge of Indiana, F&AM Nov. 1948; June 1984

Jackson, Joseph Abram, *Masonry in Alabama,* Grand Lodge of Alabama, A.F. & A.M., 1970

Masonic Service Association of the United States, The, Various Publications

Newsletter of the Northern Masonic Jurisdiction of the Scottish Rite, 1945

Nixon, Richard, *The Memoirs of Richard Nixon,* Grosset & Dunlap, NY, 1978

Noland, Mary Ethel (Miss Ethel), Oral History, Harry S. Truman Library, MO.

Officer, The, Official publication of the Reserve Officers Association, Truman dedication edition, May, 1984, D.C.

Ohrvall, C. Warren, Editor, "Information on Harry S. Truman's Masonic Career", Harry S. Truman Library, MO., 1983

Proceedings, Grand Lodge of Missouri, AF&AM, various years

Robbins, Charles, *Last of His Kind:* An Informal Portrait of Harry S. Truman, William Morrow and Co., NY, 1979

Roberts, Allen E., *Freemasonry's Servant,* The Masonic Service Association, MD, 1969

_______, *Freemasonry in American History,* Macoy Publishing & Masonic Supply Co., VA, 1985

_______, *Frontier Cornerstone,* Grand Lodge of Ohio, F. & A.M., 1980

_______, *G. Washington: Master Mason,* Macoy, VA, 1976

Royal Arch Mason, "Going to the Dogs", article by Jerry Marsengill

Smith, Dwight L., *Goodly Heritage,* Grand Lodge F. & A.M. of Indiana, 1968

Sulzberger, C.L., *World War II:* The American Heritage Picture History of, American Heritage, NY, 1966

Texas Grand Lodge Magazine, June, 1945

Truman, Harry S., *Memoirs,* Two volumes, Doubleday/Time, NY, 1955-56

200 Years: A Bicentennial Illustrated History of the United States, U.S. News and World Report, DC, 1973

INDEX